BODYPOWER

BODYPOWER

By Ralph and Valerie Carnes

THE COMPLETE GUIDE TO
HEALTH CLUB
EXERCISE MACHINES
AND HOME GYM EQUIPMENT

St. Martin's Press
New York

 For information, address St. Martin's Press, 175 Fifth Avenue, New York, N.Y. 10010.

Library of Congress Cataloging in Publication Data

Carnes, Ralph L.
Bodypower.

1. Weight lifting. 2. Weight lifting—Equipment and supplies. I. Carnes, Valerie. II. Title.
GV546.C37 688.7'641 81-8896
ISBN 0-312-08734-9 AACR2

Design by Manuela Paul

Everyone has at least two families:
the parents who nurture them through childhood,
and the family of close friends
who enrich their adult years.

This book is dedicated to our families.

Lettie and Robert
Valerie and Ross
Petros and his brothers
Junius and the memories we share

Acknowledgments

Unless otherwise noted, all photos of exercise machines were made at the Sports Fitness Institute, Glen Ellyn, Illinois. Special thanks are due to the owner, Dr. Miles Pohunek, for the many insights he gave us, as well as for the pleasure of his company.

Special thanks are also due to Al Phillips of the Chicago Health Club, and to Carl Silvani of Houston's Presidents First Lady Health Club, for their contributions to the section on health clubs and gymnasiums.

Former Mr. America, Mr. U.S.A., and Mr. Universe, Robert Gajda of the Sports Performance and Rehabilitation Institute provided crucial material and suggestions, corrections and clarifications for the sections on strength training, program development, and PHA training.

The following people gave us information and constructive criticism on subjects ranging from cardiovascular conditioning routines to women's bodybuilding, from sports training techniques to powerlifting, from health club management to locker room gossip.

Jim Johnson
Deborah Cargal
Rick Butler
Kay Rogness
Jeanne Benson
Lindy Pond
George Radice
Andy Dumpis
Phil Classen
Pete ("The Greek") Agriotasthes
Ray York
Rosina Ravalli
Angelo Lenciano
John Kading
Beverly Rieling-Haley
Ira Hurley
Kay Hurley
Andy Jackson
Richard Hoover
Dr. Robert Weil
Dr. George Regiro
Dr. Oscar Rasmussen
Dr. Mark Pentecost
Dr. Cyrus H. Stoner
Dr. McLowery Elrod
Dr. Edwin G. Olmstead
Dr. Robert McNeill
Missy Orth
Ed Turner
Robert Griggas
The unknown young doctor at the Guantánamo Naval Base hospital who started RLC on the road to recovery
Karo Whitfield, who sold RLC his first barbell set

Valerie's makeup was done by Steve Schmid of Tondu Studios, Chicago; Marilyn Miglin Cosmetics at Paul Glick Studios, Chicago; and by Adele Rock of Facials International, Lombard, Illinois.

Valerie's hairstyling was done by Leonard Poisson, Lord and Taylor Hair Salons, Chicago, Illinois.

Equipment was provided by Dr. Miles Pohunek, Al Phillips, Ira Hurley, Bob Gajda, Paul Thompson, and Jerry Brentham.

All photography was done by Ralph Carnes.

Contents

Preface

During the last decade, weight training has emerged as the most efficient, effective, and rapid way to achieve good health, to improve physical performance and to develop the kind of strength and agility required to take advantage of the multitude of recreational activities that have become popular with non-athletes—with average people who want to be strong and fit.

Weight training is no longer restricted to men who want big muscles. Women as well as men now know the benefits of using free weights and exercise machines for weight control, figure shaping, and muscle toning. Indeed, for almost a decade, women have been lifting weights without knowing it by using the modern exercise machines now available in almost all health clubs.

With the emergence of a national fitness movement, and the parallel discovery of weight training as the optimum method for achieving physical goals, there has been a tremendous growth in the construction of health clubs, spas, gyms, and "family fitness centers." All of these clubs are designed around the use of weight training equipment, either free weights or machines.

This book tells you how to build a home gym, how to choose the right health club, and how to use modern exercise equipment for the maximum results in the shortest time. Whether you want to lose fat, build muscle, shape your figure, or just lean out and stay in top condition, you'll find a routine in this book that will show you what you need to know and do.

A NOTE ON HOW TO USE THIS BOOK

To help you use this book, we've cross-referenced the chapters on exercise machines, exercises, and muscular anatomy. There are handy indexes at the beginning of each of these chapters, as well as anatomy charts to tell you which muscles are which.

The main index is on pages 168-71, at the beginning of the exercise chapter. It's set up according to muscle groups, and it will tell you where to look for a description of the muscles themselves, for machines that will work them, and for free weight exercises that will also work them.

You want to give your upper arms a workout? Look up the biceps and triceps on page 169, and you'll find that the muscles are described on page 153, upper arm machines are listed on pages 186, 187 and 190, and free weight exercises are described on pages 174 through 190.

How about a workout for your abdominal muscles? Look up the abdominals on page 170, and you'll find that the abs themselves are described on 154, the appropriate machines are listed on page 196, and the appropriate free weight exercises are to be found on page 196.

And if you don't know the names of the muscles, look at the anatomy charts on pages 151 and 161, locate the muscle you're after, and you'll find a key that will tell you where to look in the chapter on muscular anatomy.

If your health club has a machine you want to learn to use properly, look it up in the index to the machines on pages 65 through 67 and you'll find the page numbers in the machine chapter where detailed, simplified instructions are given for the machine and the exercises that you can do on it.

The exercises are illustrated with photographs. You'll find the machine photos in the machine chapter, and the free weight photos in the exercise chapter. We've also provided a photo of the equipment you'll need to outfit your own home gym, as well as a diagram for a bench press rack you can build yourself.

It's all there, in easy-to-follow language: everything you need to know to make the maximum progress with the most efficient use of your time. Whether you belong to a health club or just work out at home, this book will tell you what you need to know to get what you want.

Good luck, good reading, and have a terrific workout!

—RALPH AND VALERIE CARNES

1

RUNNING ON EMPTY, LIVING ON BORROWED TIME: *RALPH CARNES'S STORY*

November 3, 1938, in Tallapoosa, Georgia, was a cold, damp day with misting rain and fog. Our apartment behind my father's radio shop was small and overheated. It had been raining for three days, and when it finally stopped I wanted to get out of the house.

My mother finally agreed to let me visit a friend, on the condition that we stay inside to play. I threw on my sweater, cap, and jacket, and bounded out the door with the kind of uninhibited exuberance that is natural for healthy seven-year-old boys. But I didn't go into my friend's house to play. Instead, with a delightful sense of getting away with something, my buddy and I stayed outside all afternoon in the misting rain.

We kicked cans, climbed trees, threw rocks, jumped gullies, chased cats, wrestled, and searched for hickory nuts in the woods down the road. It was one of those golden childhood days. The fog and drizzle dampened our shoes but not our spirits. The cloak of mist that hung over the pine woods only made the day more mysterious and more fun.

My friend had a terrible cough. It started deep in his chest and exploded out of his mouth in a rough bark. He could feel his chest vibrating when he coughed. He sweated a lot, although it was cold. We didn't think anything about it. In fact, sometimes he coughed on purpose, just so we could hear the bark.

At dusk, we finally went to his house and dried our shoes under the potbellied stove in the kitchen. I went home and got a spanking. I hadn't really gotten away with anything at all. My mother found out that we had played outside all afternoon from the little girl up the street. It was her cat we had chased. All in all, though, it was a good day: I was tired, happy, and now warm in a pair of cotton flannel pajamas. We ate supper, listened to "Inner Sanctum" on the little Stewart Warner radio, and went to bed.

The next morning, my throat felt scratchy. I had a slight cough and my nose was running. Two days later, I had my friend's deep, rattling cough and a temperature of 103. By that time, the little boy down the street had what was called "whooping cough," and I had it, too. He got well in a week or so. Mine wouldn't go away.

Then, one morning in early December, I woke up and discovered that I couldn't straighten my right leg. It was bent at the knee, and the knee itself was swollen and tight. I called for my mother.

This was a time when physicians still made house calls. Our family doctor was a kindly, well-meaning country sawbones. He dropped by in the afternoon, took my temperature, looked into my ears and down my throat, thumped my chest, and tried by force to straighten my leg. It didn't work, and I screamed bloody murder. He stopped, reached into his bag, and ladled out a tablespoon of truly foul-tasting brown medicine, and said that he would stop by the next day.

The next morning, my right hand had begun to stiffen, large lumps were forming under my armpits, and my elbow joints were swollen. The doctor concluded that I had whooping cough, acute tonsillitis, rheumatism, and bad teeth. A week later, I was taken to a hospital in a neighboring town, and my tonsils, adenoids, and six baby teeth were removed. My right leg was still bent double, I had lost the movement of my right hand, and the lumps under my arms were as big as goose eggs.

Weeks later, when I could neither walk nor feed myself, our family physician finally concluded that I had a hopeless case of rheumatoid arthritis. I ran a low-grade temperature all the time; I was weak, sick, and had lost all the energy that I had enjoyed that day my friend and I had played all afternoon in the mist.

One day, I overheard the doctor tell my parents that my joints were calcifying, and that I would have to decide whether I wanted to spend the rest of my life sitting or standing. I chose to sit, so I could ride in the car. I always slept on my side anyway. By this time, my right hand was completely immobile, and I had not walked for almost four months.

I eventually learned to feed myself and to write with my left hand, but the doctor thought my leg was beyond recovery. I was taken to Atlanta and examined by the staff of a crippled children's hospital. They didn't admit me as a patient, however, since I had not been crippled by an injury.

We moved to the second floor of a house at the edge of town. It was owned by a kind and gracious lady, Katherine Hayes, who let me lie in her "sunroom" (our doctor prescribed sunbaths). The pattern that my life would henceforth take seemed set. Each day, I listened to all the radio dramas, read everything I could get my hands on, and lay in the sunroom, watching the other kids run and play between the houses.

Then, everything changed. (I am not a folk medicine advocate, although I am aware that digitalis was discovered through an analysis of an English herb-woman's foxglove brew. I tend to put my faith in the scientific method and pragmatic philosophy. I like the guys with a solid background in math and physics, physiology and biochemistry, and who contribute to medical journals instead of sprinkling them around, unread, on their waiting room tables. This story takes a strange turn at this point, and I want you to know where I stand on these things.)

My mother was in poor health and had to have someone to help her with the housework. Most of her attention went to me anyway, because by this time she had come to blame herself for letting me out in the rain to play, back in November. The person who helped her was a wonderful black lady named Maybelle McDaniel. She came to our house three times a week to do the wash and the ironing and the heavy cleaning (my mother had had osteomyelitis as a child, and it had left her with a permanently weak left leg). Maybelle brought not only help but a kind of stern, radiant strength to our household.

Then, one day, even Maybelle got sick and sent her cousin Lou instead. Lou took one look and demanded to know what was wrong with me. She harrumphed at the doctor's diagnosis and declared that she could cure me in a day.

My father was a hard-nosed, no-nonsense newspaper editor. "Who, what, why, when, and where" was more than a writing format, it was the way his mind worked. But by this time, he was grasping at straws, trying to save his son.

He asked Miss Lou what should be done, and she laid out the procedure. They went to the nearby woods to dig up pokeberry plant roots, while our landlady brought huge pots upstairs to cook the chopped roots. They made poultices from the hot mush that resulted and applied them to my hands, arms, and legs. They started at noon and continued until twelve that night. I still remember vividly the pungent odor of the boiling poke salad roots. I drifted off to sleep shortly after midnight and dreamed of being captured by cannibals and boiled in a pot.

The next morning, almost six months after I had awakened to find my knee swollen and bent at right angles, I awakened to find my right leg straight, the swelling gone from my knees and elbows, and the fingers of my right hand weak but movable! I lay in bed not daring to move anymore, for fear that the swelling and pain would return.

My father and mother were in the kitchen. I could hear them talking about what had happened to me. I had to get up and tell them that I was all right. I sat up in bed very carefully. There was no pain. I swung my legs off the side of the bed and slid down to the floor. My knees and legs were weak and rubbery from six months of bed, and I could hardly stand. But stand I did, and I hobbled along, keeping my balance with my hands against the wall, and headed for the kitchen.

I'll spare you the scene. It's impossible not to be sentimental about how happy they were. For a brief moment, the troubles seemed to be over. What we didn't know was that although the rheumatoid arthritis was in the process of a total remission of symptoms, the damage inside was already done.

What the crusty old family doctor had missed was the real cause of the illness. It went undiagnosed for one and a half more years, while a variety of medicines were prescribed for the malaise that now seemed to be constant. I could not gain weight. The swelling and stiffness were gone, but I remained weak. I had no stamina whatever and couldn't walk more than fifty feet without getting out of breath. I missed the second half of the second grade at school and stumbled through the third.

On Monday in the second week of September 1940, I was sitting at my desk in the third row from the door of a dingy fourth-grade classroom. For the first time, my chest had begun to hurt when I breathed. It had been hurting for two weeks, but I hadn't told anybody because I didn't want to go back to the hospital. Now it was worse, and I was having difficulty breathing. I raised my hand and asked the teacher if I could go home. She replied that I would have to wait until lunchtime. Lunchtime was almost an hour away. By the time I finally got away and headed for home, I was dizzy and had trouble walking. The teacher accused me of faking in order to get out of school.

I collapsed on the sidewalk about a block from school, was discovered by one of the high school students who played football in a field by the sidewalk, and was carried home.

This time, our family doctor brought his son, who had recently finished an internship in an Atlanta hospital. He examined me thoroughly, looked at my records, and went out in the hallway to confer with his father. I could hear them talking. They said that I was having a heart attack (which was very interesting, medically, given my age), but there was nothing to be done for me. They told my mother and father that there was no hope.

My mother refused to believe it; called Fred Glisson, our minister; and arranged for me to be admitted to the Henrietta Egleston Hospital for Children in Atlanta. When we got there, there was no room in the boys' ward, and they put me on the other side of the bookcases in the girls' ward. Dr. Aram Glorig examined me for about ten minutes and correctly diagnosed the illness: I had had rheumatic fever for two years. The earlier bout with rheumatoid arthritis (which is often associated with rheumatic fever) should have been a sufficient tipoff for the old family doctor. Unfortunately, it wasn't.

Dr. Glorig told my mother that

there wasn't much hope, given the length of time that the disease had gone undiagnosed (why do these people always assume that the patient is out of earshot?), but that they could give me morphine for the pain and they could put me in an oxygen tent to make my breathing easier. I was pumped full of various medicines late into the night.

The next day, I awakened to find a host of girls in white robes, standing around me and singing songs. I thought I was in heaven. I really did. And then a burly nurse flipped up the oxygen tent flap, turned me over, and gave me a shot. I hadn't really made it after all. I learned later that it was a tradition for the girl patients to sing for the kids who were seriously ill. To me, they were angels. They still are.

With the expertise of Dr. Glorig and his staff, and with a boost from my angels, I improved rapidly and became an item of interest for the local medical community. The story of the poke root poultices was met with polite indulgence, and our old family doctor's failure to diagnose the illness was swept under the rug.

Evidently, the rheumatic fever had finally run its course. I spent the next year in bed, with strict orders:

Don't sit up without help.
Don't raise your arms up over your head.
Don't lie on your left side.
Don't lift your legs up.
Don't reach for things, ask for help.
Don't make any sudden movements.
Don't get up and don't get out of bed.
Don't get excited about anything.
Don't try to walk, ever again.

I was told that I would be an invalid for the rest of my life. I had a damaged valve in my heart, a "textbook" murmur (caused by oxygenated blood backflowing through the damaged valve), and a dangerously enlarged left ventricle (the result of overwork as my heart had tried to make up for the backflowing blood). My blood pressure was chronically low; I had no energy reserves. I was literally running on empty.

I was also living on borrowed time. By all rights, I should not have recovered from the rheumatoid arthritis. Moreover, I should not have been able to survive two years of rheumatic fever. Further, having a tonsillectomy, an adenoidectomy, and six teeth pulled was hardly the prescription for keeping rheumatic fever under control (in fact, it assured that the disease would take a firmer hold). Prognoses were updated on a monthly basis. To project further than that was pure guesswork. Our old family doctor went on to other patients, Dr. Glorig and his staff were efficient and kind, and Maybelle's cousin Lou knew what she knew.

I spent the year reading the 1910 edition of the *Encyclopedia Britannica* and making a pest of myself, as I mistook a good memory for erudition.

A year later, in September 1941, I was allowed to take a few tentative steps. By October, I was allowed to stay up for fifteen minutes at a time. By December, I could sit up for almost an hour, but I still had to be carried from room to room. When the Japanese bombed Pearl Harbor, I was lying on the sofa in the living room, reading the Sunday funnies. When I followed my father into the kitchen as he ran to tell my mother the news, it was the longest trek I had made since I started home from school that September day over a year earlier.

I went back to school in September 1942, got a couple of double promotions, and finally finished grammar school in 1944. I lost half a year in 1946 when I spent a year with my father, who by that time was a communications technician for the Civil Aeronautics Administration at the Naval base at Guantánamo Bay, Cuba. I lost a half year of school, but it was worth it. I was again at one of those critical points in my life where everything thereafter would be changed.

By 1946, I had been out of bed for five years. I was fifteen years old, five feet ten inches tall, and weighed eighty-four pounds. I hated those Charles Atlas ads in the back pages of the comic books: I was thirteen pounds skinnier than the guy with the sand in his face. My current orders were:

No walking for over ten minutes without rest.
No fast walking.
No running.

RALPH CARNES AT 5′-10″ 84 POUNDS

No climbing stairs.
No bicycle riding.
No roller-skating.
No baseball.
No football.
No basketball.
No swimming or diving.
No scary books!
No scary movies!!

My physician, an eminent Atlanta cardiologist (now long dead of a heart attack), told me that I should not even sweep a floor, else the movement of my arms might trigger another heart attack. The good news, then, was that I couldn't help with housework. The bad news, of course, was that I couldn't do much else either. He was quite frank. He told me to be brave and face the fact that it was unlikely that I would survive into my forties; and that if I did, I would have to be reconciled to the life of a semi-invalid.

Well, he scared the hell out of me. I retreated as far into my shell as I could. I was three years older than my classmates, but I was the school sissy. The rest of the boys thought I was afraid to play baseball because I was afraid of competition. Not so. I was afraid to play ball because I was convinced that I would drop dead on the spot if I did. I wasn't afraid of mixing it up with the other kids as much as I was afraid of making a morbid spectacle of myself between third base and home plate.

The fact that my reading skills were those of a college junior only made things worse. I was a freak both ways. I was too weak and too scared to play ball, and I was too glib not to be obnoxious to the kids who made fun of me. I used my mind as a weapon. On a good day, I could alienate not only my classmates, but a couple of teachers and the principal as well.

When I reached high school, I dreaded recess time each day because I knew that several of my classmates would make me run a daily gauntlet as they punched my shoulders. It was a game they played, and I had no defense against it. Every day, I would go home with fresh bruises. I hated it, I hated them, and I hated the supercilious wimp I had become.

So when I arrived at the Naval base and my father suggested that I get a checkup from the Navy cardiologist, you can understand my reluctance. I didn't want to hear the bad news again. I had heard it for five years, and all I wanted to do was sink back out of sight. My father goaded me until I went in for a checkup. The doctor was young, bright, and fresh out of a cardiology residency at Johns Hopkins. He gave me the most thorough going-over I had ever had and then told me something I had never heard before. My new orders were:

Get some exercise.
Learn to swim, and swim every day.
Be active; get out of the house.
Take long walks.
Get some sun.
Get a bicycle, learn to ride it, and ride it every day.
Learn to do calisthenics.
Eat more; get off the light diet you're on.
Stop being such a little snot and try to find more constructive ways to get along with your peers.
Come out of that shell and don't get back in it.

That was my first day in Guantánamo. I was scared to death. My father told me that I should give it a try. If I died in six months, at least I would have lived a little. Later that week, he had to return to the States for an operation, and I was alone for the first time in my life. That was when one of the kids decided to take on the new boy. He beat the hell out of me.

I decided to take the doctor's advice.

During the year I spent in Guantánamo, I worked at the corral, learned to ride horses, play baseball and football, dive—first from the diving board at the pool and then from the cliffs that ringed the shoreline—ride motorcycles, and lift weights. I also learned how to box and worked out with both bags every day until I got pretty good at it. The last day I spent in Gtmo, I looked up the kid who had given me a licking a year earlier. I thanked him for the inspiration and then flattened him with one punch.

When I returned to Atlanta in 1947, I had gained almost forty pounds. When I went out on the recess yard at Brown High, some of the old gang came up to give me my licks. The fight that followed didn't last long, and they never bothered me again.

On the day after Thanksgiving 1947, I lost my left eye in a hunting accident. I also lost my hard-won coordination, my stereoscopic depth perception, and the edge that I had gained over illness. I spent a year learning to catch a ball again, this time computing changes in perspective instead of relying on direct depth perception. My stepfather spent months working with me, helping me through the rough spots of adjusting to a changed visual world.

I bought my first barbells, a York 110-pound set, in 1948. Up to that time, I had worked out with everything from truck springs to cast-iron dumbbells, but without much progress. I was determined to become strong and healthy, and I set out on a cautious program, increasing weights and repetitions at about half the rate called for in the courses that came with the weights. I was determined to make progress, but I also wasn't going to take any more chances than I had to. That bedridden kid was still too close for comfort.

Within two years, my military press was up to 160 at a body weight of 160. According to an article in *Strength and Health,* that put me

RALPH AFTER TWO YEARS OF WEIGHT TRAINING: 160 POUNDS AT 5′-10″

among the population's 10 percent of persons who could press their own weight overhead. I couldn't believe it. My arms had grown from ten and a quarter inches to fifteen inches, and my chest had grown from thirty-two inches to forty-two inches. When I graduated from high school in 1950, I had to pay extra for the rented tuxedo fitting: I had a forty-four-inch chest and a twenty-six-inch waist.

I'll always be indebted to Bob Hoffman, and to John Grimek, Steve Stanko, Jack Dellinger, Harry Johnson, and Harry Smith, and all the other guys who propounded the philosophy of strength and health in Hoffman's magazine. None of them knew me, but I was inspired by them to hang in there—especially by Stanko, whose phlebitis kept him in constant pain, but who became an Olympic champion.

In 1952, I decided to get back into high diving. The prosthesis that had replaced my left eye had a startling tendency to come out in the water, so I sealed it over with adhesive tape. My timing was off, and before I could practice enough to get it back, I hit the water at an odd angle and seriously injured a disc in my lower back. That accident almost ended the weight training for good.

It was eight years before I could lift again without pain. But by that time, I was a graduate student at Emory University, working full time, attending classes full time, and spending my weekends doing what all the hip, intellectual philosophy grad students did in 1960: I drank a lot of cheap mountain red, smoked bushels of Mixture 79, and stayed up all night listening to folk singers on the hi-fi. Weight training sort of got lost in the shuffle between booze and smoke, Russell and Whitehead, folksinging and existentialism. There was almost a commitment to poor health, inspired by the mistaken notion that you couldn't be an intellectual and a jock at the same time, and also sustained by a subconscious reconstruction of what we all thought the Bohemian life must have been.

As a consequence, in 1965, when I started taking karate lessons from Takiyuki Mikami, a chief instructor and fifth-degree black belt with the Japan Karate Association, I couldn't do ten sit-ups.

I got into karate for several reasons. I had a young student, Bob McBride, who recommended it as a way to stay in shape and learn something potentially useful at the same time. I also had an old friend and Marine officer, McLowery Elrod, who had used karate to turn a skinny, awkward body into a genuine killer machine. It had its appeals. Besides, I was thirty-four years old, and I had begun to realize that most of my sedentary colleagues in the academic world were through physically by the time they were forty-five. Time to get back into shape! *Kiai!*

I was pretty bad as a *karateka*.

Job changes and attendant relocations made it impossible to go up the promotions ladder in the JKA. I wound up at the University of North Dakota in Grand Forks, teaching philosophy and humanities. The nearest JKA dojo was in Minneapolis, operated by Bob Fusaro, the highest-ranking non-Oriental in the Japan Karate Association. Whenever I had a chance, I went to Minneapolis for several days of training with Bob, then returned to North Dakota to practice alone.

Eventually, I founded the karate club at the University of North Dakota and taught its classes for about two years. I still have the trophy my students gave me when I moved to Chicago.

Roosevelt University is in downtown Chicago, at 430 South Michigan Avenue, right across from the Buckingham fountain and Grant Park. The nearest JKA dojo was miles north and many blocks west. There just wasn't enough time in the week to teach classes, do research, serve on committees, write articles, give papers at scholarly conferences, and get to the dojo three nights a week for the requisite number of workouts. The logistics simply didn't work. Consequently, karate fell by the wayside as I immersed myself in the details of a new job, and receded even further when I found myself appointed Associate Dean in 1971 and Dean of the College of Arts and Sciences in 1972.

I began to look more and more like the other executives I saw walking down Michigan Avenue every morning: paunchy, stooped, harried, and preoccupied. I made a few attempts to get back into shape, but it was not a sustained effort. On my fortieth birthday, I dragged the old York set out of the storage room and tried to do a few squats. I couldn't get one hundred pounds to my shoulders, let alone do squats with it.

I got my karate uniform out of the closet, put it on, and tried to do the fourth kata (a formalized fight sequence used in rank-promotion tests). I moved like an old man. It was nothing short of pitiful. I had allowed myself to get completely out of shape again, this time not because of illness or injury, but because I had adopted the role of the Great American Middle-Management Mensch.

I began a long, cautious climb back up. Don't think I did it without help. This time, my wife Valerie was beginning a weight training program that would enable her to lose seventy-five pounds and would become the basis for our book, *Bodysculpture: Weight Training for Women* (St. Martin's Press, 1981). She'll tell you more about her program in a later chapter.

Valerie and I had learned to work together on our writing and our scholarly papers. It seemed only natural that we learn to combine our talents in working out weight-training programs. We reinforced each other's resolve to stick with our respective exercise routines, and we began a long period of experimentation into the best methods for achieving success.

I began to trim down (I had crept up to a Danish-roll-and-cream-cheese 212), and my strength and endurance began to return. I worked out in my karate uniform and interspersed katas with my lifts. I arbitrarily established a slow pace, resting between sets, and checking my pulse before and after I did specific exercises. I was still cautious, even though I had been told by one of Chicago's leading cardiologists that I had made a completely functional adjustment to the murmur and the enlarged heart. I knew the medical details. I also knew that I'd better take it easy and establish my own pace.

Soon we added a combination bench press/leg press/calf raise machine to our equipment, as well as some additional 25-pound plates. We bought the stuff at the Bodybuilder's Sport Shop in Chicago. Behind the counter was Sergio Oliva, the former Mr. Olympia, who handed me the 25-pound plates as if they were pizza platters. More inspiration, since Sergio was only a few years younger than I was.

It wasn't long before I felt the weights beginning to work their old magic on me. The poundages and repetitions continued to rise, people began to notice the changes, and I began to realize what an idiot I had been. Given my medical history, I was doubly guilty of neglect: The last thing in the world that a cardiac patient needs is to let himself get run down and out of shape. When I'm running on empty, I'm living on borrowed time.

As my development progressed, my spirits rose. The karate exercises had cured the back problem for good. There was no cardiac problem, either. The more I worked out, the stronger I got. The faster I worked out, the more endurance I developed. I watched my diet with the same care that I scheduled my workouts. And I found that the older you get and the less you eat, the more important it is to operate on a truly balanced diet. I found that I was sensitive to changes in sugar and salt intake, and that I was stronger when I ate beef but lost fat faster when I ate chicken or fish.

Valerie and I caught up on the weightlifting and bodybuilding scene by buying all the special-interest magazines, such as Bob Hoffman's *Strength and Health* and *Muscular Development,* Peary Rader's *Iron Man,* Joe Weider's *Muscle Builder,* and Dan Lurie's *Muscle Training.* We also bought up hundreds of back issues of these magazines, dating all the way back to 1931, and did a complete survey of all the claims, counterclaims, exercises, foods, and pieces of equipment that had been advocated by various editors and muscle stars down through the years. At the 1976 Bicentennial Conference of the Popular Culture Association, I gave a lengthy paper and slide show commentary on the history of weight training and bodybuilding in America.

By 1976, Valerie had made herself over completely, I was back in good condition for the first time since 1969, and we were both looking for ways to get out of the academic world. More accurately, we were trying to get up enough nerve to leave tenured professorships and the Dean's position so we could strike out on our own. We finally took the plunge in January 1977; did some consulting for a few months; then formed our own communications company, Words Unlimited, and started to write full time.

VALERIE CARNES AT AN ALL-TIME HIGH OF 185 POUNDS

I don't think we would have had the nerve had we not been given a whole new slant on ourselves through the improvements that weight training made possible.

We joined a health club for the first time in 1977, and we haven't missed over a dozen workouts since then. We've also spent the last three years experimenting with various types of exercise equipment and especially with modern exercise machines, drawing together the compendium of exercises in this book.

We're presently members of Al Phillips' Chicago Health Club, and we hold workshops and consult at the Sports Fitness Institute in Glen Ellyn (a suburb of Chicago), where athletes and ordinary folk come from all over the country for training and injury rehabilitation. Given the limited space in our apartment, it's terrific to have access to the latest equipment available, without having to keep it clean and in order. It makes me look forward to the workouts.

Another reason I look forward to the workouts is that each time I finish a rigorous routine, each time I feel the flush of vitality that comes from a good solid workout, I remember that little boy trapped back there in bed, watching the other kids play. I think about how far I've come since then, and I think about how lucky I've been down through the years since that anonymous young Navy doctor told me to get out and get some exercise. I think about all the other kids who are in the same shape I was in, and I want to tell them all to hang in there, don't let it wear you down, don't stop moving.

I also think about all the reasons that people use for not exercising. You can find every one of them in my story: chronic illness; injury; overwork; laziness; indifference to health; overindulgence; and the feeling that it is too late, that you're too old to get back into shape. I'm an expert on these excuses. I've used them all.

There's another dimension to the story, however: With a little gumption, a little knowledge, a little nerve, and a lot of encouragement, there's practically no limit to what you can accomplish. Had my father not goaded me into seeing the Navy doc-

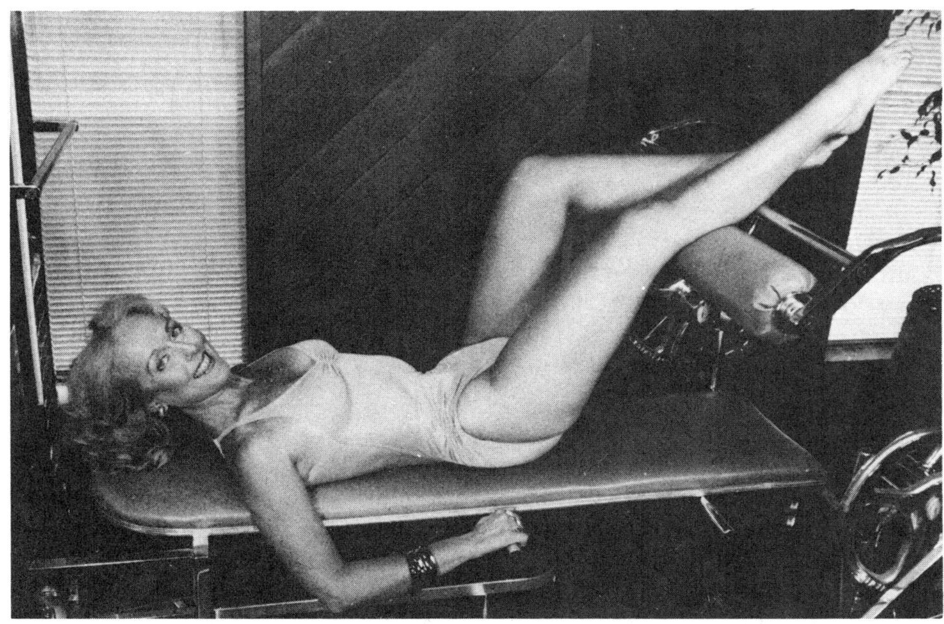

VALERIE AT 110 POUNDS

tor, I wouldn't have known that I could improve my physical condition. Had the doctor not spelled out in the sharpest terms what a wimp I had become, I might not have had the nerve to try. Had that kid who beat me up not made such a fool of me, I might not have become angry enough to go ahead and do what the doctor advised. Had Takiyuki Mikami and Bob Fusaro not been the kind of perfectionists they are, I might not have reaped the benefits of karate training. Had Bob Hoffman not founded *Strength and Health* magazine in 1931, I might never have discovered the extent to which systematic weight training could make me strong and healthy. And had Valerie not shown the perseverance that went into her own training program, I might not have stuck with it myself.

The point is: No matter how far down you may be, you don't have to stay there. If you commit yourself to trying to be strong and healthy, and if you take advantage of the thousands of sources of information that are available to you, and if you have the kind of support from people you love that I had, you'll succeed. You have to start out on your own. Nobody can make the decision but you. Once you're on your way, you'll be surprised how many friends will give you moral support. But the determination has to come from inside.

What are your excuses?

Chronic illness: I have a friend in Houston who had paralytic polio. Today, he's a father, a brilliant young lawyer, and he works out every day. Don't use this excuse around Jack Emmott. He'll straighten you out in a hurry.

The gang I run around with thinks exercise is dumb: Get into another gang. This one won't last. The odds are against them. Ask any actuary.

I don't have time to exercise: From the time I leave the apartment to the time I return, I will have driven to the health club; gone through a solid, fast, heavy workout; showered; gotten dressed; and driven back to the apartment. Elapsed time: two hours. Most people get up at around 7 A.M. and go to bed at around 11 P.M. That's fifteen hours, or one hundred and five hours a week. If you spent six of those one hundred and five hours going to the gym and working out, you'd get more out of the other ninety-nine hours. Whaddya mean, you ain't got time to work out? How much time do you need?

I'm naturally strong and healthy, so I don't need to work out: Well, that's one that I've never used, but I've heard it used by many of the people I used to take to the hospital when I drove an ambulance. Careful: You can't coast on high school and college phys. ed. forever. It usually hits you when you're about thirty-seven or thirty-eight. Now you'll know what to look forward to. And when.

I'm too out of shape to go to a gym. I'll get into shape at home, and then I'll join a health club: OK. That's like the lady who cleaned house before the house cleaners arrived, so they wouldn't see how dirty her house had gotten. If you really have the determination to train at home, more power to you. But you'll find a hell of a lot of psychological support at the gym. Don't forget, most of the people, especially at the modern family fitness centers, are there for precisely the same reasons you are. Besides, you learn from the experienced people at the gym. I did.

I'm too old to start: I didn't start to get back into shape until my fortieth birthday. And I have a heart condition. I didn't join my first health club until I was forty-six years old. I'm in the best shape right now I've ever been in. John Grimek, Mr. America in 1940 and 1941, got back into shape and won the Mr. USA contest against Steve Reeves and all the young guys when he was *forty-one years old!* Roy Hilligen, a Mr. America in the 1950s, recently came out of retirement, got back into shape, and placed among the top five in the Mr. Canada contest. How old is he? Fifty-four! It works for women, too. A fifty-nine-year-old friend recently lost thirty pounds in the women's program at the Sports Fitness Institute, entered the "Family Olympics" at a local county fair, and won four blue ribbons! She's streaked her hair, bought a new wardrobe, and shamed her sixty-three-year-old husband into joining the club. Check out the self-improvement contest winners over the years in *Strength and Health* magazine. A healthy number of them are over sixty. Let's hear it for us old guys!

Weight training is the most versatile of all the forms of exercise. Weightlifters use it to build strength, as do football players, hockey players, and a host of other competitive athletes, both male and female. Male bodybuilders use it to build big muscles, and female bodybuilders use it to trim their body fat all the way down to a few percentage points. Ordinary people can use weight training, whether with barbells or with modern exercise machines, to trim down, shape up, build cardiovascular fitness, and generally condition their bodies.

Weight training is not a panacea. I certainly wouldn't advise anybody with a heart condition to buy a set of weights and start pumping iron without getting a complete medical workup from a competent cardiologist. No person should begin an arduous workout program without first seeing if there is anything wrong inside that vigorous exercise would worsen. Lifting weights won't cure all your ills.

On the other hand, most men and women can benefit tremendously from systematic, progressive exercise. And weight training is the most versatile kind of exercise known to mankind. Further, with the advent of the modern health club, with its variety of scientifically designed exercise machines, getting into shape and staying in shape has become easier than ever before. The efficiency of any exercise is measured on the basis of the amount of good you get out of it as compared to the amount of effort you have to put into it. Weight training, especially if you judiciously combine machine exercises with free weights, is the most efficient way you can exercise.

It's not a panacea, but it's the next best thing to it. That's why all of the modern health clubs and family fitness centers use both free weights and exercise machines, whether they are offering programs in strength building or fat loss. The experts know what works, and the investors who finance the modern clubs know what pays off. The machines, whether Dynacam, Paramount, Iron Company, Universal, Nautilus, Safety Gym, are all mechanical devices for training with weights. All of the top body-building stars now use the ma-

RALPH AND VALERIE TODAY

chines. The top beauty contest winners have been using them for years. It's their secret weapon.

This book is for the average person who wants to build strength and stamina, who wants to trim the fat away, who wants to stay young and vital, who wants to enjoy the activities that being strong and healthy make possible. So when you think about it, it's only fitting that this book should be written by a former fat girl who left the classroom to found a women's programs in a fitness institute, and a former rheumatic fever cripple who founded a university karate club.

We've both been there. And we can show you how to get from there to here.

2

KEEPING YOU ON THE ROAD AND OUT OF THE JUNKYARD

A. GETTING STARTED ON THE RIGHT TRACK

All right, you're out of shape. You're flabby and fat, or flabby and shapeless. Or you're too thin (remember: thin doesn't always equal healthy) and still shapeless and out of shape. Or you're just about the right size, but you *still* puff and pant when you run for a bus or a cab, find climbing stairs a major exertion, and classify lawn mowing or leaf raking as "violent exercise." The question is what to do about it.

The first step is to make an appointment with a doctor. If you're serious about the shape you're in and want to do something about it, you need to see a cardiologist or an internal medicine specialist—preferably one with special training or interest in athletic medicine. "Sportsmedicine," by the way, is the word currently in vogue. You'll need a man or woman with this particular set of credentials because medicine, like any other profession, is a highly specialized field. You shouldn't expect a topflight obstetrician, allergist, or ear/nose/throat specialist to be an expert in athletic medicine. So go to the expert and get yourself some topflight advice before you begin.

Where can you find this kind of doctor? It may take a little research on your part, but you can call your largest local health club or gym, the athletic department of the nearest college or university—even a high school, for that matter. Or find out who is the "official" MD for your city's football or baseball team (in Chicago, for example, a safe bet is Dr. Bates Noble, the noted team doctor for the Chicago Bulls). Also check out sources like Dr. Gabe Mirkin and Marshall Hoffman's *The Sportsmedicine Book* (Little Brown, 1978). The appendices of this book list doctors who are members of the American Orthopaedic Society for Sports Medicine and also the American Academy of Podiatric Sports Medicine, all in a state-by-state alphabetical listing. Another tactic: If you know a friend or relative who is a seasoned athlete and is pleased with his/her doctor, ask for a referral. If you're a member of an athletic association or club, such as the Road Runners Club, or subscribe to a journal for a sports specialty, be on the lookout for MDs who are also members of the group or write for the journal. They're likely to be simpatico souls since they themselves are into the sport. If both you and your physician run, train with weights, jog or play racquetball, chances are you can communicate better about your special problems or sports-related injuries.

Why have a medical checkup before you begin to work out? Yes, we know: Every exercise program gives this warning and you're weary of hearing it. It's all too familiar, rather like the warning on cigarettes or saccharin or diet sodas—and you're ready to ignore it and go ahead. Well, don't!—not unless you've had a thorough physical exam within the last six months and passed with flying colors.

Here's why: Exercise is both safe and beneficial for the great majority of us. But there's always the chance that you have some undiagnosed ailment—high blood pressure, a heart condition, incipient diabetes—that could impose special restrictions on your workout or might require you to limit certain forms of exercise. Not everyone can or should run, jog, swim, or train with weights; some should do one or two of these activities, but not all. So be on the safe side. Get a thorough medical checkup, and *then* head for the gym or track. With your fears about your health all laid to rest, you can concentrate on the exercise itself and consequently get much more out of it.

There's another kind of medical exam you should consider getting in addition to your visit to your cardiologist or internal medicine specialist. A popular mistake, in fact, is to assume that the only exam required is a cardiovascular exam or general diagnostic workup.

If you want to take on a moderately strenuous program, however, an equally important second examination is a structural examination that involves bones, joints, and muscles. Possibly you have, without being aware of it, a structural defect which could limit you in the types of exercise or range of movements you can engage in, according to Dr. Robert Weil, former consulting physician for the Sports Fitness Institute in Glen Ellyn, Illinois. And if this is the case, you might find yourself injury-prone in serious—or minor—ways that keep you from profiting from and enjoying your sport to the fullest. For example, you may have had a disease of the joints such as rheumatoid arthritis, as Ralph did, and find certain movements difficult or impossible to do. Doctors who specialize in this type of examination are usually orthopedists, rheumatologists, or other professionals in fields related to the bones or joints.

Don't assume, then, that because you're healthy and sound from a cardiovascular point of view, you should start on a new sport or activity. Jogging, for example, is a simple activity but has a relatively high injury rate—over 80 percent, according to Dr. Weil. These jogging-related injuries in most cases could have been avoided had the joggers had a structural exam to determine the strength of those stabilizing muscles that lock the knee during exercise, for example.

One more possibility: If you're very much overweight—say fifty pounds or more over "normal" or desirable for your height and bone structure, and have no serious medical problems—you might consider seeking psychological help as you begin your new regimen. If you're a compulsive overeater who eats for emotional rather than physiological satisfaction, the money you invest in analysis might just be the key to permanently solving your eating problem. If the problem isn't serious enough to warrant psychotherapy, you might try some of the dieters' self-help groups like Overeaters Anonymous or Weight Watchers. Often the camaraderie and support furnished by such groups and their members can get you through difficult periods and plateaus, and start you back on the road to being permanently trim and shapely.

That brings us logically to our next step: identifying *your* specific problems. Let's say that you've just received a clean bill of health from your internist or cardiologist. Your orthopedist has pronounced you structurally sound. You're not a compulsive eater, but you have put on, little by little, thirty pounds of extra weight; you huff and puff when you run for the bus or a cab; and your Saturdays are spent in front of the TV instead of on the bike trail or track. How do you identify exactly what your specific problems are so that you can start to work on them?

Let's begin with a tapemeasure, an accurate set of scales, a full-length mirror, notepad and pen. Pick a time when you won't be disturbed, strip down to your birthday suit, and weigh yourself. Record the reading, no matter how grim the news. Next, measure the following places: neck, upper arm, wrist, chest or bust, waist, mid-abdomen, hips, upper thigh, knee, calf, and ankle. Now record all the figures.

Next, take a good long look in the mirror. Like what you see? Are there "wattles" of flabby skin, folds, bulges, a little pot or "beer belly" in front? Are your hips in proportion with the rest of your body, or do you have a shelf sticking out behind you? Women should take special note of the upper-thigh area where "saddlebags" or "pones" often form, and men, of the sides of the waist where "love handles" are prominent.

Remember that the tapemeasure and mirror are often more accurate measurements of "fat" and "lean" than actual weight. A man or woman may be "normal" in weight, yet, because of peculiarities in bone structure or distribution of body fat, look overweight or underweight. Much, too, depends on what percentage of your actual weight is muscle and what percentage is fat. If possible, as part of your medical workup, have a body fat test done with calipers or a water-displacement tank (preferable to the calipers because it's more accurate). These tests can determine fairly accurately exactly what percentage of your weight is muscle and what percentage is fat. Lacking that, however, tapemeasure and a long, hard look in the mirror will tell you quite a bit. Remember that athletes store fat in their muscles and non-athletes under the skin. Which are you, and what kind of fat do you have?

Once you've decided to get—and stay—in shape, you need to set some goals for yourself. It's important that these goals be realistic ones in order that you not end up feeling frustrated and abandon the project of getting into shape altogether. We've all had the experience of trying to go on a crash diet for a week or ten days in a vain effort to lose ten unwanted pounds for a vacation or special party. Often we lose the pounds, all right, if we go on a crash diet that's low-calorie enough. But the weight comes right back the moment we commence eating normally, because the weight loss is 80–85 percent water, muscle tissue, and waste products, and 20 percent or less fat loss. The advantage of exercise, obviously, is that it helps you increase the proportion of fat loss and decrease the amount of muscle tissue loss—which means you lose not only pounds but inches of measurement as well.

So decide on an achievable goal in terms of weight gain or loss. A loss of two to three pounds a week is excellent. A gain of one to one and a half pounds a month for muscle builders is more than satisfactory. If your emphasis is on shaping up and losing inches rather than pounds, let the tapemeasure be your guide. Same applies if you want to add muscle size—it may take several months, even longer, to add a quarter of an inch to your biceps. So much for the myth that weight training can build big, bulging muscles overnight!

If you're happy with your shape and weight, but want to lower your resting pulse rate and blood pressure and generally work toward cardiovascular fitness, make a chart and keep these readings daily or weekly. If you plan to diet at the same time you start an exercise program, get a small diet diary and form the habit of writing down everything you eat, the time and place it was eaten, how you felt when you ate and why. Often, noticing your own eating patterns will help you break bad habits—tasting dishes in preparation for dinner, finishing leftovers after a meal, noshing in front of the TV or in bed at night, putting away a giant box of popcorn at every movie.

What are realistic goals for *you,* and how should they be measured? Here it helps to remember a time in your life when you looked and felt your best. Aim for that set of measurements or weight, and then try to go one better: Firm up and shape even that "ideal" figure. If you have never been happy with the way you look—have always been too fat, thin, shapeless, or flabby—then lose, gain, or build slowly. Let your mirror be your guide. Slow down when you look the way you want to look, and go on a maintenance program. But again, let that goal be a realistic one. Women especially set unrealistic goals for themselves. Women with naturally muscular, "athletic" builds want to look like Twiggy; naturally fleshy types try to emulate Cathy Rigby or Peggy Fleming. Impossible—and frustrating as well. The goal shouldn't be total emaciation, but a trim, shapely body, the ultimate development of your own particular body type. So set a rough goal for yourself—something that is your ideal weight according to an updated height-weight chart, give or take a few pounds—and bring yourself to that figure. *Then* you can decide if you need to gain or lose, shape, build, trim, or tone, and the goal will seem less stringent because you're already so close. (Remember, by the way, that the height-weight charts are based on averages; they tend to run a few pounds heavy for women, a few pounds light for men. Especially if you're small-boned, as Valerie is, you may find charts as much as ten pounds heavy.)

One effective psychological trick is to break down your fitness goals into small, manageable segments. If you're a man, try not to think in terms of gaining three inches on your upper arms and taking four inches off your waist. Instead, set smaller month-by-month goals and enjoy some small victories before the big ones come. If you're a woman, plan to lose no more than eight pounds and perhaps an inch and a half on each of the "crucial measurements"—waist, upper thigh, and hip—rather than thinking about those big, overall goals. And don't be afraid to revise upward or downward when the time comes to go on a maintenance routine. You may find that you look good several pounds or inches away from the initial goal. If you're happy, trim, shapely, and healthy, why be a slave to figures that at best were only theoretical?

Once you have set your goals, it's time to zero in on creating a program to fit your particular needs. This program should be designed specifically for you, with your particular goal in mind. Remember the principle: *To lose both pounds and inches, use lighter weights, more sets, higher repetitions. To gain in size and strength, use heavier weights, fewer sets, fewer repetitions.* Billy Arlen, a former Mr. Texas and a recent Mr. America contender, advises weight trainers never to drop back on weight but to continue adding poundages, even if they can only do one or two reps. While this may be extreme advice, it does remind us that the key to progressive resistance exercise is found in the word *progressive.* To be of value, exercise must not only be consistent, it must also be progressively more demanding on the body. Each workout, you should add a few more reps, or increase the weight, depending on the exercise and on your own goals.

In formulating your program, you'll want to review some of the suggested regimens in chapter four of this book. Once you're past the stretching and limbering phase, you'll want to do a three-day-a-week routine, either on Monday, Wednesday, and Friday or Tuesday, Thursday, and Saturday. Initially, you'll want—and need—those extra days off to give your muscles a chance to recover, although later you might want to do light warmups, jog, or even go for a short run on "off" days. In any case, do plan to take off one day a week and give your body a chance to rest. You'll feel better, progress faster, if you do.

Pacing is an important factor in any program, whether it's a regimen to gain, lose, firm, trim, or build larger and denser muscle. Everyone—male, female, fat, thin, or muscular—can overtrain, whatever your sport and the intensity of your workouts. It's sometimes hard to know when you're overtraining, but Dr. Gabe Mirkin in *The Sportsmedicine Book* (pp. 33–34) lists these symptoms: persistent soreness and stiffness in muscles, joints, and tendons; and a "heavy-legged" or "heavy-armed" feeling. Also look for loss of interest in training, nervousness, depression, and the inability to relax. More extreme physical symptoms are headache, loss of appetite, fatigue and sluggishness, sudden loss of weight too sudden to be explained away by your diet, swollen lymph nodes, and cessation of the menses in women. A high resting pulse in the morning is often a sign of overtraining; so is a sudden tendency to small injuries such as pulls or sprains. The only cure, alas, is to cut back on training days for a week or so until you begin to feel better and the symptoms disappear.

On the other hand, there's the new fitness devotee who takes it slow and easy—too slow and easy, in fact, to make the gains or losses he/she counts on. While overtraining is to be avoided, be sure you're not "undertraining." You should leave your workout with a comfortably tired feeling so that you *need* to sit down, drink a glass of juice or have a light snack before you go on with your day's work. Don't make haste so slowly that you lose the training effect altogether. Remember that Wednesday's workout should be a little more difficult than Monday's if you want to make any progress at all. Don't get stuck in the rut of the same sets, same reps, same amount of weight, and then wonder why you've reached a plateau.

Speaking of plateaus: In even the best and most ambitious of programs, they're inevitable. If you're dieting, as your body first begins to lose weight and after that big, wonderful water loss of five pounds or so, you'll begin to compensate for the fat loss by hanging onto whatever free water remains. So although your measurements continue to drop, the scales may remain constant, and you get depressed with the feeling you're getting nowhere with your program. The only solution: Hang in there, stay with the diet, step up the exercise program a bit, and soon you will be rewarded by a sudden drop of several more pounds. The same goes for a slow gainer who is trying to add a half-inch to his bicep but just can't seem to break a sticking point. Increase poundages if you can, add some protein to your daily diet, and see if you can break the plateau.

Beginning fitness buffs often don't know how marvelously adaptable the human body is. The first few days of a rigorous diet or exercise regimen, we show improvement because our bodies are literally shocked by the change from our normal sedentary habits. We exercise and grow sore—a sign that the muscles are responding to training. Or we restrict our food and grow thinner, meaning that the body has taken notice of the lessened food supply. But when we hit a plateau, it's a sign that the body has adapted to the new treatment. To make further gains or losses, we have to surprise, literally *shock* the body with a new and different routine: different exercises, more weight, a changed combination of sets and reps, new activities (such as running or cycling), a different diet. Even changing the time of day when we work out or changing the order of the exercises can sometimes do the trick. Just a year or so ago, diet experts were studying the relation of mealtimes and weight loss and were suggesting that we breakfast like kings, lunch like princes, and sup like paupers. Now the matter seems more controversial—but it's a scheme worth trying if you need to break a sticking point in your diet. Certainly the time of day when you exercise *can* affect your progress: Barbara Huttner of the Vail Club Health Spa states that "exercising before breakfast squeezes a hormone, called ILA, from the muscles. This regulates blood sugar throughout the day and provides a constant level of energy—no high and low swings so you don't feel tired" *(Harper's Bazaar).*

The biggest danger in exercise routines—as with marriages and small businesses—is that they tend to founder about midpoint. That's when most people get discouraged, frustrated, overconfident, or just too busy and too involved with work and other activities and begin to slough off. There are two (seemingly contradictory) syndromes that contribute to this phenomenon. The first takes place when the new fitness devotee gets discouraged, decides that his/her gains or losses are too small and insignificant, and concludes that "this isn't doing me any good." So he/she begins to backslide, eats a little more or eats some forbidden goody that isn't on the diet, takes a day off, then two days, then a week more. The first thing you know, our fitness buff has become a fitness dropout, and all the good resolutions are forgotten. If he or she goes back on the program, it will take a long, painfully sore week or two to get back to the point where the dropout occurred and progress can begin again.

The opposite situation: Gains or losses are too fast, too dramatic, and the exerciser is lured into thinking that he or she is just about to reach the goal. So there's just one little slice of pie or cake to reward oneself, just one more day off "because I've been so good"—and soon this champion is backsliding, too. Either way, it's a self-defeating syndrome which takes its toll in false starts and re-starts when the shape-up process begins again.

Obviously, everyone gets tired at

some point in any sustained program. It takes effort, will power, dedication, and stamina to crawl out of bed on a cold morning and head for the health club or gym, or to pass up the invitations to the local watering hole at 5 P.M. in favor of hitting the running track or weight room. One effective trick is to reward yourself liberally—not with food or layoff days, but with a new book or record, an evening at the movies, a day spent antiquing or shopping or museum-hopping—whenever you reach some important goal in your program. But the secret is always in steady, sustained effort over a period of months, even years. Don't overtrain, but don't make your training too light or spasmodic either. Keep to a consistent three or four workouts a week, and the scale and tapemeasure will reward you by giving back those magic numbers every time!

B. WHAT YOU'LL NEED IN THE WAY OF EQUIPMENT, CLOTHES, AND ACCESSORIES

One of the great pluses of resistance exercise is that, unlike many other sports—skiing, scuba diving, even racquetball or tennis—it is among the cheapest forms of fitness training available today. It's virtually inflation- and recession-proof. The equipment is inexpensive, long-lasting, easily replaceable, and the clothing and other gear required are simple and sturdy.

First the basics: You'll need shoes, socks, a warmup suit or sweat suit. Women may prefer leotards and tights, or a tank or T-shirt with shorts. Whatever combination you prefer, that's all you need to get yourself started in home or gym workouts.

The warmup suits and sweat suits come in every style, color, and price range imaginable. There are both men's and women's suits available—some of the women's suits are a wonderful velour-like fabric and can double as lounging outfits or casual wear after the workout. The most basic suit, of course, is the standard gray or navy track suit, which sets back your budget by less than twenty dollars in most cities. Often you can get good buys in these suits for even lower prices if you haunt Army-Navy, surplus, and large-volume sporting goods stores. The suit is composed of comfortable sweat pants with elasticized legs, a drawstring waist, and a sweat-shirt-style top, hooded or not as you prefer. The suit washes well, wears forever, and seems to withstand any sort of abuse. The only drawback: The navy and red colors tend to fade, so in the end you may be better off with old reliable gray.

One versatile style of the men's workout suit, manufactured by Head and other large sportswear firms, is the two-piece suit with jacket-style top and pants with elasticized waist. The advantage: You can wear the jacket with a tank or T-shirt underneath and shed one layer as you begin to work up a sweat. Put the jacket back on after you finish the workout minus the now-wet T, and you can head for the juice bar or coffee shop in fine style. These suits are also good choices for running gear on those in-between coolish days in spring and fall when you start the run feeling chilly and end it soaked in sweat. The suits are also a good choice for biking, since they narrow towards the ankle and have zippers to fit snugly over your sock.

Many women who work out in gyms or health clubs prefer leotards. In fact, many gyms such as the Chicago Health Clubs make them mandatory for women members. They're great workout gear: The cotton ones are washable, stain-resistant, stretchy, flexible, and comfortable. There's just one problem: If you're overweight and just beginning to work out, a tight-fitting leotard emphasizes every curve and bulge and makes you feel all the more self-conscious about your extra pounds. One solution: wear a dark, nonshiny, nonstretch leotard with fairly heavy opaque tights (the Danskin dancers' tights are excellent). Top it all with a long, loose T-shirt that falls to about the top of the thigh. If most of your weight is in the rear, get a pair of short, loosely fitting boxer-style shorts and slip them over the leotard. You'll feel a little less exposed and still be comfortable and properly dressed. Plus, there's an extra thrill of accomplishment when you're finally able to shed that extra layer of camouflage.

What kind of leotard is best? That's almost entirely a matter of taste. Danskin makes some excellent standard models, while Capezio's Rudi Gernreich-designed line of dance gear is both innovative in design and colorful. The plain cotton (or cotton-blend leotards) are adequate for any workout, but if you're going in for competition, planning to attend a special event, or just feel like sprucing up for your daily workout, the shiny stretch materials look new and different.

Tights come in two varieties—the stirrup-footed toeless variety that dancers wear and the full-footed tights. If you go for the first kind, the club or gym may require that you wear ballet slippers or socks over them to comply with the usual "no bare feet" code. The full-footed type is usually less trouble for general wear, unless you're after a particular look or want to use the tights for dance class also.

One addition that's functional as well as attractive is a pair of leg warmers—those long, tubelike, knitted "half-stockings" that dancers wear. They're very practical for cold-weather workouts and help protect against muscle pulls if you aren't always careful to warm up adequately. You might also use them, as Valerie does, to help increase perspiration in the lower thighs and calves in order to prevent water retention. And in the winter, in a cold gym or studio, they're lifesavers for the woman who is prone to muscle pulls and other small injuries.

What about shoes? Runners and joggers, of course, are traditionally hypersensitive to shoe-related problems. But weight trainers and body builders also need good shoes, especially for such lifts as the squat and calf raise. You need the firm footing provided by shoes that won't slip but grip the floor and increase your stability in the lift. Trying to do a lift like the calf raise or rise on toes with bare or stockinged feet on a slippery gym floor is asking for trouble. And with both hack and regular squats, you need shoes that provide good heel support so that you don't lose your balance as you come up from the "down" position.

Unlike the sweat suit or leotard, the shoes won't come cheap. You can expect to pay thirty-five to fifty dollars or more for a good pair of sports shoes. But they are probably the single most important investment you can make in your fitness wardrobe. Good shoes can make the difference between comfortable, injury-free workouts and hours of misery or petty injuries.

As for choosing the right shoe, much depends on how you want to use the shoe: for what sports, when and where you want to use it. If you want a unidirectional sport shoe (for running or jogging in a straight line, moving straight ahead), you'll have different needs from the fitness devotee who wants to do weight training, aerobic dancing, and also try tennis, martial arts, and other multidirectional sports that involve varied movements (including side-to-side motions).

Regardless of the type of activity you're engaged in, certain general criteria apply. Dr. Robert Weil of Aurora, Illinois, a former consultant for the Sports Fitness Institute, suggests the following criteria:

1. Choose a name-brand shoe. Look for a recognized brand name, such as the "4-star" or "5-star" shoes that received such good marks in the most recent *Runner's World* survey. Be prepared to spend some cash for one of these name brands, but remember that, with proper care, they will last for a long time.

2. Consider comfort as an important criterion for your shoes. Don't be overpersuaded by elaborate sales pitches or advertising. One shoe may be right for your foot and wrong for your friend's, and vice versa. Individual feet "fit" some brands of shoes and not others. The best way to test a sports shoe is the same way you'd test an everyday walking shoe—by wearing it and walking in it on a carpeted floor. Once you've bought it, Dr. Weil suggests breaking the shoe in by wearing it around your living room or in another carpeted area before you take it out to the gym or running track.

3. If you intend to use the shoe for running or jogging, make sure it has a rigid heel counter (that's the part of the shoe that hits the ground). The rigid counter slows down excessive mobility in the heel and increases stability.

4. The ball of the foot should be padded and flexible, with at least three layers of shock-absorbent material under the arch and the back of the heel. Dr. Weil finds a difference "of ten-fold or more" in the shock-absorbing capacities of a quality shoe and a less expensive brand.

5. Before you buy, test for heel stability. Put the shoe on a counter or other flat surface, heel facing you, toe pointing front. The heel box should be perpendicular to the back of the heel, not tilted in one direction or the other.

6. Check the toe box for proper size. This is especially important if you have a problem with easily bruised toenails. Make sure the toe box is deep enough and round enough not to rub or split the nails.

7. Finally, make sure the shoe you pick matches the history of any foot problems you might have had. For example, if you have a problem with the balls of your feet, get a shoe with extra padding. Wide, flared heels on running shoes are good for stabilizing turning ankles but might easily aggravate a lower back condition. Make sure the shoe works to correct any specific problems that you might have now or have had in the past, and you'll find your workouts enhanced and your progress faster.

Style and color choice are, of course, strictly matters of taste. But if you, like many of us, live in your workout gear during off hours and casual weekends, you might consider buying a shoe that coordinates with your jeans and other weekend gear. You might want to buy two pairs—one more expensive name-brand pair for serious running and workouts, another less expensive "fun" shoe for weekend and home wear.

Socks are another essential part of your fitness wardrobe—they help prevent blisters and provide further insulation and cushioning for the feet. Although most sporting goods stores will push thick athletic socks, experienced runners like Dr. Gabe Mirkin (in *The Sportsmedicine Book*) advocate a thinner sock, to allow room for the foot to move freely inside the shoe. Valerie has also found that a thinner stretch sock works better for her thrice-weekly run—more toe room and hence less danger of bruised toenails.

No discussion of athletic gear is

complete without at least a reference to all the sweat-producing gear that you find in sporting goods stores and in ads in the back of the weight training magazines. Some are legitimate devices; other really are as dangerous as they're reputed to be.

There are several varieties of sweat-producing uniforms: the rubberized "Panther suits" (usually sleeveless and about mid-thigh length) for both men and women; the thinner rubber "sauna suits" sold in ballet shops (usually two pieces, separate top and pants); and the waist and thigh wraps which are often simply pieces of elasticized cloth or rubber to slip around your waist or over the upper thigh.

As with any other kind of equipment, good sense and caution should be your guides with this gear. Yes, it *does* work—but only in a limited sense. It *does not* cause you to "lose weight" in the sense of losing body fat. But it does cause you to lose water through increased perspiration and to that extent can be called effective. *Never* wear a rubber suit or sauna suit on a long run and never outdoors—you could become seriously dehydrated, especially in summertime. Also stay away from this gear if you suffer from any form of heart trouble, high blood pressure, or diabetes.

Where the suits and wraps *are* useful is for the person with a chronic water-retention problem, especially a highly localized one. Valerie for years suffered from severe edema in her lower legs and ankles. She finally found that the problem could be controlled without diuretics as long as she stayed on a low-salt diet, followed an intensive leg routine, and ran or jogged three times a week while using the leg wraps. Her solution: A thin layer of plastic food wrap is wrapped around each leg under her tights, with sauna pants or leg warmers to increase the perspiration.

A word of caution on the waist wraps: The pull-on kinds are so tight that often they can send your blood pressure soaring. Better to find the wrap or buckle variety that fastens with snaps or buckles (Sears Roebuck has a good, inexpensive model) so that you can adjust it to fit your own waist size. With both leg and waist wraps, be sure to check with your doctor before using them on even a limited basis; you don't want to aggravate an undiagnosed medical problem. On the other hand, if you're a diuretic dependent, the sweat gear may allow you to reduce or drop the diuretic dosage and increase natural perspiration.

If you're into serious training and are using very heavy weights, you may also want to consider investing in knee pads or knee guards for protection of the knees during the squats and other heavy lifts. Other essentials: a lifting belt (simply a wide leather belt that circles the waist completely and provides extra support for the back), and a pair of lifting gloves to help you get a better grip on the bar (you'll see old-style weightlifters put chalk on their palms for the same reason—to dry up perspiration and assure that you have a firm grip before you start a lift). The belt is a particularly good idea and an essential investment for anyone, male or female, who is doing serious work on the squat. Women may have trouble finding their correct size (after all, weight training *does* trim down waists in record time!), but a size S or XS from the boys' sporting goods department will usually work. Punch an extra hole or two if necessary.

A gym bag or "workout bag" is almost as essential as the suit and shoes. It's a convenient way of getting your gear together and keeping it all in one place. Adidas, Puma, Head, Nike, and other shoe or suit manufacturers make some excellent bags. Or, if you prefer, get one with your club insignia or logo. Small airline carryalls or totes work well, as do the new nylon Sportsac bags (Valerie is addicted to her purple Sportsac with the matching cosmetic case). The bag should be roomy enough to hold all your workout gear, the clothes you plan to change into, and ideally should have a zip top and a small zippered or lock compartment inside for holding keys, change, your health club card, bus or train tokens, and cosmetics for the women.

If you plan to shower and dress for work or social engagements after you leave the club, you might also want to invest in a lightweight nylon suit bag just large enough for your day's outfit. A shoe or boot compartment is a nice extra and saves schlepping a tote with boots on cold winter days.

In addition to your workout gear, your bag should also contain a large towel and washcloth or sponge; soap (unless it's provided by your club); small travel-size bottles of shampoo, rinse, and conditioner; a small pack of safety pins and a needle and thread for last-minute repairs; and some Band-Aids for cuts, scrapes, or blisters. A small compact blow-dryer is a handy addition, too. Women may also like to add a compact curling wand or a set of travel-size hot rollers. A small comb, brush, cosmetic or shaving kit, and deodorant complete your outfit. Women might also want to carry some extra elastic bands or combs to hold back hair, some napkins or tampons, and extra tights and hose in case of runs and snags.

Women who are just getting into sports or fitness are often dismayed at the damage that hot gyms, running tracks, saunas, and locker rooms can do to hair and makeup. Sure, the main purpose of the workout is to slim, trim, and increase fitness; but you also want to leave the gym looking good for the day's activities.

The solution? If possible, schedule your workout either for the beginning of the day and use your post-workout cleanup as dressing time, or schedule it for the end of the day when you're ready to go home and relax anyway. Start the morning workout with only minimal makeup—a touch of tinted moisturizer and a dab of lip gloss is all you need at 8 A.M. Pull your hair back into a ponytail or a simple knot or braid. Don't try any fancy coifs; instead, concentrate on getting the hair out of your face. A terrycloth headband helps; so do combs, barrettes, and big plastic hairpins. Ten minutes before the workout ends, plug in your curlers or curling iron—they'll be hot and ready to use by the time you've showered and shampooed your hair. While your hair is drying and setting, refresh your makeup, using the tinted moisturizer as a base for a light foundation, blusher, concealer, and a touch of eye shadow. Refresh your lip gloss, add mascara, and you're off and running. The total time from shower stall to the door is about ten minutes; on really busy days, you can cut the time still further by setting and conditioning your hair under a terry turban or pretty scarf while you work out. And if you can develop an attractive braid, knot, roll, or chignon that works for sports-into-daytime-into-evening, you're way ahead of the game.

In general, the more you can minimize the dressing/undressing routine, the more you'll enjoy and profit from your workout—and this goes for men, too. If you go directly from home to the club, it helps to leave home dressed in workout gear, carry your "work clothes," and change in a one-step process as you leave the gym. If you go the club at the end of the day, change out of your business clothes, and after the workout, go home to shower still wearing your sweat suit or leotard. Or carry along a pair of jeans or some other casual clothes to avoid "dressing up" again after the workout. Women especially will find that leotards and tights make great casual clothes for an evening at home or on the town—just take along a fresh one to change into, freshen your hair and makeup, slip on pants or a skirt, and you're ready for the evening. Remember: Locker rooms are crowded at peak hours—morning and evening—and whatever you can do to minimize the dress/ undress/ shower/ shampoo/ change/ routine will make your workout easier and more enjoyable.

A word or two in closing about workout clothing and gear in general: There's a tendency in these inflation-ridden times to relegate workout clothing to the old-shirt-and-cutoffs school of dressing. In other words, we sometimes save money by using our grungiest casual wear for the workout and save our discretionary funds for business and dress wardrobes.

If funds are really tight, it makes sense to go in that direction. But often the sloppiness of your outfit carries over into the workout itself. A simple sweat suit or leotard is inexpensive, attractive, professional-looking, washable, and multifunctional. It also encourages you to make the most of your workout because now you look the part of the athlete you want to be, the fit, trim, lean woman you admire. Often if you're really in the doldrums, a new top, leotard, or pair of shorts can give you a psychological boost. We all seem to run better in red, lift more weight in bright blue or yellow. Don't underestimate the psychological effects of color and style in your workout. It might just pay to retire that grungy old college-track-team shirt and buy a red/jade/purple/orange one before you try to tackle the next bench press or squat!

C. WHAT TO BUY IF YOU PLAN TO WORK OUT AT HOME: FREE WEIGHTS AND OTHER HOME GYM EQUIPMENT

What you should buy depends on two things: how much money you are willing (or able) to spend, and how much room you have to hold the equipment. When Ralph first started weight training at home with free weights (barbells and dumbbells) he bought a 110-pound York barbell set, put the plates on the bar, and rolled it under the bed when it wasn't being used. Later, when he got back into weight training, he added a bench press/leg press/calf raise machine to the original equipment. Today, if we had room, we would set up a complete gym at home, but two-bedroom apartments in Chicago aren't that spacious. Remember, however, that Valerie went from 185 to 110 while working out with only the old York 110-pound set and the bench mentioned above. It was crowded in the spare bedroom, but it was worth it.

At the other end of the spectrum, Hollywood stars such as Clint Eastwood work out every day in their own fully equipped home gyms. An article on Eastwood's gym appeared in *Esquire* magazine a couple of years ago. Ole Clint has the works: a multistation pulley and leg-press machine, and a complete set of weights and accessories.

If you've got only a spare corner, you can still do a lot of work. One end of a garage is sometimes ideal. If you've got a spare room where the temperature can be regulated, you're well on the way.

The cost of equipment varies tremendously, depending on how far you want to go and what kind of iron you want to buy. Let's start at the bottom and work our way up.

Almost all of the major department stores, sporting goods stores, and some of the variety stores now carry weights. Oshman's, Sears, J. C. Penney, Montgomery Ward, and many other national chain stores sell everything from plastic-coated concrete or shot-filled sets all the way up to high-quality Olympic Standard barbells.

The best way to approach the problem of outfitting a home gym is first to spend some time doing research in the body-building magazines on what kind of equipment you need. If you merely want to do a little lifting and get into shape, then the investment is not very great. If you want to add pieces of equipment, then the price goes up, and it becomes more critical how you spend your money.

Look through the advertising pages of *Strength and Health, Muscle*

THE BASIC HOME GYM: bench, barbell, curling bar, dumbbells, iron shoes, assorted barbell plates

Builder, and *Iron Man*. Learn the names of the pieces of equipment, and learn to recognize good, solid, heavy-duty equipment, as opposed to the junk that some of the department stores sell. Ralph once bought a bench-press rack at a nationally based store and had to return it when he found that it wouldn't support a hundred pounds!

When you've armed yourself with the terminology of weight training, when you know all the names of the pieces of equipment, then go down to your local sporting goods store, department store, or bodybuilders' supply shop. Here's what to look for when you buy equipment:

FREE WEIGHTS

Many family fitness centers, health clubs, and gymnasiums have a full range of free weights and accessories as well as the latest exercise machines. However, many of the modern clubs will tell you that you don't need to work out with free weights, that the machines are all you need and do the job better than free weights besides.

Don't believe them. While exercise machine technology is developing at almost the same rate as health club PR, a simple law of exercise physiology will demonstrate them to be wrong. *Exercise is specific to the muscles being exercised.* That means, simply, that a certain movement will develop a certain set of muscles. Other movements will develop other muscles. No machine *precisely* duplicates free weight exercises. Any physical movement involves vastly complex combinations of muscle contractions and nerve transmissions. The more varied your exercise routine, the more muscles you will develop. The more varied your movements for a particular exercise, the more varied the effect will be on the muscles you are trying to develop. If you want to develop heavy lifting capacity for the bench press, do the bench press.

While you're developing such capacity, the more exercises you do to develop the muscles that balance and coordinate these complex movements, the more poundage you will be able to handle.

Further, part of the beauty of free weights is that they force you to find *your* power groove: that coordinated movement that is peculiar to your specific bone, ligament, tendon, fascia, and muscular structure. As you find your power groove, you will find greater strength in the exercise you are doing, and your development will be consequently greater.

Machines, on the other hand, limit the range of movements (although most machine companies will tell you that their products make possible a full range of motion for the first time). [Remember, the range of motion in any exercise movement is a product of at least five things: the mechanical structure of the joint involved; the way that the ligaments are formed around the joint; the condition of the fascia that surrounds and interleaves the muscles that are being worked; the tendons that fasten the muscles to the bones; and, finally, the muscles themselves. Add to this the constricting involvement of blood vessels, nerves, and skin, and you have the major elements that make up any movement.]

Although some machines are designed so that they can be adjusted for height, most of them are designed for the "average" person. The movements possible with any machine are those that are designed into the machine. Most machines began with an attempt to duplicate the motions of free weights while getting rid of the dangers of falling plates, etc. Then machines were built with cams and levers, pulleys and counterbalances, so that it was possible to go through the machine's range of motion while keeping constant tension on the muscle.

The important thing to remember, however, is that it is the range of motion of the limb being exercised that should determine the nature of the exercise, *not* the range of motion of the machine itself. The ideal machine would be one in which the effective range of motion of the limb being exercised is exactly duplicated by the mechanical range of motion of the machine.

Further, since the machine exercises are determined by the machine's range of motion instead of your own, unless your range of motion approximates that of the machine, you will never find your "power groove." You will be forced by the design of the machine to move in whatever direction it calls for. As a consequence, you will not develop the strength that you need in the muscles that help you to balance and coordinate your body through the movement of the particular exercise.

So to say that the machines are "just as good as or better" than free weights is false, not only for practical but for logical reasons as well. Machine leg presses are not the same as squats. The muscles developed doing machine leg presses are not developed in the same way as they would be doing the squat. The same is true for the bench press, and a host of other exercises.

Besides, such claims miss the point. The machines are of great value, *not as a substitute* for free weights, but as the next logical step in developing more and more varied ways to develop the body. There are thousands of things you can do on the machines that are impossible, improbable, or dangerous with free weights. A good health club will have a full range of both kinds of equipment.

BARBELLS AND DUMBBELLS

The basic piece of iron is still the barbell. You'll find three basic types in health clubs: Olympic barbells; fixed-weight, preloaded barbells; and curling barbells.

The Olympic barbell is a plate-loading bar, with rotating tips, used for Olympic weightlifting. Every club that's worth its salt will have at least two Olympic sets, one on a bench press setup and one on squat racks. You'll find the really serious people congregating around these two pieces of equipment. Since the Olympic barbells get so much use at a health club, they show wear fairly quickly, especially along the ends of the bar where the plates slide back and forth when loading. Consequently, the surface of the bar is polished supersmooth, and the plates can slip right off if you become unbalanced during the lift.

If the plates slip off, it can not only hurt anybody standing nearby but can also result in serious injury for the person doing the lift. If you're doing either squats or bench presses, not only is there danger that the plates can fall on you, but you can wrench your back, arms, legs, or chest when you instinctively try to catch the falling bar. Make sure that the collars are on the ends of the bar and that they are tightened properly. It takes a little longer, but it's worth it in the long run.

The second type of barbell is the preloaded, fixed-weight barbell, usually found leaning against a rack designed to hold a dozen of them in varying weights. They are handy for a variety of lifts that do not involve using weights heavier than you can pick up from the floor (or the rack). Weights rarely go higher than 125 pounds.

The third type is the old-fashioned curling bar, which is bent at slight angles along its length in order to prevent tightening of the forearm muscles while doing biceps exercises. Although such bars are still popular, the current trend is back to the straight bar for biceps work. Since the straight bars force the hands to supinate (or turn palms upwards) through the complete range of motion, the biceps achieve a greater contraction than they would with the curling bar. Try the two types of bars and see for yourself.

Most people, incidentally, use the curling bar for triceps exercises. The angle at which the bar is bent makes it fit comfortably in the hands for triceps extension exercises and various forms of the two-arm pullover. Again, try the bar and see for yourself how it feels.

Health club dumbbells are usually one of two types. First, there is the chrome version of the old plate-loading dumbbell, which consists of a knurled bar with thin, chromed plates and collars on the ends. The plates are usually large in diameter but thin in cross section, so that they can be held close to the body.

The other type of dumbbell is also chromed, with a knurled handle, but with plates on each end that are bolted with Allen-head bolts to the handle instead of being held on by collars. These dumbbell plates are usually all the same diameter, regardless of weight, with the consequence that heavier plates are thick, and really heavy plates are too thick to be used with ease. While a 20- or 30-pound dumbbell of this type is comfortable, an 85-pounder is really cumbersome, with a 6-inch-thick chunk of metal on either side of the handle. You have to hold the dumbbells out from the body to keep the ends from hitting your thigh as you bring them up into a curl. Also, there is so much mass out at the ends, the dumbbell becomes a chore to handle in exercises that bring it overhead or to the sides. Not a very practical design, but it looks terrific in the rack!

Chrome plating causes problems, too. The advantages of chrome-plated exercise equipment are chiefly aesthetic, as any health club employee responsible for polishing the stuff will tell you. It looks great, but it collects visible fingerprints, and it flakes off when it's hit too hard (look for the little pile of flakes under the pulley machine sometime). The worst disadvantage, however, is that the chroming makes the handles slippery. Add the combination of sweat and heavy weight, and you're in trouble. There have been many times when we could have handled 20 or 30 more pounds, but the bars or handles simply slid right out of our hands.

Another kind of dumbbell that you probably *won't* find in the modern health club is the old cast-iron, spherical-end dumbbell. They are rare enough to have become collectors' items in some parts of the country. If you run across a pair of fifties, try to buy them.

KETTLEBELLS AND SWINGBELLS

Kettlebells and swingbells are simply variations on the dumbbell, designed to make certain exercises easier and more effective. A kettlebell is made by placing a special handle on a dumbbell bar between the center of the bar and the plates and collars. You hold the kettlebell handle instead of the dumbbell handle. It looks vaguely like the kind of handle that was used on old cast-iron kettles in the nineteenth century. The advantage is that you can change the center of gravity of the dumbbell and thus attack the muscle from a different angle.

Swingbells are made by taking a dumbbell handle, loading a plate or plates in the center of the bar instead of at the ends, and fastening the plates with collars on each side. You then grasp the swingbell at each end of the bar and swing it overhead or between your legs.

IRON SHOES AND ANKLE WEIGHTS

Iron shoes are dumbbells for the feet. They are actually cast-iron "sandals" that fasten to the feet by leather straps. The shoes have holes through which you can slide a dumbbell handle so you can add weight. Slap a few plates and collars on the ends and you're ready to do leg curls, leg extensions, leg presses, and a variety of anterior, posterior, and lateral leg raises. If the straps ever wear out, they can be replaced with leather dog collars.

Former Mr. America (1966) Bob Gajda has invented a dumbbell for the feet (the D.A.R.D.) that requires no straps or collars but relies on cleverly placed handles and a simple lever principle. It can give you as vigorous a workout as you would ever want, as many pro ball players have discovered.

Ankle weights are usually canvas or leather, are filled with shot or sand, and strap or lace around the ankles. They are clean, neat, don't rust, and are very popular with women. They can be bought in weights ranging from a few pounds to ten or twelve pounds apiece. They can be used for any of the exercises ordinarily done with iron shoes.

"CRUSHERS," CABLES, AND SPRINGS

"Crushers," cables, and springs go a long way back in strongman history. We have a treasured 1937 issue of *Strength and Health* magazine that carries ads for "The Giant Crusher Grip: the only exerciser made that positively will develop the crushing muscles of the body," and "Super Cables: 10½ inch strands! FREE set to any man who can stretch them to arms' length! Can you?"

The crushers are like giant nutcrackers, hinged together at one end, with hand grips at the other. There is either a coil spring in the center of the bar against which you squeeze; or the bar itself, instead of being hinged, makes a loop in the center. Whatever the configuration, the point is to bring the ends together and crush that imaginary walnut. The crushers develop the arms, shoulders, and pectorals.

Cables are usually either wide, thick rubber bands or coil springs, strung parallel to each other on metal handles. They are usually used to develop the upper back, posterior and lateral deltoids, and (by hooking one end with the feet) the back, legs, and hips. The cables were a bargain at $3.50 in 1937. Today, they're still a bargain at $8.50.

TORSION BARS AND SPECIAL APPLICATION BARS

These pieces of equipment all involve some variation of a twisting motion, using a bar as the resistance. They work exactly the way the front suspension on a VW microbus works: no springs, just a long bar that resists being twisted when rotational force is applied. Such movements develop strength in the arms, wrists, shoulders, back, and chest, depending on the particular exercise.

WRIST ROLLERS AND NECK HARNESSES

Wrist rollers consist of a rope or chain, fastened on one end to a large wooden dowel. Barbell or dumbbell plates are tied to the other end. The object is to roll the rope around the dowel by bending the wrists. Roll it up, and then roll it back down. Many modern gyms have wrist-rolling machines, which are nothing more than new versions of the old wooden dowel and rope.

The same piece of rope can be used in conjunction with a harness or set of straps that fits around the head or the neck. By moving the head in various motions, you can develop the muscles of the neck. The various neck machines are updates on the same principle, using pulleys and weights instead of ropes and leather.

Sadly enough, the probability of

BOB GAJDA SHOWS VALERIE A TENSION BAND EXERCISE FOR THE SARTORIUS

finding these odd pieces of equipment in a modern health club is remote. Some of them have them, but most of them do not. We include them here to drive home a point:

> *There is no single collection of machines or free weights that will give you everything you need or want in the way of bodypower. The more variety you give your workouts, the better developed you will become.*

Remember, there are "fashionable" exercises in the same way that there are "fashionable" body parts. During the fifties, huge pectorals became a must for any serious bodybuilder. Then there were high, peaking biceps. And monster quadriceps. Right now, Frank Zane has taken bodybuilding away from the excesses of "beefcake" and back to a slimmer, more symmetrical physique.

As long as there are fads in muscle groups, there will be fads in exercises. But size and shape aren't everything. Function and utility are of equal if not greater importance. The more subtle your approach to weight training, the more lasting and satisfying your progress. Don't make the mistake of thinking that you're in shape just because you work out three times a week, bombing and blitzing your pecs and delts.

If you don't believe it, if you want proof and a little fun to boot, here's an experiment you can try. Write to Ira Hurley for one of his Unique Tension Bands. They're little rubber bands, about an inch and a quarter wide, and long enough to put around your wrists, ankles, or knees. To use them, you simply loop one end of the tension band around your hands, feet, or legs and anchor the other end to a stable object. Then, pull against the band. Do all the rotational movements that are ineffective with free weights. Then, get the biggest Neanderthal you can find at the local health club and talk him into going through the entire tension band workout. He'll be skeptical at first, and then he'll learn that his 450-pound squat and 335-pound bench press don't mean a thing when it comes to pronating or supinating his foot or doing terminal flicks (rapid, repetitive movements through the last ten to thirty degrees of a range of motion) during the hip-abduction routine. In plain language, he'll be rotating his foot along a longitudinal axis and then rapidly bringing his leg up from the floor to the side. But he'll be doing it with resistance, which makes the difference.

The next morning, he'll be sore where he didn't even know he had muscles. Which muscles? All of the muscles that give us balance and collateral stability, which coordinate those big slabs of meat that everybody down at the gym spends so much time developing. The usual run of weight-training exercises—whether free weights or machines—neglects them. The old pieces of equipment, such as crushers, cables, and various harnesses; and the new equipment, such as Hurley's Tension Band and Hydra-Gym's rotational movement exerciser, all give you the polish you need to be really in shape, really strong and healthy, with *real* bodypower.

Few people think about the small, obscure, but absolutely vital muscles that provide stabilization to the big, showy, attention-getting slabs. But neglecting these exercises is like spending a fortune on a paint job and nothing on the engine.

BENCHES AND BENCH PRESS BENCHES

First of all, they should be sturdy. Don't bother with light-weight, tubular stuff that's put together with one-eighth-inch or three-sixteenth-inch bolts. You'll outgrow this sort of stuff in a hurry, and the money will be wasted. Besides, it becomes wobbly and rickety quickly, and some of it is downright dangerous.

Also, check the upholstery. The best-grade benches are covered with a heavy mylar or mylar-type material, most of it with a metallic flake underpattern. This material is practically indestructible. The bench we bought in 1972 has been in constant use and still shows no wear at all.

Make sure that the joints are welded and that the welding is of good quality. If there are sharp edges in the weld, it means a sloppy job of finishing, which may indicate a sloppy job of welding under the thick coat of paint.

The pipe or angle iron that is used for bench construction should be heavy enough to support your own weight and the weight of the barbells and dumbbells that you will be using. Better to err in the direction of massiveness than in the direction of flimsiness.

Lastly, lie down on the bench and see if it's comfortable. Some benches are so wide that they cut into the shoulders when you do bench presses and flying exercises. Others are so narrow that they threaten to tip over at any moment. Lie down on the bench and go through the motions of a bench press, using varying widths in your hand grip. If they won't let you try out the equipment, go to another store.

Some companies, such as Rick Adams Products in Healdsburg, California, manufacture bench-press benches with built-in safety stops to keep the weight from coming down on your neck if you can't make that last rep. You will probably be able to find local outlets for equipment with such safety features. It's worth looking into, especially if you work out at home and have no one to spot you in such exercises.

PULLEY MACHINES

Here, the sky's the limit. All the major muscle magazines list ads for pulley machines; you can also find them in the company brochures or catalogs from Universal, Paramount, Nautilus, or Dynacam. The small ones that are advertised in the muscle magazines run anywhere from $50 to $150. You can spend several thousand at the Nautilus plant in Deland, Florida, or at the Dynacam plant on the Gulf Freeway in Houston, Texas.

Again, the thing to look for is quality in manufacturing and reasonable cost. Paramount's multistation gym features several kinds of pulleys, both low and high positions, along with graduated resistance that will enable you to concentrate on perfect form at the point of maximum contraction. The same is true of Nautilus and of some of the Dynacam equipment. Few of the small pulley machines have this feature.

You'll also want to consider where and how you will mount the pulley equipment in your home gym. The Paramount, Nautilus, Universal, and Dynacam pulley machines are free-standing. Most of the smaller units need to be mounted to a wall or to the floor. If you know where the studs are in your walls, and if you have a wooden floor instead of slab, you're in good shape and you can mount away. On the other hand, if you're not good at carpentry or masonry, you may have some difficulties tying the pulley machine down. If it's wobbly or if it is in danger of coming loose during a lift, you may have built yourself a potential accident. Further, some of the smaller pulley units fasten to the ceiling. Be sure you know what kind of load your ceiling will take before you attach a pulley to it and 200 pounds to the cable at the other end. You don't want to bring the house down during the first workout.

SAFETY GYMS AND POWER RACKS

Many of the combination exercise machines have leg-press stations. Few of them have any way that you can use them for squats. Rick Adams' Saf-T-Gym has a squat rack built into the rest of the piece of equipment. Many power racks are available at local sporting goods stores. Most of the power racks and safety equipment feature a system of bars or crosspieces that can be adjusted for height and which will catch the loaded barbell for you if you can't make that last repetition. If you're unsure of your leg strength and you don't have a spotter at home, an adjustable power rack is the best investment you can make. In fact, most of the power racks can also be used as safety bench press racks simply by placing a bench under the rack and setting the crosspieces so that the bar comes almost to the chest in the bottommost position of the lift. This way, you can lift the bar off the pegs with your arms extended, then lower it to within an inch of where you would if you were not using the racks, then set it off on the pegs when you are finished. If you can't make it back up to the pegs on the last repetition, then let the barbell rest on the safety bar or crosspiece and slide out from under it.

LOW-COST MULTISTATION GYM EQUIPMENT

The popularity of multistation, multipurpose gym equipment has led some manufacturers to merchandise smaller versions of their professional gym machines to the general public. The Dynamic DC 115 multistation machine features a bench press station, incline bench slant board, leg press/calf raise, leg extension/leg curl stations, in heavy chrome and mylar, with pin-loaded plates for ease in changing settings. The leg press station is rated up to 450 pounds, the bench press at 250, with a 60-pound leg curl and leg extension station.

Check your local sport shop. There are many modestly priced versions of multistation machines on the market, some locally manufactured. You'll need a room set aside for them, but if you have the space, these relatively low-priced universal-type gyms give your home gym a lot of versatility. They're clean, easy to use, don't require a spotter, and have built-in weights that don't clutter up the room.

At the other end of the scale, if you want to go Clint Eastwood style, Universal, Paramount, Nautilus, Dynamics, Hydra-Gym and Mini-Gym have all you could ever conceivably want in the way of exercise machines. For the average citizen, the best place to buy such equipment would be at a going-out-of-business sale or auction. Occasionally you can find some real bargains in the classified sections of the various muscle magazines. If you've got the cash, then the sky's the limit. A few examples of multistation stuff:

DYNAMICS

The No. 215 Dynamic Gym can be built to order, incorporating a wide variety of stations into a general-purpose weight rack. Typical configurations include a bench press, a leg press, two pulley pulldown stations, a shoulder press, a double pulley for the legs, high and low pulleys for the lats, a chinning bar, and a parallel dip station—all in heavy chrome and mylar, with pin-loaded plates for instant weight changes. The entire setup includes about 2,000 pounds in weight (best put in a room that rests on the slab!), is 96 inches wide, 104 inches long, and 90 inches high.

PARAMOUNT

Another deluxe piece of multistation equipment is the Paramount "Duoflex" gym, which is ultra heavy-duty and features cams for the pulley stations. The typical configuration consists of the following stations: leg extension, leg press, pulley pulldown, military or seated press, leg curl, chinning bar, parallel bar dips, and bench press. One of the unique features of the Paramount machine is the independence of right and left arm and leg movements. In everything but the parallel bar, chinning bar, and pulley pulldown, each arm or leg works separately, thus simulating the action of a dumbbell set instead of a barbell set. The Dynacam machine can be adjusted for either independent or combined movement, while the Paramount machine is for independent movement only.

UNIVERSAL

Universal Gym is the granddaddy of all the multistation gyms, and their products can be found in most colleges and high schools. A typical Universal Gym configuration consists of the following stations: leg press, calf raise, pulley pulldown, low pulleys, military and behind-the-neck press, incline bench/abdominal board, parallel bar dips, chinning bar, and bench press.

NAUTILUS

Nautilus does not manufacture a genuine multistation machine but instead limits its machines to a few related exercises. A good example is the combination leg press/leg extension machine, or the bench-press flying exercise machine. Nautilus got started in the exercise machine business with research on physical therapy machines. Hence, the Nautilus machines tend to be precision-designed pieces of equipment, aimed at specific muscle groups.

HYDRA-GYM

Hydra-Gym of Belton, Texas, produces a multistation gym that is a combination of all their individual machines. Each machine is bolted onto the others to yield a compact, efficient, and comprehensive multistation gym, suitable either for a health club or for a basement home gymnasium.

MINI-GYM

Mini-Gym does not make a multistation gym, but instead offers an extensive line of machines that simulate actual sports movements.

Again, if you want to go the high road, you can either contact the six major companies—Dynamics, Paramount, Universal, Nautilus—Hydra-Gym or Mini-Gym and strike whatever deal is possible; or you can haunt the classified sections of your local newspaper or the bodybuilding magazines and stay on the lookout for bargains. If you have the money, you'll never regret having bought the machines. At the end of the book is an index of manufacturers.

FREE WEIGHTS: HOW MUCH AND WHAT KIND?

The price range in free weights is astonishing. Again, it all depends on how much you want to spend and how far you want to go in outfitting your home gym. Let's start with the basics:

THE BARE-BONES BARBELL

Stores such as Sears Roebuck, J. C. Penney, and Oshman's now sell low-cost, decent-quality barbell sets for under forty dollars. You can start with the "Princess Set" that Foley's in Houston markets for women: It's an 80-pound set, with a barbell that you can take apart if you want to take it with you on vacations, plastic-coated plates that neither scar the floor nor make a lot of noise clanking the way the cast-iron plates do, and a set of two dumbbell handles with appropriate collars.

Oshman's now carries a full-fledged Olympic-type barbell, complete with ball-bearing bar, 45-, 35-, 25-, 10-, and 5-pound plates, and good-grade knurling on the bar for a little over $350. The bar is not chromed, but it is a solid, serviceable outfit.

If you really want to go first class with your bare-bones barbell set, there is the York Olympic-International 310-pound set, which has been the standard for Olympic competition equipment for the last forty years. The set features a 45-pound high-tensile-strength bar with revolving sleeves; two 5-pound, leather-lined collars; two 45-, four 25-, four 10-, four 5-, and two 2½-pound plates. The set was advertised at $298.50 in the April 1980 issue of *Muscular Development* magazine. If you're interested, you should get in touch with the York Barbell Company in York, Pennsylvania. Be sure to ask about shipping charges.

COMBINATION BARBELL SETS WITH ACCESSORIES

York also markets what it calls the "Big Twelve Special," which consists of a 5-foot-long barbell with wrenchless collars; a chrome sleeve for the bar (in the "Aristocrat" set); four each of 1¼-, 2½-, 5-, 10-, and 25-pound plates; a pair of dumbbell bars, with sleeves and collars; a pair of iron boots (for leg exercises); a headstrap (for neck exercises); a wrist roller (a thick wooden rod with a rope that attaches to a plate), a pair of bars for the iron boots; two hand grip exercisers; and four different sets of courses.

The Weider company, in Los Angeles, California, competes with their "Big 16" set, which consists of a barbell, dumbbell, kettle bell, iron boot, headstrap combination, with weights ranging from 120 to 340 pounds.

Other companies have similar sets. Check with your local sporting goods store to see what's available. You'll save shipping costs.

If you decide to buy your free weights locally, and if quality equipment such as York isn't available, here's what you should look for:

1. Make sure that the bar is straight, that the ends have been machined, and that it is not simply a piece of cold-rolled steel that has been lopped off of a longer piece.

2. The bar should have knurling (crisscrossed grooves) on it where your hand grips it. The knurling should be either on the bar or on the sleeve that comes with the bar.

3. Collars will be cast-iron. Make sure that the pins used to tighten the collars turn freely. Sometimes, especially when the equipment is shoddy, the threads aren't cleaned out with a wire brush after they are tapped, resulting in pins that bind—a little thing, but a source of frustration in the middle of a workout when you don't need any distractions.

4. The plates will be either plastic (or vinyl), filled with shot or concrete; or they will be cast-iron. If they are the former, make sure that none of the seams are split in the plastic or vinyl and that the plates of identical markings weigh the same. Sometimes, especially with cheap equipment, the manufacturer doesn't always fill the plates equally. If the plates are cast-iron, make sure that there are no ragged edges along the mold lines. If it's a cheap set, like as not the manufacturer did not go to the trouble of making sure that the burrs were filed off. Also, the iron plates should have a good coat of paint on them. Good paint will chip soon enough. If it's bad, you'll wind up with black flakes all over the floor.

5. If you buy an Olympic-style set, make sure that the ends of the bar where the plates slide on are free in their movement. No Olympic set should be made without bearings. Make sure that they don't bind. Also, if you are buying a used bar, especially a used Olympic bar, be sure that the bar is straight. Olympic bars usually get a lot of heavy use, and the probability of a bend is likely.

6. Count all of the advertised features and make sure they are actually present. Some manufacturers will call their set the "X Number" outfit, and half of the items that comprise the set are made up of collars, wrenches, and sleeves.

SOME MACHINES YOU CAN BUILD YOURSELF

Many bodybuilders have built their own equipment. Mr. America 1974, Ron Thompson, a rarity among competitors, did most of his pre-contest workouts in a home gym. Ron even built a massive leg press machine, reminiscent of the Nautilus cam-loaded combination leg press and leg extension machine.

You probably won't want to be that ambitious at the beginning, and you probably don't know enough about metal work to build a full-fledged "machine" right off the bat. There are, however, a number of items you can build out of wood, if you have some power tools, some room, and a little bit of imagination.

Here's an isometric drawing of a bench press rack that can be built out of stock lumber. The "outriggers" feature holes through which you can position steel bars (the cold-rolled stuff you can buy at any metal yard) so that you won't have to worry about dropping the bar on your neck. Also, there is enough room between upright members of the outriggers to allow you freedom of movement during the exercise.

The bench is 5 feet long and 4 feet 5 inches tall. The outriggers make it 5 feet wide. The bench itself should be covered on the top with a piece of ¾-inch plywood, cut to the dimensions of the bench, and upholstered with naugahyde (or some other durable material) over a layer of foam rubber.

You should assemble the rack with both ½-inch bolts and ⅜-inch wood screws. Get the screws with bolt heads on them. Use the bolts where you can bind two or more boards together; use the screws where you fasten one board to another, but don't come out on the other side of the board.

It's a large piece of furniture, and you should build it so that it can be taken apart. A good idea would be to glue the structural members of the bench itself and the outriggers, while bolting or screwing on the outriggers to the bench. Make sure that you fasten the outriggers securely to the bench, so that you don't get any wobble.

You should also use heavy-duty metal shelf braces where the outriggers join to the bench and at the top inside of the outriggers. This will assure you of a solid piece of equipment.

When you finish building the rack, you'll probably have ideas of your own about additional projects. All you have to do is look through the magazines and adapt the metal equipment to wooden construction. With a few variations, they're pretty much the same. After all, the pur-

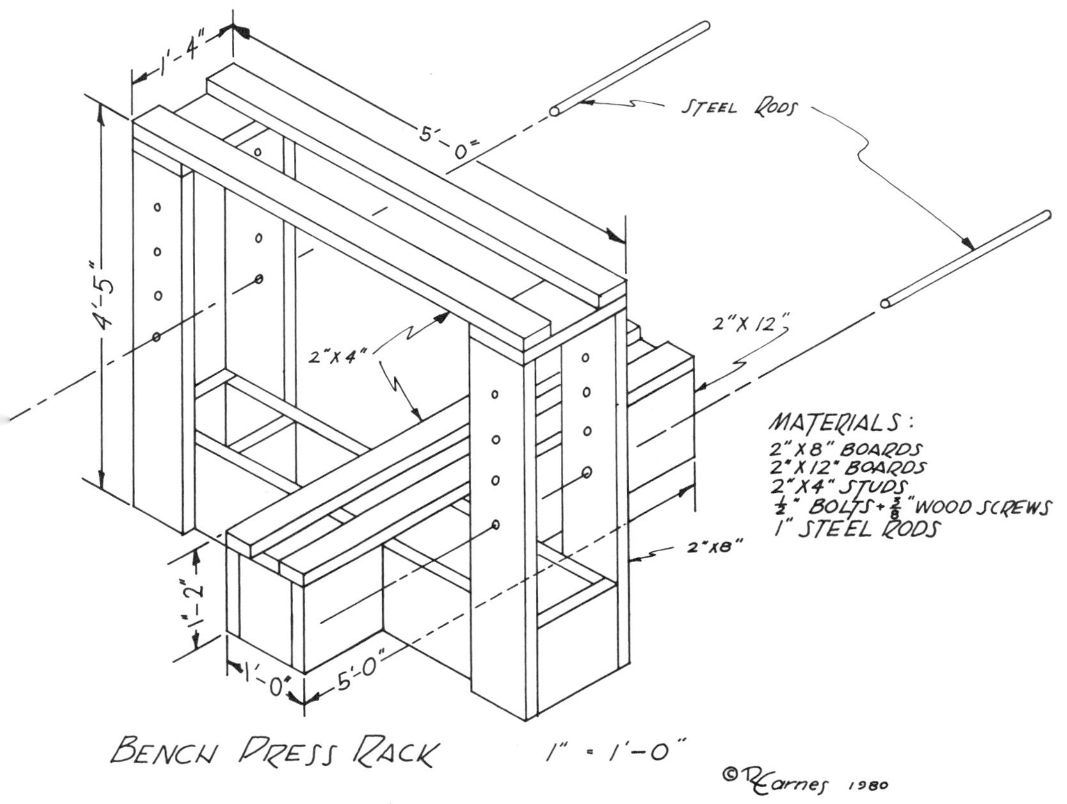

A BENCH PRESS RACK YOU CAN BUILD YOURSELF

pose of all the machines is to allow you to work muscle groups and individual muscles.

Now you're ready to put together your own home gym. You know what kind of weights you need, what kind of machines you can build, and the range of equipment available to you. It's a sizable investment, but it carries with it the convenience of being able to work out at home.

No matter how elaborate your home gym may become, there are distinct advantages to joining a health club. In the next section, we'll explore these advantages, both in terms of cost and in terms of the zillions of fringe benefits that come with having all the modern equipment just sitting there waiting to be used. Unless you have a lot of capital, you can't beat the modern health club when it comes to equipment.

D. THE BODY SHOPS: WHAT YOU NEED TO KNOW ABOUT HEALTH CLUBS, HEALTH SPAS, GYMS AND FAMILY FITNESS CENTERS

Let's get one thing clear to begin with: You do *not* have to join a health club, gym, or spa to stay in shape. That's the first question we're often asked when we lecture to audiences on fitness and related topics. It's a legitimate query for both the new fitness buff and the pro. Advertisers and health club owners—not to mention some of the members themselves—would like to convince everyone that belonging to one of these fitness emporia is the only way to stay in shape. But as you've already learned in an earlier section of this chapter—and as any owner of a $29.95 barbell set will tell you—there are literally hundreds of people who stay fit year in and year out without access to a health club or gym.

So membership is not one of the prerequisites to keeping fit. On the other hand, there are many, many advantages to health club or gym membership. Let's try to define and discuss them so that you can more readily weigh the pros and cons for yourself:

1. First and foremost, being a member of a health club or gym helps to give a formal structure to your workout and thus increases your will power and/or makes it easier to stay on the routine. You get into a pattern of working out each Monday/Wednesday/Friday for an hour before work, on your lunch hour, or immediately after the office closes for the day. Your body and psyche come to depend on the workout. You learn to count on—and relish—that time in the gym, away from the demands of home, family, job, and friends. You get caught up in the rhythm of the club's schedule. Club owners, instructors, and other members look for you and are disappointed when you miss a session. You feel that the other women in your 9 A.M. exercise class (or the men you always spot on the bench press) depend on your support and help. Soon it becomes a matter of real personal pride to make that early-morning or lunchtime workout three days a week.

2. It's a way of assuring that you'll always have the equipment you need when you need it. Let's face it—nothing is cheap these days. And although most exercise equipment is relatively inexpensive (remember: complete 110-pound sets of weights can cost as little as $29.95), the more complicated equipment, especially the machines, will set you back quite a few bills. A set of safety squat racks, a heavy-duty calf raise machine, and a strong, sturdy bench press bench are basics—but few home gym owners can afford them. The more serious you become about your training schedule, the more you'll find that you need that heavy-duty club equipment to supplement your barbell set and slant board. Add to that the extras that your club may provide—sauna, pool, steam room, inhalation room, running track, tennis or racquetball courts—and you'll probably decide that the membership fee is well worth the money. In today's inflationary market, that $25 or so a month is probably the best health and recreation bargain going.

3. It's a way of containing the workout and equipment, of separating all the exercise and exercise gear from the rest of your life. Pathologist and psychiatrist Dr. Edwin Olmstead of the University of North Dakota medical school likes to remind students that scientists have a distinct advantage over liberal arts types: The scientist has a lab smock, a laboratory, test tubes, equipment—all the "props" that spell legitimacy in the natural sciences. The writer or artist, on the other hand, gets up each morning and starts creating his/her universe from nothing on paper or canvas.

The gym for many of us serves the same function as the scientist's lab. It provides the props we need to make us feel like working out and staying in shape. It also keeps the weights, machines, and other equipment distinct from the rest of our lives so that we aren't tempted to work out for one set, go and check on dinner in the oven, come back, do another half-set, load the washer, answer the phone, take a look at the TV soaps, yell at the kids, drink half a soda, and then wander back to finish the set. It's a way to compartmentalize the fitness part of our lives so that we concentrate our energies fully on the workout, *then* go about our business for the day or evening.

4. Being around other people who are working out inspires healthy competition and a kind of camaraderie. The woman who is twelve pounds overweight and self-conscious about appearing in public in a leotard suddenly feels better about herself if she's in an exercise class with other women who are anywhere from five to fifty pounds over *their* limits, and also trying to lose. And the presence of one or two slim, svelte beauties in the class doesn't hurt, either—so much for inspiration! Men, sometimes even faster, develop a sense of fellowship in the gym as they spell one another, spot on the bench press, "work in" between each other's sets, and compare notes on their best and worst lifts.

Now that couples' gyms are the latest thing—a real trend, we think—"his and her" workouts are growing more common. Al Phillips, one of the owners of the Chicago Health and Racquet Clubs, points with pride to the coed gym in the new Oak Lawn Club, while Carl Silvani, owner of the Presidents/First Lady chain in Houston, encourages men and women to mix and mingle in the large, mirrored gym-in-the-round at the Sharpstown shopping center.

There are many reasons why the coed workouts are catching on. It's fun to duplicate one another's routines (we do), using slightly lighter weights for the woman, heavier poundages for the man (women take note: you may well outstrip him on some of the leg lifts!). It can be a fine mixing and meeting ground for singles; for couples, it's an excellent, inexpensive way to work and play together at the same time. You can encourage one another and keep up your partner's morale while you do your own routine. And if it's a family fitness center, including the kiddies will save baby-sitting costs and also start the little ones on a program that will give them a head start for life.

5. Finally, health club membership in a good club puts you in touch with new developments, ideas, and research in the areas of fitness, diet and nutrition, sports medicine, and exercise. You'll learn from talking with other members, instructors, owners, managers, visitors. Brochures, newsletters, diet plans, new routines, articles, announcements of meetings and contests, and other material distributed by the club can help you solve some of your special problems and also keep you informed about the latest trends in fitness research. Some research-oriented clubs, like the Sports Fitness Institute (Glen Ellyn, Illinois), devote a percentage of their time to research and study in the newest areas of fitness—biomechanics, simulative training for specific sports, proper form in various activities. Many sponsor seminars, films, speakers, and special classes for members and guests.

This is an important aspect of health club membership, for, like any branch of knowledge, exercise, nutrition, bariatrics, physiology, and related subjects are constantly growing, changing fields. New discoveries are being made every day. Some are directly applicable to you and your particular interests or problems. Your health club, if it's a good one, will certainly help keep you current and informed on these topics.

Now that you know the potential advantages of health club membership, let's talk about some of the liabilities. Some you already know, thanks to media coverage and the general grapevine: steep fees, inadequate equipment, misleading or false contracts, inconvenient locations and bad hours, indifferent or incompetent instructors. So let's take a hard look at the different kinds of health clubs, gyms, and spas and learn how to screen them, study them, and otherwise test them out. It's the best way to minimize the risks and maximize the benefits of membership.

There are several kinds of "health clubs" (or "spas" or "gyms") currently operating in this country. Probably the most common type is part of a large chain, such as the Chicago Health and Racquet Clubs or the Presidents/First Lady. (Incidentally, both of these chains are affiliated with the IPFA, or International Physical Fitness Association, which has over 2000 affiliates nationally—the advantage being that members of one club can use their membership cards at an affiliate club in another city if they travel or move to another location.)

There are also other large chains such as Nautilus of America, and these often vary greatly from city to city. A chain may have a fine reputation in one city and do badly elsewhere, depending on local management and backers. Check out each club and each chain for its local standing—don't automatically assume that if it's good in Milwaukee, it's also good in Dallas.

If you feel that membership in a large chain is not for you, check out the smaller local exercise studios, such as Jeannie's Gym or Rena's (both in Chicago). Some of these are exclusively for women and often offer good fringe benefits—exercise classes, free massage, dance or yoga lessons, seminars or workshops. These, again, vary greatly—some are excellent, others a complete disaster (remember, you don't need special credentials in many cities to open your own "studio" or exercise class). Consult your local chapter of the IPFA or check with the Better Business Bureau or Chamber of Commerce if you're uncertain about the owner's or instructor's credentials or background.

If "name" programs or classes are your thing, then seek out a studio connected with a big-name exercise program, book, fitness expert, or celebrity. Head for Elizabeth Arden's and get a workout designed by Bonnie Craig, or sign up for a Nicklaus or Lotte Berk class. If you're a star watcher and live on the West Coast, try Ron Fletcher's or Jane Fonda's gym and work out in the company of the best bodies in Hollywood. A plus here: You can usually read all the press first, get a copy of the program or book on which the program is based, thoroughly familiarize yourself with the technique, and *then* call and make an appointment to see the gym.

If weight control and diet are high on your list of priorities, you might consider one of the spas or "fat farms," such as the Greenhouse, Main Chance, the Golden Door, Rancho la Puerta. These places are usually fairly expensive "diet retreats" where you can be assured of rest, relaxation, and a totally calorie-controlled diet to help you whittle away the pounds. Exercise is usually included but is often a secondary concern—although some spas, such as the Ashram, now stress workouts quite as much as diet and nutrition. Check out your choice of places carefully before you sign up. If weight loss in terms of pounds is your primary goal, the "fat farms" may just do the trick. But if shaping up on a long-term basis is more important and you lack the discipline and stamina to duplicate those pre-dawn walks and noontime calisthenics at home, a week or ten days of regimented living will do little more than start you toward reshaping your body and changing its muscle/ fat ratio.

For excellent fitness bargains, check out the local YMCA/YWCA. The facilities differ radically from city to city and town to town, but many of the Y's offer fine facilities for men and women alike, and at bargain prices. City Y's are often sex-segregated, but many suburban centers are "family fitness gyms," with gymnastics, simple dance training and games for the kiddies, exercise and ballet classes for Mom, and a weight room and team sports for Dad. Also, check out your local community center, high school, or junior college for more fitness bargains. Often at the least you'll have a weight room, a pool, perhaps a running track, some classes or exercise groups, and friendly instructors, good hours, and low prices to boot. Don't expect the latest in shiny chrome machines or an Olympic-size pool, but you may find perfectly adequate equipment and training, especially if you're a beginner. And we repeat: Go visit your local Y before you sign on anyone's dotted line. Houston, Texas, boasts a downtown YMCA which is quite literally the standard for the entire city: machines, free weights, powerlifting equipment, running tracks, tennis and racquetball courts. Unfortunately, it's not yet coed, so Astro City women will have to wait for the new additions before they can enjoy this most completely equipped of Y's.

For serious weight trainers, the pro or semipro body building gyms—those of the caliber of Hank's in Houston or Gold's in L.A.—are perhaps the best bet. They tend to be no-nonsense, businesslike places with all the heavy-duty equipment, complete sets of Olympic weights, every kind of machine available, and heavy-duty benches and squat racks in abundance. The membership is usually small in comparison to the mass-market clubs, and the atmosphere serious. One drawback: Some won't allow women (Hank's doesn't, Gold's does). If you're a woman who has been in weight training for some years, however, it doesn't hurt to ask. Many of these places will try to make some accommodation for women who are seriously into the field. But they're not places for beginners, male or female. Wait until you've had at least a year of concentrated work with weights before you attempt this kind of gym.

All right. Let's say that you've now surveyed the local offerings. You've narrowed your choices down to two or three clubs, and you're ready to make a decision. How do you tell the good clubs from the bad or indifferent ones? Here's a brief, rough-and-ready checklist to consult before you make your final decision:

1. First, find out what the IPFA-affiliated clubs are in your city. Go visit the club closest to your home or office. Also, check out some of the smaller, local gyms or exercise studios, the town body-building hangout, the Y, community center, or family fitness center. Ask questions, compare rates, and, if possible, go through on a "guest pass" for a sample workout. (So much the better if you know someone who is actually a member—often he/she can get up to three free passes for you.) The good places will respond positively and openly. They're usually delighted to have a guest (some may charge a minimal fee of $3–$5, especially on weekends) and are pleased to show the facilities to a prospective member. Beware of the clubs that are reluctant to allow guests or refuse outright to let you visit. They may be hiding shabby equipment, inadequate facilities, or a downright "scam" such as "magic machines" (usually passive equipment) or a methodology that doesn't work.

If you get suspicious and have a question about a club's business practices, contracts, fees, liability coverage or insurance, or membership policies, consult the local Better Business Bureau or Chamber of Commerce. They can usually tell you which clubs in the city, if any, have numerous complaints against them. These organizations can't tell you which equipment is superior or which methodology is most effective, but they *can* give you some clues as to which clubs are legitimate and which are simply hustles to transfer money from your pocket into theirs.

2. In these inflationary days, nothing's cheap, and health clubs are no exception. But, as with everything else, it pays to shop around and do some price comparison before you sign on the dotted line. Prices vary so widely according to the section of the country, the facilities, the benefits covered by membership, and the clientele that it's nearly impossible to quote an "average" rate. Big-city membership in most large clubs will run in the neighborhood of $200–$400 for an individual and $450–$600 per couple for the first year. Often there's a sharp drop in price for the second year—the Presidents/First Lady chain (Houston and Dallas, Texas), for example, will drop second-year fees to an annual fee of $55 a year per person plus a small monthly fee. The third year, you pay only the annual renewal fee and no monthly charges. Some body-building gyms charge by the month—Gold's is a flat $45 a month as we go to press. Big-city YMCA's are usually quite expensive because of their downtown locations and the many extras they offer, but women's and "family membership" Y's are often quite modestly priced. Check out bargains like the small but well-equipped Body Shop at the Chicago

Loop YWCA—a real fitness bargain with classes in everything from *tai chi* to weight training.

The small, privately owned gyms differ greatly in price. Some are reasonably priced; others are quite expensive (the owners have to cover that soaring overhead and make a profit in order to stay in business). Much depends on size, location, clientele, and the "extras" offered. In general, not surprisingly, the posher the club and the more famous the celebrities who endorse them, lend their famous names, or even work out there, the more dollars you can expect to part with.

3. Unlike other amenities—clothing, shoes, jewelry, gourmet foods, cars—in health clubs a higher fee doesn't necessarily represent an "investment." Here you frequently don't get what you pay for. Often the no-frills, large-volume club will offer well-maintained machines, competent instruction, and good hours—the basics you need—because it's large enough to maintain these essentials with decently low fees. The serious body-building gym can often keep its membership fee relatively low because there are no saunas, Jacuzzis, inhalation rooms, yoga instructors, masseurs/masseuses to add to the overhead cost. It all depends on what you want, and how you want to use the club.

One helpful way to decide whether you want to go for a no-frills package or take the high road of "luxury" or "prestige" clubs is to visit several examples of each. Then carefully assess your own workout patterns. If you find that you use only the basics—equipment, locker rooms, showers, running track, or pool—then you can have that three-times-weekly workout without going broke. The larger clubs will often have a number of membership "specials" each year. If you keep up with the newspaper and TV ads, read the fine print on the contracts, and do some serious shopping around, you can often pick up some surprisingly good bargains in holiday/"shape-up-for-summer/couples-only, or other special fitness plans. (A word of caution: Just make sure you pay attention to the details of the deal and compare regular and special prices before you buy.)

If, on the other hand, you use the sauna, steam room, whirlpool, or inhalation rooms on a regular basis—or if you need them for rehabilitative or therapeutic reasons—then by all means find a club that offers them along with the membership package. If you're likely to use the club for social or business purposes or simply as a place to relax and mingle with friends, the elegant reception area, members' lounge, juice bar and restaurant will be worth the additional fees to you. Just make sure that you aren't paying for frills or "hidden extras" that you'll never use.

4. The "rights" and "privileges" of membership are touchy subjects for many health club members (and former members). Many people have misconceptions about what a membership is supposed to mean and to what it entitles members. Again, the contract that you sign when you join should be your guide. You can (and should) expect it to be followed to the letter. It should state which facilities the membership that you bought entitles you to use, the hours for both weekdays and weekends, the amount and kind of instruction available, the nutritional or diet counseling that's offered (if any). Remember that the time to ask questions is *before* you sign, not after. If there are special concessions or conditions, make sure you get them in writing. (For example, if you're a woman and want to use equipment on the men's side, make sure your salesperson has the manager put in writing your permission to do so—otherwise, expect a nasty hassle every time you cross over the Line of Demarcation that separates men's from women's sides.)

Also, if special hours, alternate days (for men and women), child-care facilities, access to the running track or racquetball courts, or sauna/steam room are your concerns, have them specified in the contract as well. And if you come into the club on a "special" membership fee or reduced rate, make sure your contract reflects it. If there's a change of management or even of salespersons during the year, you may get charged the full fee. Again, remember: The time to negotiate is *before* you sign, not after. *Get it in writing* if you feel you need or want more equipment, different hours, counseling or instruction over and above your contract. Otherwise, what you sees is what you gets.

Now let's talk about the club's side of the deal for a moment. The club management or instructors can ask you to leave if you are creating a disturbance, annoying other members or instructors, using machinery in a dangerous or destructive way, eating or drinking on the premises, smoking outside the lounge areas or locker rooms, or using facilities not specifically covered in your contract. Most contracts will include some statement on dress and conduct. Some, for example, say that men must wear shirts with arms (no tank tops or bare chests) and that women will wear leotards.

Most clubs also say no bare feet (tennis or running shoes, footed tights, and ballet flats all fill the bill), and some frown on shorts for women unless tights are worn under them. Don't join unless you agree to abide by these rules. Most clubs won't allow women to color their hair in the shower and specify that bathing suits must be worn in saunas or steam rooms. Others specify that you cannot allow children to wander among the weights unattended. These are health and safety precautions, some of which are necessary for insurance purposes. Other regulations are just there to protect both you and the club or its management from undue risk. Comply with them unless they're really foolish or discriminatory. And if you have a legitimate complaint that deals with safety or sanitation, go directly to the management. Don't waste time airing your grievances to the receptionist, instructor, or locker-room attendant—often he or she really can't correct the situation.

5. While we're on the subject of health and safety regulations, remember that it's up to you to take care of yourself, your own body, and any possessions you bring along with you. The clubs have an almost impossible task in trying to safeguard the life, health, safety, sanity, blow dryers, cosmetics, fur coats, and assorted underage children of every member who comes in. They do a surprisingly good job. But don't leave your prized fox jacket, your favorite bracelet, or even a set of hot rollers in plain view of everyone who comes into the locker room and expect them to survive for very long. The locker-room attendant can't spend her entire time watching your gear—she also has to distribute towels, sell juice and shirts or bags, replenish the soap and shampoo, and readjust the temperature of the sauna rooms. Keep your things locked up if you value them.

By the same token, pay attention to those signs in the weight room that warn you that "this equipment is for use by serious weight trainers only." The warning isn't meant to scare you or to intimidate women who have never lifted before. It *is* meant to warn away children, people with severe injuries, and anyone who isn't serious and careful about training. If you're a novice trainer or if you are injury-prone, try to work with a partner—it's a good habit anyway. Certain lifts, such as the bench press or squat, should not be done without a "spotter" (that is, someone to catch the weight if you reach a sticking point and need help in getting the bar back on the rack). It's especially helpful to train with someone when you're just getting started. We're strong advocates of coed gyms for just that reason—women can use husbands, brothers, or friends to get them past sticking points in the heavier lifts.

Whatever the rules in your club, however, the responsibility for your safety is largely yours. That's not as scary as it sounds. Weight training and work on machines are among the safest forms of exercise. Injuries are relatively few and minor in comparison to, say, skiing or Grand Prix racing. But take the responsibility yourself. Learn proper form and make sure you can handle the weight you select. If you want to handle very heavy weights, work up to the poundage—don't start out with more than you can comfortably lift. The Chicago Health and Racquet Clubs post a good reminder: "If you can't set it down easy, *don't pick it up.*" And if you *are* injured, don't automatically assume that the club provides first aid. One large chain refuses to treat even minor cuts or bruises. Sometimes it's a legal or insurance-related problem—the club's legal counsel or insurance firm may have warned management that to treat even a minor injury is inviting litigation from members. Other considerations include local and state laws regarding liability, the club's past history of injury and lawsuits resulting from such accidents, the particular language of the club's contracts and advertising or PR materials, and, often, the persuasion of its owners, managers, and/or investors.

What to do in case of personal injury? Obviously, your first thought is to get treatment, so do notify an instructor or receptionist. Some clubs will have a staff physician or a local MD who is affiliated with the club or accepts its members on a referral basis (the type of arrangement that Bud and Bill Halbert of Houston's Omega Club have with Kelsey-Seyboldt physicians, for example). Even if you're not a regular patient of the referral physician, if it's an emergency, he or she will usually make room for a person referred by the club because of injury or illness.

Once you're cured and contemplating a lawsuit, however, matters can get more complicated. Most clubs are protected against "self-inflicted" injuries—that is, the pulls, sprains, and bruises you get by handling a weight that's too heavy; spraining an ankle or wrist on the tennis or racquetball courts; or running into a machine or free weight. The marginal cases are those that involve faulty or damaged machinery—broken cables, pulleys that pull loose, a dumbbell that comes apart in midair. If you're injured and want to sue, your lawyer must first determine if the injury was actually due to the club's negligence or failure to provide safe conditions for its members. Even if the equipment is damaged or improperly maintained, the club can counter that nowhere in its contract or promotional materials does it promise machinery or free weights in good repair. (Your lawyer, on the other hand, may counter that this is implicit in the contract even if not so stated.) In any case, your best defense is normal caution in using the equipment—and a sharp eye in reading your contract and other materials. The more injuries you can avoid, the smoother your relations with the club will be. Litigation in these cases is usually tedious and the outcome "iffy," at best.

6. On to the equipment now. It varies dramatically from club to club, running the entire gamut from racks upon racks of shiny chrome free weights and chrome-and-vinyl machines all the way to the tiny exercise studios which have only a modest selection of slant boards, ballet barres, and a stationary bike or two.

Don't think that more is necessarily better. The equipment you need depends almost entirely on your personal goals. Machines are not necessary for a serious program. You may actually prefer to work exclusively with free weights. Many serious bodybuilders do; so do many powerlifters. On the other hand, you may want the variety and ease of handling that the machines provide— there are no weights to change, no equipment to lift. And if you're experimenting with a range of exercises, the machines provide you with a ready-made way to vary routines and combinations of exercises.

Still, there are a few caveats. If the club does have machines, make sure they are well maintained, clean, well oiled, and in good working condition. If you're a man, make sure the equipment includes enough weight to allow you to make real progress. If that rack of shiny chrome free weights doesn't include anything over 50 pounds, shop elsewhere for a club to join. And if you're a woman, take a long, hard look at the "ladies' side." Do they shortchange you with flimsy, lightweight equipment such as pink and blue dumbbells that stop at 5 pounds? Does your "side" omit basic equipment such as a leg press machine, squat rack, calf raise bench, or a sturdy bench and bar for the bench press? (Many clubs will omit these from the women's side and tell you, if you ask, that these machines or free weights will "build big muscles.") If you are told this, run, do not walk, straight out the door and find a club with a more enlightened management. In this day of coed gyms and women with impressive credentials in both bodybuilding and powerlifting, there's just no excuse for such patronizing attitudes.

Even if both men's and women's sides are adequately equipped with machines, both should include some free weights. Contrary to some of the promotional hype, you really can't do everything with the machines. Free weights are simply superior for certain exercises. And while a good running track, some stationary bicycles, a treadmill, and an Olympic-size pool are technically "extras," they're standard equipment in so many clubs today that it hardly pays to join a facility without at least one or more of these.

7. As the old saying goes, there are tricks in every trade, and the health club business is no exception. The number of scams and hustles is staggering, given the relative size of the industry and the length of time that fitness has been "big business" in America.

It helps at the outset to keep one thing in mind: The health clubs, gyms, and spas *are* businesses, first and foremost. The subject is health, all right, but like any other business, they must take that subject and make it profitable. The clubs are not helping you get into shape as an act of kindness to you—they can't afford that kind of charity. What the good clubs will do is to make the profit but also offer courteous, legitimate assistance to the man or woman who wants to get and stay in shape. The bad ones, on the other hand, will stop at practically nothing to get your money transferred from your pocket into theirs and will offer little or no assistance on diet, exercise, health, or fitness in return for your investment.

Most of the misleading and/or deceptive statements made at health clubs arise from that initial visit (to them it's a "sales call"). You can minimize the hassle by going to the interview as well informed as possible. Study newspaper ads, make phone calls or inquiries beforehand, ask for material to be mailed to you. The best source of information is often a friend who has been a member of the club for some time and can give you the inside story. Try to go at least once, as anonymously as possible, as a "guest." Go through a complete workout, use the pool or sauna, use the locker rooms and showers. The better clubs will permit up to three free visits for you to make your decision.

When you set the appointment to discuss joining the club, be aware that the person you see, likely as not, will be a salesperson, not the manager, and usually not an instructor. Smaller clubs will sometimes have instructors doubling as sales staff, but the larger the operation, the more likely it is that a trained salesperson will talk to you.

Some of the material presented will be straight informational stuff, but much will be pure hype. There are some common tricks and ploys to watch out for. If you go through a free supervised workout, you may also be asked to take a "fitness test" involving some simple exercises or movements such as walking or running around the track, stepping up and down on a small bench, or doing some basic exercises. Your blood pressure, pulse rate, weight, height, and measurements may be taken. It's a common practice to quote the figures a little on the high side so that you end up with blood pressure or pulse rate a few points higher than they actually are. Don't be surprised if your weight reads five pounds heavier than on your bathroom scales and your measurements are an inch or two over (or under) your own tapemeasurings. The club has to convince you that there's plenty of room for improvement—otherwise, you might not join. Some of the less honest salespeople will actually tell you that "you're in terrible shape," "grossly overweight," or "have just let yourself go" in order to make the sale. They'll shamelessly play on your feelings of guilt for those ten extra pounds or your feelings of inferiority if you're too skinny (male) or too heavy (female). They've learned through experience that there's no one more susceptible to a well-honed sales pitch than an overweight woman or an out-of-shape man who is ashamed of his/her body and the shape it's in.

We observed one southwestern club which hired super-skinny ectomorphic model types as "instructors" (actually salespeople) to weigh and measure the women prospects. The scales were carefully calibrated to weigh everyone exactly eight pounds over actual weight. Then at the end of the sales pitch, the average-weight woman would be told by the super-svelte "instructor" that she was fifteen to twenty-five pounds overweight—and here was Twiggy herself sitting sleek and bulgeless in her leotard to reinforce the woman's guilt and frustration. The really obese women were giggled and snickered at by this bevy of skinnies and made to feel even fatter when they lumbered out in the tight leotards the club provided. Some lost their nerve, paid the money, but never came back. Effective as a sales technique, yes—but we can't give it high marks for contributing to fitness.

So before you go into the club, it's wise to know your exact weight and measurements. Don't be afraid to call the salesperson's bluff if he uses the "what-bad-shape-you're-in" method on you. If you're already running five miles a day or training regularly, speak up. And be firm about goals. Don't be intimidated into using a heavier weight or doing more reps than you can comfortably handle. If you are male, you may find the "instructor" setting the machines on too heavy a weight in order to make you feel weak and inadequate. Don't feel you have to apologize. Reset the machines so that you can do six to eight reps comfortably and go on with your workout. Remember that you're testing the club, not the other way around.

As for pulse rate and blood pressure, unless the staff physician checks these readings, all you have is a lay person's figures. Don't be alarmed if that friendly salesperson diagnoses high blood pressure. But do have yourself checked by a physician—you should do this before starting an exercise program anyway.

If the interview and initial workout go smoothly, and you get to the stage of examining a contract, read both the large and fine print carefully. Better yet, ask to take the contract home for your (and your lawyer's) perusal. The legitimate clubs will say yes; those that have something to hide will pressure you to sign on the spot. Don't be intimidated by the old ploys—"our membership is nearly full" or "we have only a few openings left." Usually this is a simple lie. One way to call their bluff is to smile, say thanks, and ask to be put on their waiting list. You'll usually find that, miracle of miracles, there are still places left two weeks later. If you are trying to get in on a special offer of reduced membership, go when the offer is relatively new so that the ruse of "tomorrow is our last day on these rates" can't be used.

Remember that any special "deals" or considerations about equipment, hours, or facilities not covered in the contract need to be put in writing. Verbal promises don't count once your name is on that piece of paper. If you're promised facilities that are "forthcoming" or will be added during the year you're a member, have the contract revised and initialed by a representative (preferably the owner or manager) to reflect the additions. That way, you've a chance of renegotiating the contract and fee if those promised goodies fail to materialize. We've learned that one favorite trick is selling memberships to minimal facilities at a higher fee than the facilities warrant with a promise of new equipment, saunas, whirlpools, steam rooms, Olympic pools, gymnastics equipment, juice bars, restaurants, classes, massages, and sun rooms—all of which never materialize and are forgotten by the time renewal fees roll around again. Remember: What you see is what you get. Don't fall for the health club's equivalent of pie in the sky.

There are two other membership

scams that are worth mentioning: the pre-opening membership sale and the "lifetime membership" hustle. Both tactics can be perfectly legitimate, or they can be the purest kind of hustle. In the "pre-opening membership" sale, a month or two before opening, the club will sell discounted memberships at savings of up to 25 percent or more off the usual price. If the club is legitimate, both parties profit: The new member gets a considerable savings on his/her first year's fee, and the club gets some ready cash to cover opening costs. But there's nothing to prevent club owners from taking your money and running—to the nearest jet bound for parts unknown. Or they may simply delay the opening date long past the expiration date on your membership card, so that your January-to-January membership is worthless; the club won't be finished until *next* May. One simple way to foil this: Check with the local Better Business Bureau or Chamber of Commerce, find the identities of the owners or managers and the nature of their track record. If they operate a legitimate club already, chances are this one is also on the up-and-up. Another tactic: Insist on *seeing* the facilities. Are they really "under construction" with equipment, weights, machines, and building materials sitting around in crates? Are there workmen busy putting in showers and lockers? Is there a reception desk in the hallway and offices for sales staff and managers? Or is it just a bare storefront with no sign of any construction under way? If it's the latter, tell them you'll be back when the club is closer to completion.

The "lifetime membership" hustle is even more elaborate. With this one, a club sells (sometimes at a discount, sometimes at regular fees) a one-payment-only membership called a "lifetime fee." The question is: *Whose* lifetime? You assume it's yours, but often the fine print interprets it as the club's (or corporation's) "lifetime." That means, in plain language, that you're a member as long as the club or controlling company exists. If, however, the company declares bankruptcy or goes out of business, you are out of luck. Again, a common ploy is to sell "pre-opening memberships," get prospective fitness buffs to plunk down big bucks for what appears to be a discounted membership good for the next twenty-five to thirty years, then take the money and run. There's nothing you can do about it if the contract states that the membership is not transferable or refundable should the club go out of business. Buyer beware!

8. What about fringe benefits? Do all those frills really make one club superior to another? The answer depends on what your values are, how much time you plan to spend at the club, and how you intend to use it.

At one end of the scale are the superposh clubs like the University Club in Houston: a private dining room and lounge for members, meeting rooms, a library, an elaborate reception area and message center, special classes, a running track atop the Galleria roof, tennis and racquetball courts, a pro shop, gift shops, uniformed attendants, a full stock of current magazines and books for browsing, and elegant dressing and locker rooms. At the other end of the scale: the no-frills body-building gym or the local high school or college gym that has little else besides the weights themselves and perhaps a running track.

Are you tied to your office most of the day and therefore limited to a short workout before or after work? Your club will double as your fitness center and also a place to socialize, relax, play sports, even conduct business or take important calls. Just make sure you'll use what you pay for—nothing is more frustrating than knowing you're paying fully half the membership fee for services you haven't the time even to sample.

While we're on the subject of extras: Be careful when you read your contract to notice whether or not access to tennis and racquetball or squash courts is covered in your contract. If there's an additional fee for the use of the courts—and there often is—check on weekday, weekend, day and evening rates. Sometimes there's a real difference. And check on the waiting lists or the time needed to reserve a court. Nothing is more frustrating than to arrive at 10 A.M. Saturday morning, gear in hand and partner in tow, only to be told that the courts are already booked for the day!

9. A special tip for women only: Before you sign, be sure to check out all the equipment you're entitled to use. Often the women's contracts will exclude certain facilities such as courts, pool, or running track. Sometimes, for example, the track is on the men's side and you're kept off that forbidden turf. Don't be dazzled by the array of chrome and vinyl on the men's side unless you can use these pieces, too. Gyms differ widely in terms of policy—some gladly let the women use both sides of the gym. The best, of course, provide genuinely equal facilities for both men and women.

But other clubs, as we've already noted, don't allow women to use the men's equipment and provide inadequate facilities on the women's side. One club manager actually told us, "Oh, well, we just offer a little yoga and dance for the women—they like that sort of thing, you know. They don't *need* weights over ten pounds anyway."

If the gym is reasonably well-equipped and lacks only, say, squat racks and a bench for the press, ask that your contract be amended to include these machines on the men's side. *Get it in writing.*

10. What about instruction? How much or how little do you really need? Again, much of the answer is up to you. If you are a beginning exerciser who needs many questions answered and likes or needs the security of having an instructor present as you train, then pick a place with a good track record for stable staff and knowledgeable people. If you prefer to be left strictly alone while you work out, loathe the idea of someone standing over you telling you how to use a particular machine or free weight, find a club whose policy it is to have instructors on a request-only basis. This usually means that they're available when you need them or during exercise class hours. The rest of the time, you get the privacy you need.

If you're really a rank beginner, it makes sense to combine the two methods. Start with a series of supervised workouts to make sure that you're doing the exercises in correct form; then, when you've mastered the form, start doing your solitary sessions. Even then, it's good to have a knowledgeable coach, instructor, or fitness expert check out your form periodically.

What about expertise? Like everything else in the clubs and gyms, it varies greatly from club to club. The highest levels of expertise are found in the research-oriented clubs or in serious body-building gyms. An added plus, too: Often your fellow members in such places will be veritable gold mines of information about exercise, routines, and form; you can literally learn from hanging around the place and listening. For women, a safe bet is to go the "high road" to the "name" spots, which can afford to hire better help, as a rule, than the large chains.

The chains (such as Nautilus, Presidents/First Lady, Chicago Health Clubs, etc.) are, of course, trying to cut their tremendous overhead and so tend to hire young high school or college-age instructors with a phys. ed. background and little more. Often their only real "training" for the job is a short employees' course or seminar in the machines used in the club. As a result, some of these instructors simply don't know the equipment very well, and many have no special competence in designing programs or routines. You're safest designing your own program from a book such as this one and using the club instructors to help you work on form with specific machines.

If you need and want expert instruction or coaching, ask questions when you come for the interview. What is the instructor's background in physiology and exercise? Has he or she worked in a gym before? Does he/she work out regularly? Doing what? Has he/she trained any serious athletes or contest winners? Entered any competitions? (Incidentally, some of the better gyms will hire bodybuilding contenders or contest winners to spark some interest in the men's gym—Houston's Presidents/First Lady had in one year Billy Arlen, Danny Tobol, and Carlos Blackwell—all contenders in, or former winners of, the annual Mr. Texas competition.)

Another key: Get to know the manager, or at least investigate his/her background. The good ones are usually themselves athletes or former athletes and are knowledgeable about exercise and physiology. The bad ones are simply average hustlers who could care less about fitness or health and are often woefully ignorant about machines, free weights, and other equipment. Watch out for these types—they're out for your buck, not your health.

All said and done, all the scams, hustles, and caveats aside, health club or gym membership is still well worth the investment. In a day and age when food, clothing, real estate, medical costs, entertainment, and transportation are almost prohibitively expensive, the fitness industry—when the setup is legitimate—is still one of the most affordable items in your yearly budget.

Look back at the list of advantages at the beginning of this section for a moment. *If* your club is clean, well equipped, not oversold and therefore not overly crowded, provides help when you need it, privacy and independence when you don't, there's no better bargain in fitness anywhere. A year's membership for yourself and your family/spouse/ friend is one of the best long-term investments in health that you can make—particularly if the next year or several years bring reduced rates or lessened monthly fees with the same benefits covered. While you're saving for that backyard pool or home sauna, why not enjoy them in your club? Why not save your limited apartment or townhouse space for living, dining, and working and use the weights at the club? Just keep your eyes and ears open, read the large *and* the fine print, stay alert to changing and deteriorating conditions, and you'll get the most from that membership fee, whatever it is.

3

THE TOOLS OF THE TRADE: MODERN EXERCISE MACHINES: *WHAT THEY ARE AND HOW THEY WORK*

Index to the Machines

The Machines Themselves

In this section, we're going to describe the machines most commonly stocked by modern health clubs and how they can be used for maximum results. We'll divide the machines according to the exercises performed on them and the muscles that are worked. Then we'll point out differences between machines from various manufacturers, so that you can be on familiar ground whatever brand of machines your health club has. We'll also tell you how to avoid injuries.

We'll start with neck developer machines and proceed all the way down to calf developers. We'll identify the muscles that are being worked by the particular machines, and we'll also point out the range of motion required for specific exercises. In Chapter Four, we'll discuss the major and minor muscle groups in greater detail, so that you will know exactly what's going on when you do the exercises. When we cross-reference the exercises in Chapter Four, we'll refer you back to the descriptions of the machines given in this section.

NECK MACHINES

Dynacam's No. 433 DC Neck Developer is typical of neck-developing machines. It stands about 4 feet high, is made of chromed metal, has a seat in the middle and hand grips with which to steady yourself. A metal rod runs from a pivot point at one end to a cam at the other. A pad is located at midpoint on the rod. A cable is attached to the cam at one end and to a stack of plates at the other. To use the machine, sit on the seat so that the front, back, or either side of your head rests against the pad. Then lean against the pad until you cause the rod to pivot (and the cam to rotate). The amount of effort required is determined by how many plates you are lifting with the movement. The machine is "pin-loaded," which means that the weight can be varied merely by moving a pin up or down the stack of plates.

Nautilus also has a neck developer, which is designed so that you literally climb *into* the machine. It has handle grips for the hands, and by pivoting on the seat 360 degrees, you can work the neck muscles from any angle desired. The weight is in the form of pin-loaded plates and can be varied over a wide range of poundage.

Most other neck machines are similar in design, some utilizing eccentric cams in order to alter the relative weight at different points in the range of motion, and others using simple levers that are in turn attached to weights. The important thing to remember is that not every machine "fits" your body. Some are adjustable, and some are not. Don't strain your neck trying to fit into the range of motion of the machine if its range of motion doesn't fit yours.

Also, don't make the mistake of using too much weight the first time around. Most people neglect their neck development. The old-timers used the neck harness mentioned in the preceding section, or they did such exercises as the wrestler's bridge. If you haven't worked your neck in a long time, don't overdo it. Neck soreness is unlike soreness in any other part of the body, as anybody who has ever awakened to find a "crick" in his or her neck can testify.

BACKWARD NECK MOVEMENTS ON A NAUTILUS NECK MACHINE

TRAPEZIUS MACHINES

The trapezius muscles ("traps," for short) insert at the back of the skull, at the shoulder blades, and along the spinal column all the way down to a point just above the small of the back. Trapezius machines replace the old shoulder shrug movements with a barbell or dumbbells.

Nautilus has a machine specifically designed for traps development. It has a seat, which faces a stack of plates and over which is a padded horizontal bar that pivots at the frame of the machine and which is attached to the pin-loaded plates by a chain. An eccentric cam distributes relative resistance through the range of motion.

To use the machine, sit down facing the crossbar. Place your forearms under the bar against the pads, bend the elbows, and lift up with the traps alone. Don't try to help yourself by using the biceps or the shoulder muscles. Isolate the traps and do the movement with them alone, so far as it's possible. You'll find that you don't need much weight with the Nautilus machine to give yourself a good workout. Be careful not to strain your elbows when you make the lift.

You will also get some traps training with the Nautilus deltoid ma-

SHOULDER SHRUGS: PARAMOUNT LOW PULLEY STATION

SHOULDER SHRUGS: PARAMOUNT BENCH PRESS STATION

chine. It is impossible to isolate the deltoids completely, and when you make the movement, you will involve the traps to a certain degree. Dynacam also makes a deltoid machine in which the movement is similar to that in the Nautilus machine. The traps involvement is also similar.

You will receive further traps work with the Dynacam 435 DC vertical shoulder machine. It simulates the barbell military press and involves the traps accordingly at the very top of the lift.

Paramount, Universal and Dynacam's multi-station machines often feature low pulley stations that can be used effectively for traps work. A bar is usually attached to the low pulley cable by an "s" hook and a chain. You can adjust the distance of the bar from the floor by shifting the "s" hook from one link of the chain to another.

Stand facing the machine, with the feet about shoulder width apart. Grasp the bar with both hands, and stand with the back slightly arched to avoid injury. Most of these stations are pin-loaded, so you will have to select a weight that is appropriate for you. When you are standing in the starting position, the cable should be tight, and the plates should be about two inches off the stack. This will assure constant tension throughout the lift.

Shrug the shoulders as high as you can, then slowly let the bar back down to the starting position. Your arms should be straight throughout the lift. Don't bend the elbows. If you do, the arms will do some of the work. You can make the movement straight up, or you can rotate the shoulders. If you do the latter and you hear popping noises in your shoulders, slack off. You may injure yourself.

The Paramount multipress machine, which simulates military presses, behind-the-neck presses, and a variety of other upper-body movements, will also give your traps a workout at the top of the overhead pressing movements. Try them all, and you'll find that each works the traps from a slightly different angle. If your gym has them all (it probably doesn't), you might make the journey through them one after the other for a supersetting workout.

Finally, Dynacam, Universal, Paramount, and Nautilus all have machines that are used for other purposes (for example, the Dynacam bench press, the Nautilus calf raise, the Paramount bench press, and the Universal bench press), which can be used for a traps workout. Just grasp the bar that is normally used for bench pressing (or the harness that connects to the plates on the Nautilus calf raise machine) and do the movement that you would ordinarily do with a barbell. Depending on which machine you are working with, you may find it easier and more natural to face away from the machine while you do the exercise. Again, try it and see how you fit into the machine's range of motion.

SHOULDER MACHINES

Let's divide the development of the shoulders or deltoids into three parts: anterior or front deltoids, lateral or side deltoids, and posterior or back deltoids. Each head of the deltoid muscles has its own motion and needs a different movement to work it to the fullest.

Lateral Deltoid Machines

The most common shoulder machine works the lateral deltoids. Dynacam has one, and so does Nautilus. They are quite similar in design and seating position, so we can describe their use together. Nautilus combines their lateral-deltoid machine with a seated press, so that you can work out the lateral and anterior deltoids with a single machine.

The Dynacam and Nautilus lateral-deltoid machines feature a seat that is tilted back at a shallow angle, so that you are leaning back against the backrest. Both machines have a curved bar on each side, on which there is a padded area and a handle for the hands to grip. The elbows are bent at right angles, and the palms are facing each other at the beginning of the lift.

The movement is in an arc to the sides and ends with the upper arms slightly above a line that is parallel to the floor. Some coaches recommend that you not raise the arms higher than parallel to the floor. Others recommend with equal force that you should bring the arms as high as possible.

In either case, you should strive to do the movement with the deltoids alone. Don't help them with flexion of the arms. If you do, you will simply deprive the deltoids of the work that they would ordinarily receive.

LATERAL RAISE: NAUTILUS DOUBLE SHOULDER MACHINE

As to which set of coaches is right, our advice is to try the movement both ways and decide for yourself which of the two results in greater development for the shoulders.

This machine is a good example of the importance of matching the range of motion of the machine with the range of motion of the body part being worked. In Ralph's case, the Nautilus machine seems awkward, while Dynacam's machine is a perfect fit. On the other hand, Dynacam's seated press machine feels awkward, while Nautilus' is just right.

Anterior Deltoid Machines

For the development of the anterior or front deltoids, you have a wide range of choices. Nautilus has a seated bench press-movement machine, which is combined with what is usually called a "pec deck": a machine that allows you to bring your outstretched arms from the side to the front, thus working the pectorals. The Nautilus bench press machine features two bars that rise vertically from pivot points at the bottom of the machine.

The bars are gripped with the hands in a position that is 90 degrees from the usual bench press hand position. With the Nautilus machine, the palms are facing each other. The rest of the movement is similar to the regular bench press: Push the bars away from you, and then let them back down to the chest.

Dynacam has a similar machine, the 307 DC, in which the seating position is slightly more inclined. Both Nautilus and Dynacam machines are pin-loaded for easy use. In addition to the 307 DC, Dynacam also has the standard bench press machine that is usually found in multistation gym sets. In it, you lie on your back in exactly the same position as the regular free weight bench press and grasp the bars on either side to perform the movement. Paramount has a similar machine, as does Universal. Some of them feature separate bars and a stack of plates for each arm, which can be linked together for a simulated barbell bench press and separated for a simulated dumbbell bench press.

The value of all of the bench press machines in the development of the anterior deltoids is the same. In the bench press, the beginning and the middle of the movement works the anterior deltoids. When the bar is closest to the chest, the anterior deltoids are brought most fully into play. As the bar(s) rises, the pectorals take over the bulk of the weight, then, as the movement is completed and the bar(s) is farthest from the chest, the arms finish the movement.

If you are used to free weights, you may find it awkward at first that the bar is at the chest at the beginning of the lift when you use the machines. Only with floor-type press machines such as Dynacam's No. 107 and Paramount's Multi Press model 3250 do you simulate the exact movement of the free-weight bench press. With these machines, the bar is overhead as you lie on your back on a bench. By rotating the bar in your hands, you pull it off the pegs that hold it in the "up" position. The bar is attached to runners that fit into grooves on the sides of the machines, or it is attached by a chain to a stack of plates.

In either case, the movement starts with the arms extended and then proceeds downward towards the chest. However, the bar moves in an exactly vertical path, and there is none of the usual deviation from the vertical plane that you would ordinarily have if you were lifting free weights. Consequently, unless your own "power groove" follows a precise vertical plane, the two machines may seem awkward. Try them and see.

UPPER BACK EXERCISE ON A PEC DECK

Posterior Deltoid Machines

There is also a variety of choices for the development of the posterior deltoids. With free weights, you are usually limited to bending at the waist and lifting dumbbells out to the sides in an arc that is perpendicular to the floor. Consequently, there is always a danger of straining the lower back. Because of this danger, you are also limited in the amount of weight you can lift in the movement.

Nautilus, Dynacam, Paramount, and Universal all have machines with which you can work the posterior deltoids. Nautilus, Dynacam, and Paramount have "pec decks" that can double as simulators for the bent-over rowing motion. Sit in them backwards, and you'll work the posterior deltoids. Nautilus builds a machine specifically for this purpose.

All of the major manufacturers offer simulations of the bent-over rowing motion in their bench press machines. Instead of lying on the bench, stand over it or on it and bend over as you would for a regular free weight bent-over row. Although this is a popular lift, we can't overstress its dangers. When bowed, the back is in its weakest muscular and skeletal configuration. Bent-over rowing and the stiff-legged dead-weight lift both place the back in a bowed position. Both are among the most dangerous of all exercises.

Far better to use the pec decks or

the machines that are specifically designed for developing the posterior deltoids and the upper back. To use the pec deck for back work, simply sit in the seat 180 degrees from the way you would sit in it to do pectoral exercises. Position your arms on a horizontal plane, with the elbows bent. Put the backs of the upper arms against the pads you would ordinarily have your forearms against for pec work. Push back with the arms as far as your range of motion lets you push. You'll feel a tightening of the upper-back muscles and the posterior deltoids if you do the movement properly.

The Nautilus upper back machine is easy to use, and the seat is adjustable for torso length. The advantage of the upright machines is that they preclude the danger of lower-back injury, while at the same time allowing a good workout of the area between the shoulder blades and to the back of the shoulders.

Again, all of the machines are pin-loaded for easy use. You will have to try them for yourself to see if they "fit."

LATISSIMUS DORSI MACHINES

The latissimus dorsi muscles ("lats," for short) sweep down on the sides from under the arms to the sides of the waist. They are the muscles that give men that sought-after "V" shape. Most of the exercises for the lats are done with pulleys or with chinning bars. There are a few machines that work the lats as they also work other muscles. Let's go over them all.

Pullover Machines

The Dynacam 304, the Paramount 2110, and the Nautilus pullover are all machines designed for bent-arm pullover movements. The machines work the latissimus muscles to an extent, as well as the pectorals. In short, they work the same muscles that the free weight bent-arm pull-

PULLOVERS: NAUTILUS PULLOVER/TORSO ARM MACHINE (STARTING POSITION)

PULLOVERS: NAUTILUS MACHINE (FINAL POSITION)

over works. Depending on your own lever system, you may or may not be able to use the pullover machines to any advantage. While we've known people who swear by them, neither of the three work for us. The Nautilus is too big for Valerie, the Dynacam makes Ralph's shoulders pop, and the Paramount feels strange to both of us.

This is not specifically a criticism of the machines, it's a description of the disparity between our lever systems and those of the machines. Try them all, and you may match up.

Nautilus makes a torso machine that works the lats in two different ways. There is an overhead pulley bar that can be pulled either to the chest or behind the neck, and there are padded bars to either side that can be brought downward in an arc by the arms. To use the padded bars, place the arms straight up, elbows pointing to the ceiling, with the forearms crossed over the head. Bring the arms down in an arc, with a spot just above the elbow being the point of contact. Don't cheat, but use a weight that will allow you to go through the complete range of motion until you are all the way down at the sides. You'll need to use the safety belt to strap yourself into the machine, otherwise you will lift yourself up off the seat during the movements.

Chinning Bars

The oldest and most familiar way to work the latissimus muscles is by chinning. This is done by grasping a sturdily mounted overhead bar with the hands (either palms away from you or palms facing you) and pulling yourself up until your chin is level with the bar.

A variation is the "behind-the-neck chin," which is not a chin at all but a "neck." In this case, pull yourself up until your head is in front of the bar and the bar can be felt at the back of the neck.

By varying the way you grasp the bar and by pulling yourself up either in front of the bar or behind it, you can work the lats from different an-

LATISSIMUS EXERCISE: NAUTILUS BEHIND NECK/TORSO ARM MACHINE

gles. Remember, each person has his or her own set of muscles and levers. Try the various ways of doing the movement and see for yourself which is the most effective for you.

Overhead Pulley and "Cable" Machines

Since many people are not strong enough to pull their body weight up to the level of an overhead bar, pulley machines offer a way to do lat exercises with less than body weight. Most machines are pin-loaded and have a range from 2½–200 pounds.

The cables of such machines range from actual cables (Dynacam, Paramount, and Universal) to motorcycle-type chains (Nautilus). "Cable" is thus a generic term for a variety of machines which feature "pulldown" movements.

Some of the pulley machines use circular pulleys; others, such as Nautilus and Paramount, use eccentric cams or variable-groove pulleys in order to distribute weight over the full range of motion. The Paramount multistation gym is especially good in this respect: The cable rides down to a smaller-diameter pulley groove during the last 15 or 20 degrees of the range of motion, thus making it possible for you to complete the movement in strict form.

PULLDOWN BEHIND THE NECK: NAUTILUS BEHIND NECK/TORSO ARM MACHINE

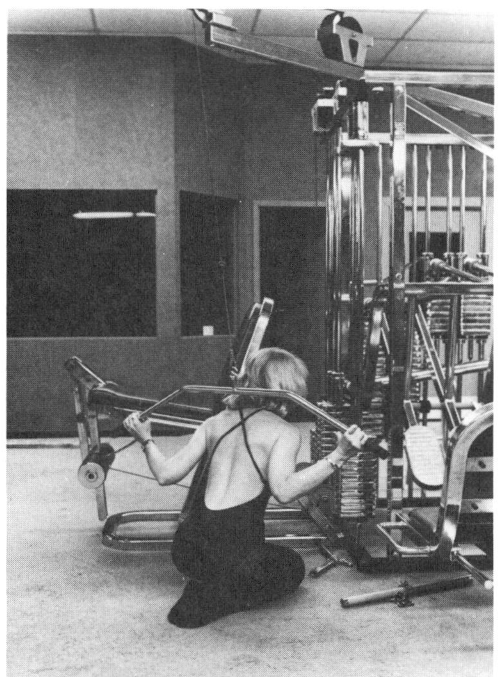

PULLDOWN BEHIND THE NECK: PARAMOUNT OVERHEAD PULLEY STATION

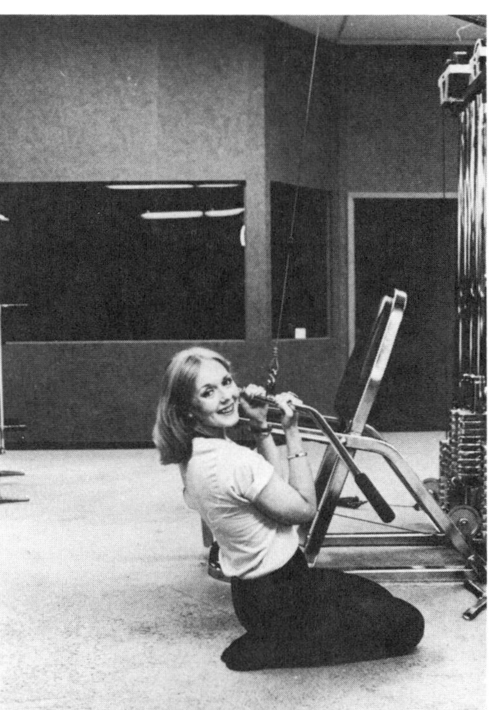

PULLDOWN TO THE CHEST: PARAMOUNT OVERHEAD PULLEY STATION

PULLDOWN TO THE CHEST: NAUTILUS PULLOVER/TORSO ARM MACHINE

Opinions vary about the position of the body during overhead pulley work. Some instructors will insist that if you don't sit on the floor with your feet in front of you, the pectorals will do all the work (this is obviously false, since the pectorals could not possibly do *all* the work of moving the arms from an overhead position to the sides of the body). Other instructors insist with equal vehemence that you should lean forward while resting on your knees, so that the bar can be brought down behind the neck.

We suggest that you try a variety of hand grips and hand positions (close grip, narrow grip, palms facing you, palms facing away) and a variety of body positions (seated with the legs in front of you; seated, with the legs crossed and brought up under the buttocks; legs bent at the knees, with the weight of your body distributed against the backs of the calves). Also, try pulling the bar down to the top of the chest, then to the back of the neck. You'll learn quickly which variation does the most for you.

Low Pulleys

Some machines have a low pulley position, so that you can perform movements for the lower lats. On these

SEATED ROWING: PARAMOUNT LOW PULLEY STATION

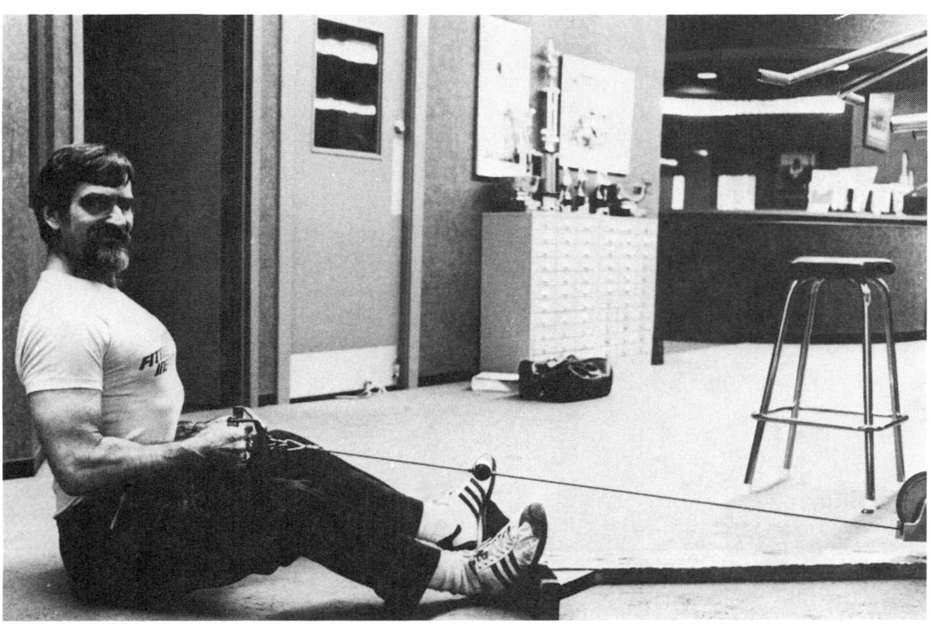

machines, the pulley is located at floor level, and the cable or chain travels almost parallel to the floor (with a slight angle upward towards you). Most people use a narrow grip in this exercise. Try a variety of grips with it and see which one does the most for you.

You should sit facing the pulley, grasp the bar with the palms facing away from you (the other way, the biceps do too much of the work), and pull back toward the body so that the bar ends up at the sternum just below the pectorals. When you do the movement, you should concentrate on making the lats do the work. Many people do arm exercises before they do pulley work, so that the arms will be too tired to help. This is called the "pre-exhaustion" principle and is a good way to concentrate the effort on the lats.

LATISSIMUS DORSI EXERCISES ON OTHER MACHINES

There are many ways to use machines for purposes other than those for which they were designed. Here are a few ways to use machines other than chinning bars and pulleys for lat exercises.

Multistation Gyms

Most multistation gym machines incorporate bench press stations. By grasping one of the machine's handles at this station, you can do one-arm bent-over rowing motions: Stand by the machine, lean over from the waist, reach down and grasp the handle with either hand. Use your other hand against the bench to support yourself. Now pull the handle up by bringing the arm to the side with the elbow bent. You will end up with the arm in a position analogous to that found in the low pulley movement.

As you've probably guessed, any piece of gym equipment that has a station or an attachment with which you can simulate a movement ordinarily done with free weights or with another machine can be used as a replacement for the other pieces of equipment. The important thing to remember is this: *Unless the movement is exactly the same, with strength being exerted exactly as it would be in another exercise or on another piece of equipment, the substitute machine or exercise will not duplicate the original.* Instead, it will become a variation on the original exercise.

We mention this as a cautionary note. Although the bench press station of a multistation gym machine can be used as a substitute for pulley work, it is not the same as pulley work. The range of motion of the handles at the bench press station is not the same range of motion found at the low pulley station. There is a wide latitude of motion possible with pulleys. There is no variation at all with the fixed range of motion of the bench press station.

The same goes for any mechanical

substitute for pulley work. So what might be easy with the pulley may be harder than expected with another machine, and injuries may result. Be careful when using machines for purposes other than those for which they were designed.

There are a few things to watch out for when working with pulleys:

Older models of one of the most popular multistation gyms have a problem with a small fitting at the point where the cable attaches to the stack of plates. The fitting is about the same diameter as the hole through which the cable runs, so that when you pull the bar all the way down, the fitting sometimes gets stuck in the hole. Most people are baffled when the plate stack doesn't go right back down, and they release their pressure on the bar. That's when the fitting pops out of the hole, the bar flies up out of their hands, and they get a nasty whack on the chin! The company has since redesigned the feature, and the new machines are perfectly safe. The old ones are still around, however, so look out for them. Just ask around the gym. Everybody will know about it.

You should also always inspect the cables on any machine that you use, even if somebody else has just finished using it. Cables wear out, and they wear out on some machines more quickly than they do on others. They also have a tendency to get down to just a few strands of wire before anything is done about them. If your gym is heavily used, be assured that the cables are worn.

ONE-ARM BENT OVER ROWING: PARAMOUNT BENCH PRESS STATION

There is danger especially to the eyes when cables come apart. Don't put yourself out of the running with a stupid injury when you can avoid it by being aware of the condition of the machines you use. If the cables are frayed or coming unwound at your gym, report it to the manager. If nothing is done about it, get hold of the owner and tell him about it. Raise hell. They're trying to save pennies on equipment, and you're trying to save your hide.

One final word on pulleys. Often, the pulleys are mounted so that you can brace your feet against the side of the machine while doing the exercise. Be careful that you don't let your toes stray into the path of the stack of plates. You can get a nasty jolt when 100 pounds of plates come booming down on your foot.

Further, some machines (such as Paramount) mount the pulley at one of the machine's corners, off at an angle, so that it's impossible to brace yourself against the machine. Consequently, if you use a weight greater than your body weight, you will simply pull yourself along the floor toward the machine.

Most gyms place a block of wood or a slab of metal against the machine, so that you will have something to prop your feet on. Be sure that the block or slab is securely positioned against the machine. If it flies up and away at the top of a lift, you may be pitched suddenly against the pulley or its mounting.

LOWER BACK/HIP AND BACK MACHINES

Let's continue down the back to the lumbar region. The muscles to be developed here are the lumbar sacral muscles, the erector spinae, which form a double column up the small of the back on either side of the spine. With the neck, they are probably among the most neglected muscles in the body. Most bodybuilders use the stiff-legged dead-weight lift to develop these muscles. Unfortunately, the stiff-legged dead-weight lift works them only at the very top of the lift, when the back is finally arched. Until that point in the lift is reached, the lumbar muscles are not fully contracted, and the spine is bent in a bow and thus at the point of its weakest.

The most common way to work the lumbar muscles is on a spinal-extension bench. This is not a machine but is usually a combination Roman chair (a traditional apparatus for situps) and spinal extension bench that has a place to hook your feet while you do the two different exercises. To use the bench for the lower back, lie on it facedown, while hooking the legs under and against the horizontal padded bar so that the backs of the calves are under and against the padding. Your pelvis will then be lying across a padded seat. Don't bend at the waist. Don't let your body bend down to the floor. That's the way most people use the bench, and it's the wrong way. Instead, never let your upper body go lower than parallel to the floor. The proper movement is up from parallel, as far as you can go. You'll feel the lumbar muscles contract. Both Paramount and Dynacam build sturdy versions of the Roman chair bench.

Dynacam, Paramount and Nautilus have hip and back machines that are specifically designed to work the lumbar region and the hip muscles that tie in to the lower back. Dynacam's model 229C is heavily chromed, well upholstered, and features eccentric cams to distribute the resistance over the complete range of motion.

To use the machine, lie on your back with your knees bent and the

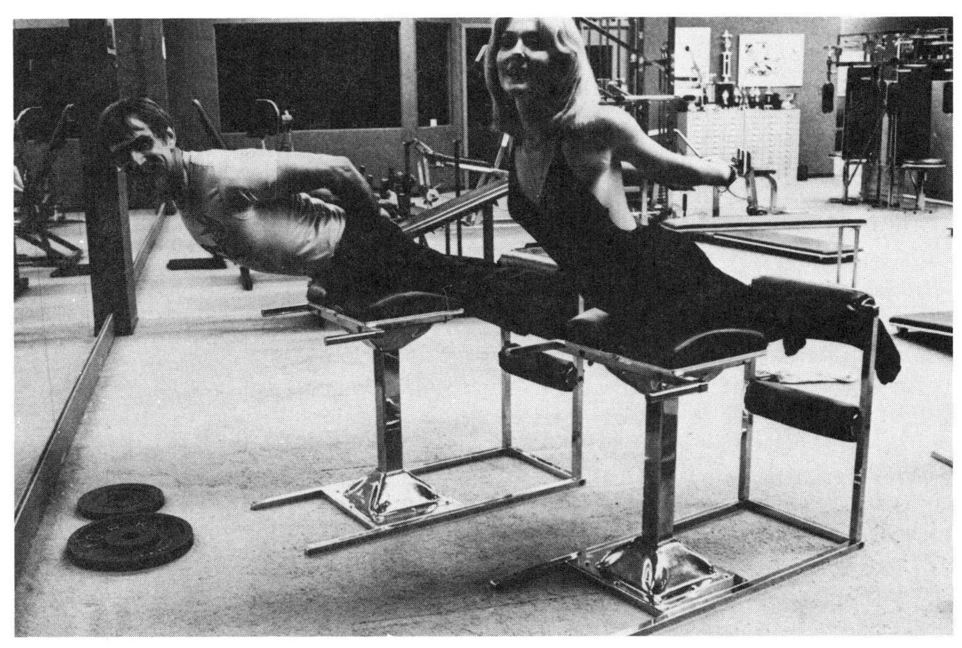

SPINAL HYPEREXTENSION: ROMAN CHAIR

HIP AND LEG EXERCISE: PARAMOUNT LOWER BUTTOCKS AND HAMSTRING DEVELOPER (courtesy, Chicago Health Club)

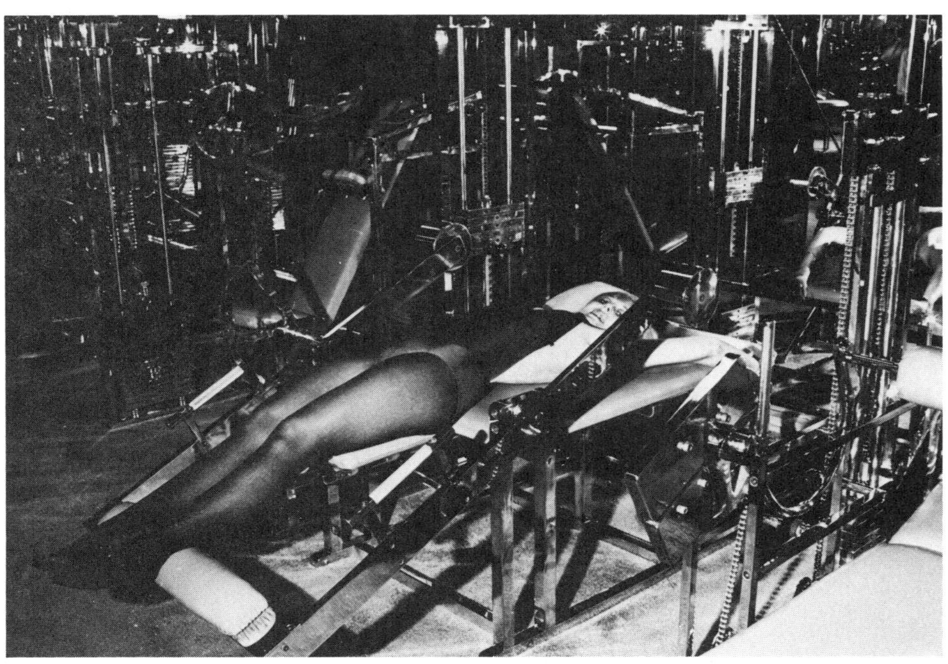

legs pulled back near your face. The backs of your knees will then be against a padded bar that is connected to the eccentric cams. The movement is done by flexing the lower back and hip muscles so that the backs of the legs push the padded bar in an arc away from you. You should continue the movement until your body is straight; then you should go a little bit farther until the back is bowed. The first part of the movement is done by the hips, and the last part of the movement is done almost exclusively by the lower back. The machine is pin-loaded for easy adjustment of the plates that provide the resistance.

Nautilus' hip and back machine works in a similar way and requires that you make the same movement from the same position. Nautilus also has a dual hip and back machine, in which the padded bar is divided into two bars, one for each leg. In this machine, the legs are pushed against the bars separately and alternately, so that the back and hips are worked from a slightly different angle than they would be with the solid bar. Both of the Nautilus machines are pin-loaded.

It is also possible to work the hips by using a leg press machine. Universal, Paramount, Dynacam, and Nautilus all have leg press machines of varying designs. We'll cover them in the section on leg machines. If you want to work the hips, you must bring the legs back toward the body as far as you can. It's in the first movement of the legs away from the

HIP AND BACK EXERCISE: NAUTILUS HIP AND BACK MACHINE

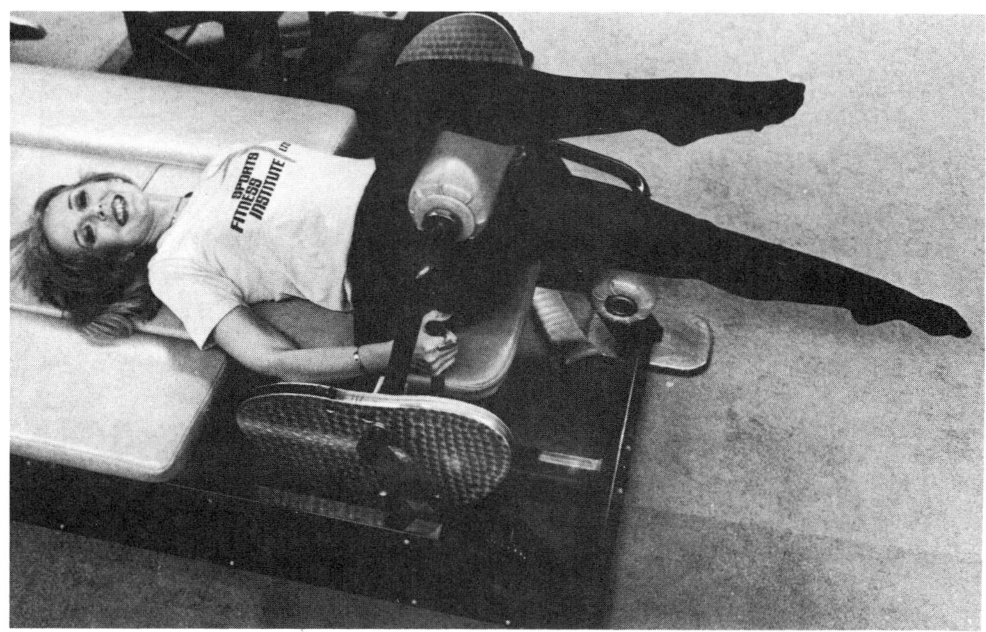

body that the hips are worked. This movement is analogous to (but not exactly the same as) the bottommost position of the deep knee bend or full squat. In the squat, the hip muscles start the upward movement; then the thigh muscles, or quadriceps, take over and complete it. Unless you go all the way down, the hips don't really get a thorough workout. Likewise, when you do the leg press, unless you bring the legs all the way back to the body, the hips never get the workout that they need.

Dynacam also has an ingenious Leg Kick machine, which features a padded collar that fits around the ankle. The collar is fastened to a pulley cable, which in turn is fastened to a stack of pin-loaded plates. By standing erect and grasping a horizontal bar, it is possible to duplicate a large number of ballet movements with the addition of the resistance of the plates. This machine can be used to work the muscles at the sides of the hips as well as the back. It doesn't take much weight at all to work these muscles, and you'll be surprised at how weak you are in these particular movements until you try the machine. Paramount also has a similar machine.

ABDOMINAL MACHINES/ SIDE EXERCISE MACHINES

There are few abdominal machines in existence. Most people still do sit-ups and variations of what is usually called the "crunch," in which the abdominals are isolated by spreading the legs as wide as possible with the knees bent. The abdominals are then flexed so that the distance between the pelvic bone (the symphysis pubis) and the breastbone (the sternum) is shortened as much as possible. This movement works the abdominals almost exclusively and is far more effective in toning the stomach muscles than the regular situp.

You should also do a "reverse crunch" for the lower abdominals. This is accomplished by keeping the upper body on the floor or slant board and bringing the legs up (knees bent and wide apart, feet together or ankles crossed) until your hips are off the floor. You can combine the two crunches by bringing the upper body and the hips up at the same time, keeping only the small of the back on the floor. Do all of these movements slowly, and pause at the point of maximum contraction.

All of the major companies manufacture some form of slant board, which is nothing more than a padded board with a hook at one end that enables you to raise the end off the floor. By lying with your head at the lower end of the board, you can put a greater work load on the abdominals.

Most of the major companies also manufacture some form of the Roman chair abdominal bench, as described above in the section on hip and back machines. These benches come in a variety of shapes and sizes but all work on the same principle:

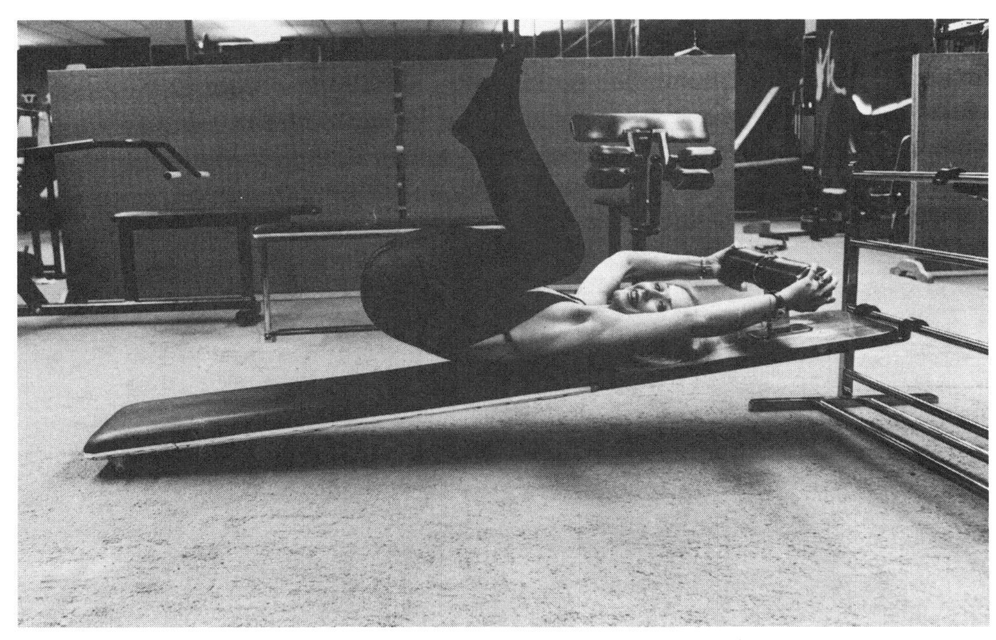

REVERSE CRUNCH OR REVERSE TORSO ROLL: SLANT BOARD

SITUPS: SLANT BOARD

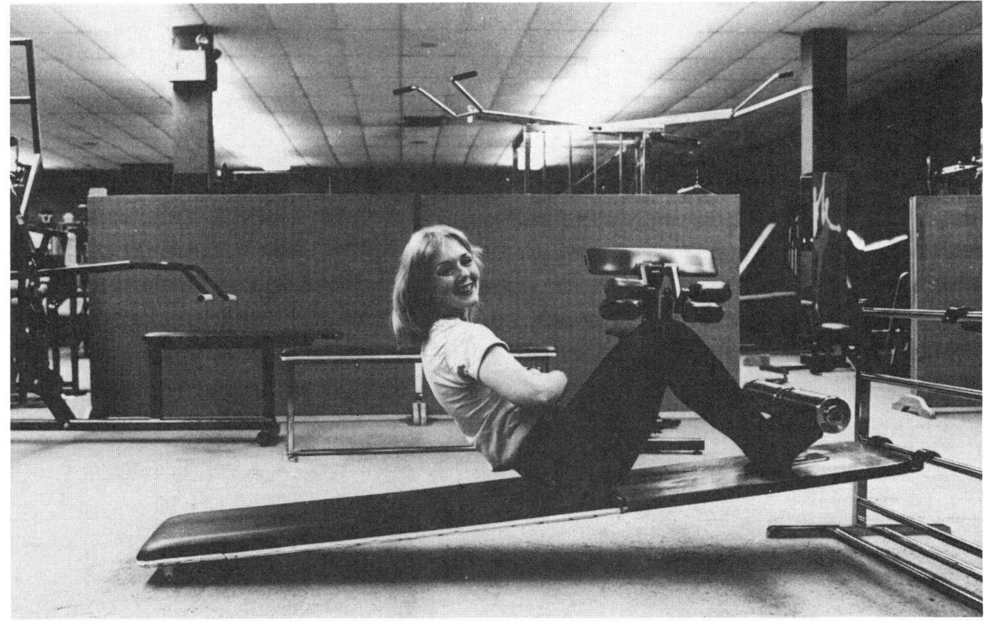

CRUNCH OR BODY ROLL: SLANT BOARD

SIDE CRUNCH: SLANT BOARD

The feet are positioned under a padded bar so that the fronts of the calves are against the pads. It is possible, then, to bend past a line that is parallel to the floor when doing situps. Most of the Roman chair benches are illustrated in the company catalogs with someone bending backwards until he is almost touching the floor with the back of his head.

Let us caution you against doing the exercise this way. In the first place, the Roman chair is supposed to be used to exercise the abdominal muscles. It does this only in the sense that the abdominals are held in a contracted condition while the movement is made. The range of motion of the spine from a point where the abdominals are relaxed to a point where they are fully contracted is actually very small. In most people, the movement caused by the contraction of the abdominals would be only a few inches. Consequently, it is not necessary to do a full situp in order to work the abdominals.

Further, when you bend backwards below a line that is parallel to the floor, you place tremendous pressure on the vertebrae and discs of the lower spine. The amount of stress is on the order of 2,000 pounds! Since such a movement has minimal effect on the abdominals and introduces the possibility of serious injury, we

SITUPS AND/OR CRUNCHES: ROMAN CHAIR

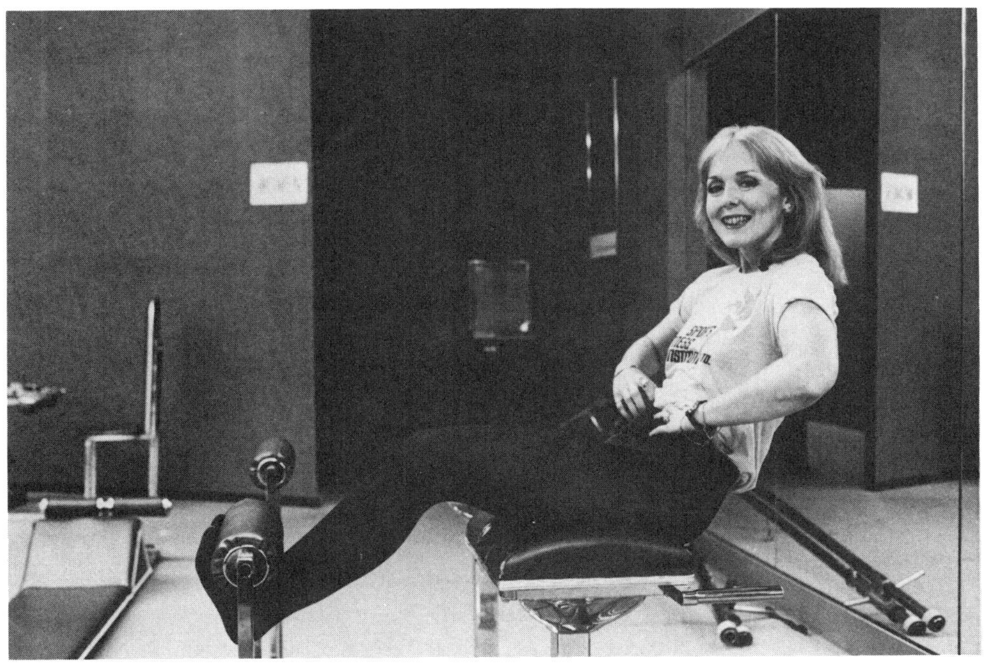

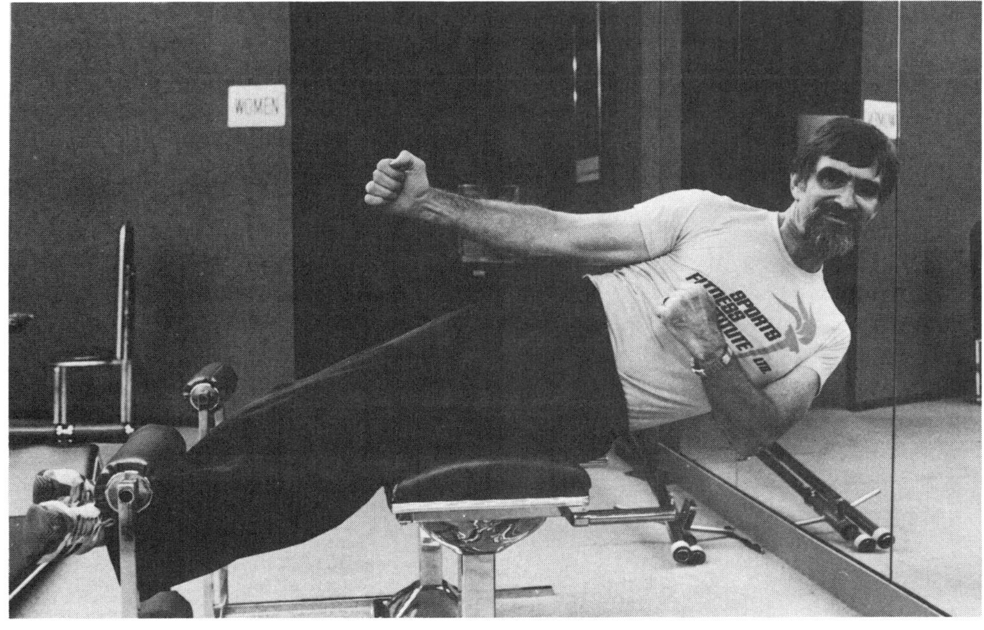

SIDE CRUNCH: ROMAN CHAIR

would recommend that you approach Roman chair exercises with caution.

Dynacam has designed a variable resistance abdominal machine, Model No. 105 DC, which features an eccentric cam, a system of pulleys, and a pin-loaded stack of plates for weight. To use the machine, sit back on the bench against the backrest and place the legs under the padded bar that crosses the top of the bench. The backrest is adjustable, so that you can vary the position of the upper body relative to the padded bar. You can pull both legs up at the same time, or one leg at a time. Bend the knee as you come up, and try to bring the leg as high as you can. Handles are provided as handgrips, so that you can isolate the abdominals during the movement. Actually, this machine is a leg-raise machine and as such will primarily work the lower abdominals. However, by concentrating on the contraction of the upper abdominals, you can give them a workout at the peak contraction position of the exercise (when the knees are closest to the face).

Paramount's Side Waist Exerciser Model No. 3570 replaces the side-bend with dumbbells. The machine consists of a short bench, with handles that come around the sides as you sit with your back to the part of the bench to which the handles are attached. There are no plates, nor is

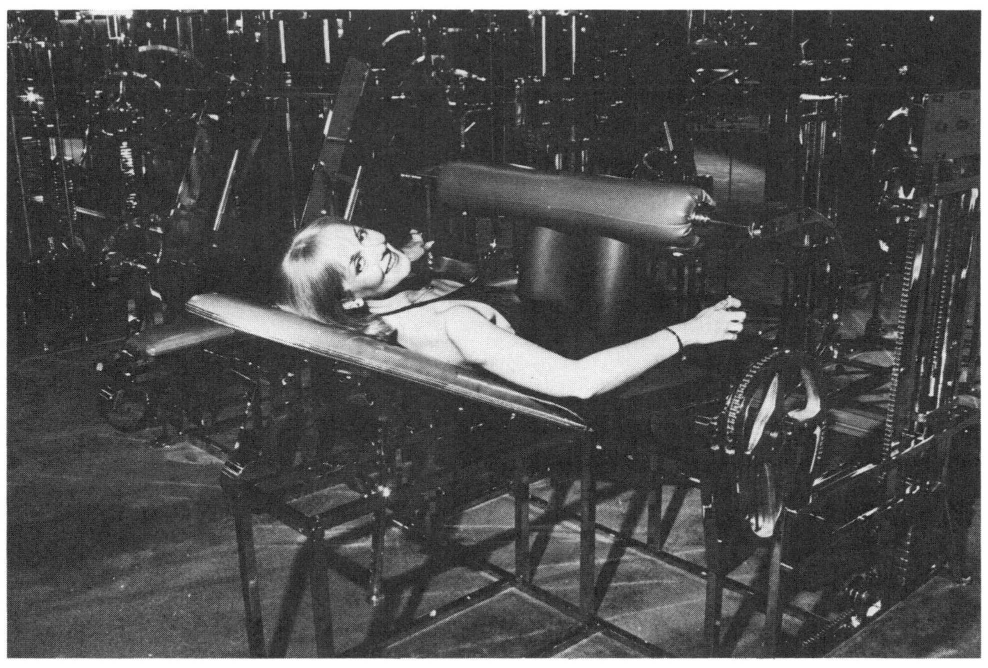

ABDOMINAL EXERCISE: DYNACAM ABDOMINAL AND WAIST MACHINE (courtesy, Chicago Health Club)

there a variable resistance mechanism. Instead, the machine uses a friction clutch which is adjustable with a small control.

Paramount, Dynacam, and Universal all manufacture some form of a basic twisting machine, which consists of a circular pedestal to stand on and a bar to grasp with the hands in order to immobilize the upper body. Remember that twisting motions don't involve much strength. Their chief value is in toning the muscles around the waist and massaging the area by the constant twisting motion. Dynacam's "Twistaway" No. 165 is a two-position twister, with the usual circular pedestal on one side and a circular seat on the other. On the standing pedestal side, the upper body is immobilized while the lower body pivots at the waist. On the circular seat side of the machine, you sit facing away from the bar, place your arms along the length of the bar behind you, and pivot at the waist. If you hold your legs straight out from the machine, you can take advantage of angular momentum, and the stress on the waist muscles will be greater, resulting in a better workout.

In using any of these twisting machines, go easy at first until you have become more flexible in the waist. If you are not used to twisting motions, you may pull one of the small stabilizing muscles that run down the sides of the spinal column. These

EXTERNAL OBLIQUE EXERCISE: DYNACAM TWISTAWAY MACHINE

muscles are usually weak, and if they are strained or torn, you will be incapacitated for several days. Remember all the stories about people who injured their backs during the craze for the twist dances? Same thing. Be careful, take it slowly, and don't try to twist too far in either direction at first.

In addition to the twisting machines, Roman chair benches, and abdominal machines, most gyms stock some form of leg raise apparatus, such as the Dynacam No. 168 Vertical Leg Raise. These pieces of equipment feature armrests on which the elbows are placed, handles for the hands to grip, and footpads to stand on at the beginning of the movement. Once you're in place, lift the feet off the footpads and swing the legs up in an arc as far as you can bring them.

A word of caution is appropriate here. When you do the vertical leg raise movement, you are bending at the hips. That is, the small of the back is curved slightly in a bow, and the legs are brought up in front of you. This approximates the movement of the legs in the toe-touching exercise. The difference is that in the leg raise, the lower abdominals and front pelvic muscles are pulling them up.

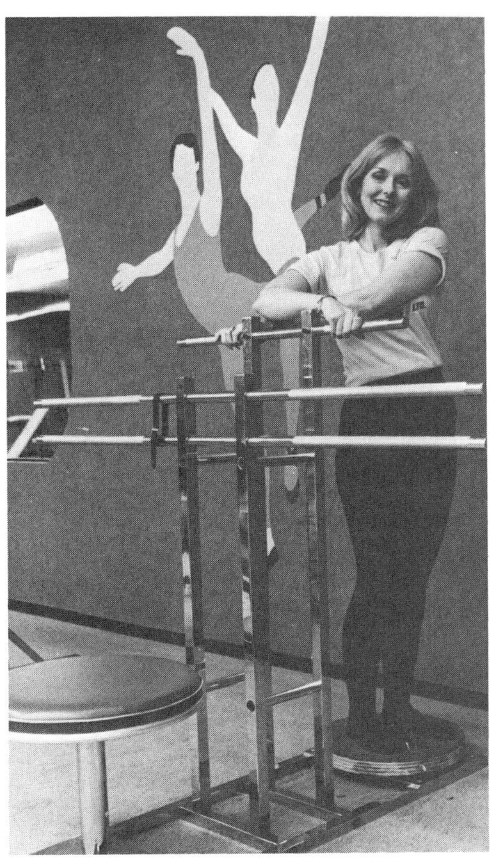

STANDING EXTERNAL OBLIQUE EXERCISE: DYNA-CAM TWISTAWAY MACHINE

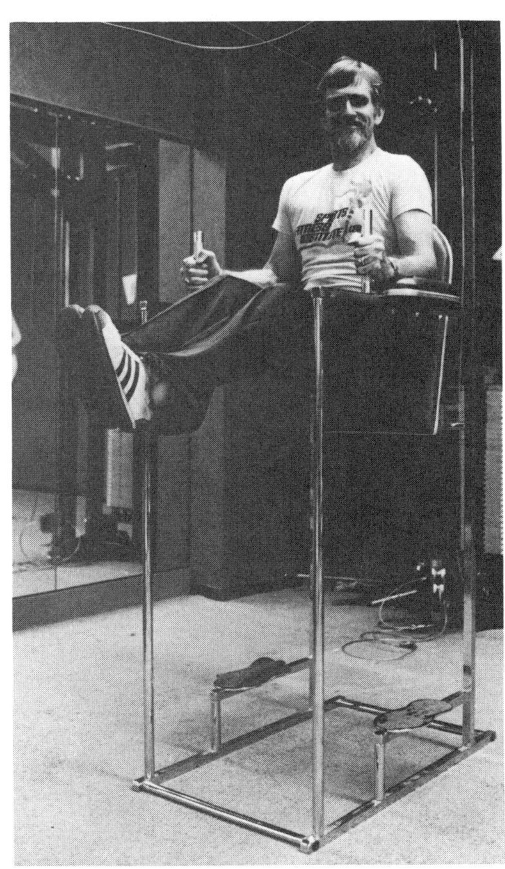

VERTICAL LEG RAISE: DYNA-CAM VERTICAL LEG RAISE APPARATUS

SUPINE LEG RAISE

However, as far as the sciatic nerves are concerned, the motion is the same: The nerves are being pulled tightly along the backside of the hips and down the legs to the feet. While muscles stretch readily, nerve bundles do not. If you try to come up too far in the vertical leg raise while holding your knees locked, you can possibly damage your sciatic nerves. Don't take a chance. Bend the knees as you bring them up. Never try to do leg raises without bending the knees at least slightly. If you're going to try to zoom your feet up above the level of your head, give your sciatic nerves a break and bend the knees. The same cautionary word is applicable to the traditional ballet-barre stretch, where you stand on one foot and bring the other foot up to the barre without bending the knees.

Many people attempt leg raises on a slant board, with the head placed at the high end of the board. There is danger in this, too, because such a position places great pressure on the lower spine. The vertical leg raise apparatus is superior to the slant board for leg raises, if for no other reason than the opportunity it offers for shifting the body backward and forward between the armrests, thus re-

SIDE LEAN: PARAMOUNT BENCH PRESS STATION

SIDE LEAN: PARAMOUNT LOW PULLEY STATION

lieving some of the lower-back pressure.

Many companies recommend that side leans be done with one handle of the bench press machine: Grasp the handle with one hand while standing to the side of the machine. Then pull up on the handle as you contract the side muscles, or external obliques. You can do the same thing at a low pulley station. Some people also do the stiff-legged dead weight lift with the bench press station of multistation machines. The same word of caution applies to all of them: Use light weight, concentrate on making a complete contraction, make sure that you are doing a natural movement, instead of letting the machine's range of motion alter your normal bodily range of motion.

MACHINES FOR THE CHEST

All of the major companies produce bench press machines. They are always one of the favorite stations on the multistation machines, and the popularity of the lift has prompted some companies to design machines especially for the bench press. All of the machines are pin-loaded; most of them feature eccentric cams to distribute the resistance over the entire range of motion.

The bench press stations on the multistation machines are pretty much alike, with minor differences from one manufacturer to the next. They all feature a separate bench that is placed in front of the station between the handles. The handles are attached either to sleeves that run up and down vertical bars or to a pivot point inside the machine. The sleeves or the pivoting bars are attached to pin-loaded plates, which are usually numbered (and which numbers sometimes have little to do with the weight being lifted).

Depending on the manufacturer, the machine's handles may or may not allow you to work in your particular power groove. For Ralph's bone structure, Dynacam's handles are too short (as found in the No. 215 DC Dynamic Gym) to allow comfortable, natural movement, while Paramount's handles are too close together. By the same token, Universal's handles are the right width but too short. This is no criticism of the machines themselves. It is merely an illustration of the fact that you must try the individual machines yourself

BENCH PRESS: PARAMOUNT BENCH PRESS STATION

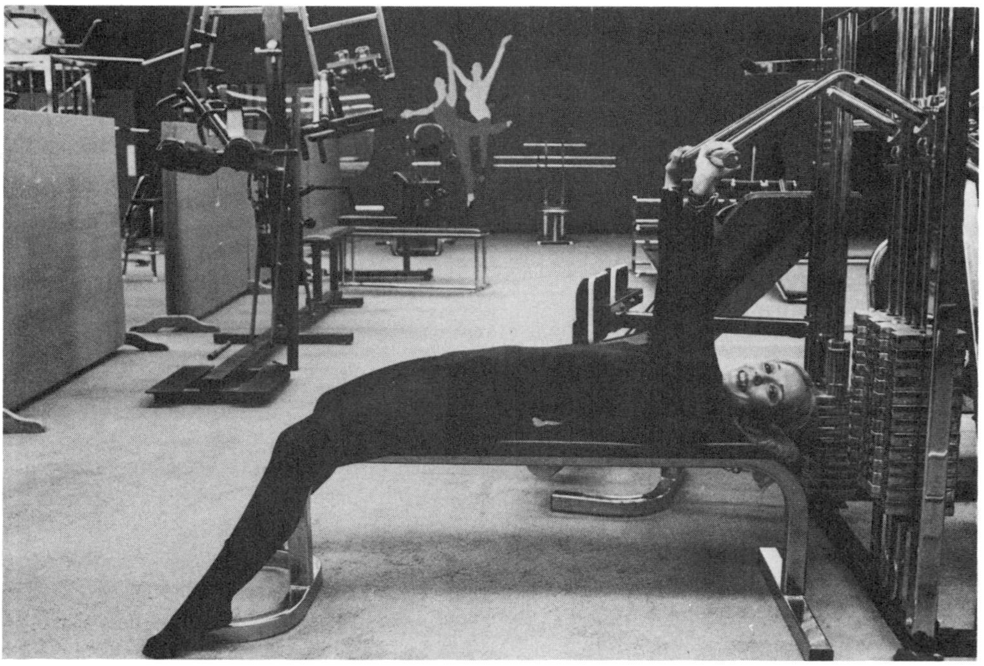

BENCH PRESS: NAUTILUS DOUBLE CHEST MACHINE

before you can be sure that your own range of motion approximates that of the machine.

In all of the multistation bench press machines, you should lie on your back with your head toward the machine. Grasp the handles and push them upwards towards the ceiling in a smooth, steady movement. When you reach the top, don't pause but instead continue the smooth motion back down to the starting position.

Dynacam and Nautilus have similar seated bench press machines, as mentioned earlier in the section on anterior deltoid exercises. Both feature vertical bars at the sides and a seat position that tilts the body back at a shallow angle. There is also a footrest on both machines that doubles as a pedal arrangement, so that you can help squeeze out those last few reps with a little help from your legs. You can concentrate on either the upper pectorals or the lower pectorals by placing your hands high or low on the vertical bars. You'll have to experiment to see where your hands should go to work your muscles from the best angle. If the gym instructors tell you that there is only one correct place to put your hands, tell them that their advice assumes

BENCH PRESS: PARAMOUNT FLOOR-TYPE PRESS MACHINE (courtesy, Chicago Health Club)

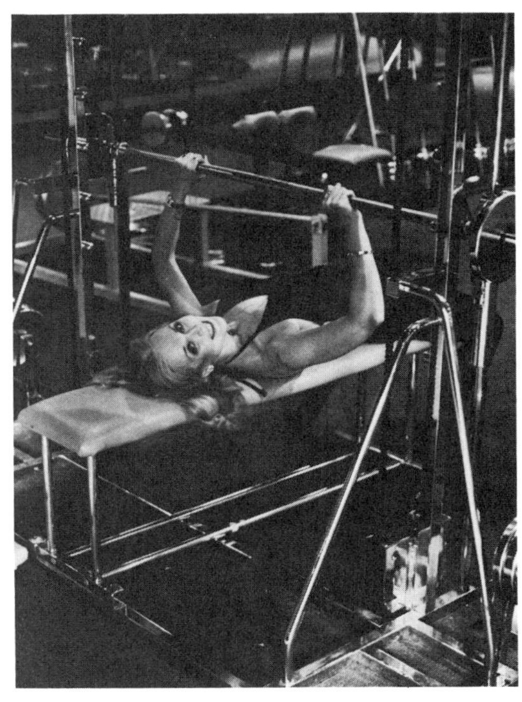

that everybody is built exactly the same. If they persist, tell them where to get off.

Another type of bench press machine was also mentioned in the section on anterior deltoid exercises. It is the floor-type pin-loaded machine that has a horizontal bar which approximates the "feel" of a regular free weight bench press. These machines usually have a built-in bench that pivots away from the machine so that you can use the apparatus for squats.

Also, the bars usually have room at the ends for additional weight to be added in the form of plates. These are extremely versatile machines and can be used without a spotter when you want to force a few more repetitions with only partial movements. The pegs on which the bar hooks run all the way down the sides, so you can always hook the bar on them and slide out from under the weight if you can't make that last rep.

The only drawback of these machines, as we pointed out earlier, is that the bar moves in an exactly vertical plane. In the free-weight bench press, the bar travels from the chest to the top of the lift in a slight arc toward the direction in which the head is pointed. It would be rare indeed if you bench pressed in a perfectly vertical line. Further, there is no universally acceptable evidence that it is better to bench press in a vertical plane than with the slight arc. The body is an organism, not a machine, and so has peculiarities that are missing in purely mechanical designs.

Another type of chest developer is the "pec deck" that we mentioned in the section on the posterior deltoids. Both Dynacam and Paramount call it a "butterfly" machine. Nautilus includes it in the combination bench press and pec machine. All of the machines have the same motion: The arms begin bent at the elbow, out to the sides at right angles, and end in front of the chest with the palms together or facing each other. This motion duplicates the old flying exercise that is done with two dumbbells. The exercise works both the anterior deltoids and the pectorals. All of the machines are pin-loaded for easy weight changes.

PECTORAL EXERCISE: DYNACAM DOUBLE VERTICAL BUTTERFLY MACHINE

PECTORAL EXERCISE: NAUTILUS DOUBLE CHEST MACHINE

Paramount manufactures a seated bench press machine unlike any mentioned so far. It features a vertical seat back, two short handles in the form of bars, and two long pieces of metal that are rectangular in cross section and which are fastened by a cable through a pulley to a stack of plates. The vertical pieces are attached at a pivot point at the base of the machine. Thus, the short bars move in a slight arc away and downwards.

Dynacam makes what they call a "Prone Butterfly" machine, which is a butterfly machine on which you lie instead of sit. The weight is varied by sliding a cylindrical piece of metal along a bar underneath the bench. Another version of the machine is pin-loaded so that more substantial weight can be used. It's amazing that both are called "prone" butterflies, since the proper position for the body in both of them is supine, not prone. This is simply a continuation of an old mistake: People used to call the bench press the "prone press" until somebody finally pointed out that the name was 180 degrees off.

In all of the bench press machines, the anterior deltoids do most of the work when the bar is close to the chest; the pectorals pick up the load as the bar gets farther away from the chest; and the arms finish the lift as they straighten completely.

In the butterfly machines, the arm muscles are isolated so that they can't help in the movement. When the arms are out to the sides at the beginning of the movement, the anterior deltoids do most of the work. As the arms are brought in an arc to the front, the pectorals pick up the load and finish the movement.

Depending on the length of your arms, you may or may not be able to use the pec decks or butterfly machines effectively. There is usually some leeway for shifting the position of the arms, but there is little opportunity for adjustment of the machine itself. When you try the machine out for the first time, shift your hand and arm positions until you feel comfortable in the machine. You don't need much weight with the butterflies. They are pectoral and bust shapers and trimmers, not muscle builders. Use light weights and high repetitions. You'll get all the bulk you need from the bench press.

ARM MACHINES: TRICEPS

All of the bench press machines are in fact arm machines, at least in the last one-third of the lift when the arms straighten out away from the chest. There are many other machines that work the arms. They are usually the most popular machines in the gym. Let's start with triceps exercises first.

Military Press Machines

The traditional barbell press was called the military press, because you were supposed to stand with the chest out, belly in, looking straight ahead as you did the lift. The barbell was placed at the top of the chest, then lifted in front of the face to a position overhead and in line with the back of the head. At the top of the lift, the arms were to be locked.

The lift is as much an anterior and lateral deltoid developer as it is an arm developer. If you've never done this lift before, you'll find that the real burning sensation will be in the shoulders instead of the arms. It, like the bench press, is a compound lift; it involves more than one muscle group.

There are three types of military or overhead press machines: overhead press stations on multistation machines, single or compound units designed especially for the press and for shoulders, and the rack-type machines such as the Dynacam No. 107 floor-type bench press.

The first type is the most common, simply because more gyms have multistation machines than do not. Many companies, such as Dynacam, offer the same overhead press apparatus found in their multistation machines in a single unit model. Whatever the manufacturer, the machines are essentially the same. They have two bars coming out of the machine, which bend about a foot from the ends and offer a grip that is analogous to a regular barbell's. The other ends of the bars either pivot on a structural member of the machine or fasten to the pin-loaded plates by sleeves. The motion is upward, starting at the top of the chest.

If the bars pivot on a structural member of the machine, the movement will be in a slight arc away from you if you stand facing the machine as some of the catalogs depict. This, of course, would be the opposite of the way that the military press is done with free weights, and it calls for a motion of the torso that would lead you to lean "into" the lift instead of finishing the movement with an arched spine. Easy to correct. Stand facing away from the machine if the bars pivot on a structural member. It's not the way some of the catalogs show it, but it's the best way to do the lift.

The Dynacam machines feature sleeves that run up vertical bars and

SEATED MILITARY PRESS: PARAMOUNT PRESS STATION

STANDING MILITARY PRESS: PARAMOUNT PRESS STATION

which connect to the bars that you grasp with your hands. Since the action of the machine is direct, with no pivot or arc, the movement of the bars is exactly vertical. You can approximate the slight backward arc of the free weight military press by facing away from the machine and allowing the torso to move slightly forward as you finish the lift. The effect will be almost the same as if you were using free weights, with one important difference: The machine will be "balancing" the weight, not you. If you haven't done the military press with free weights, don't try to hop from the machine to the barbell without dropping the amount of weight you're lifting until you get used to balancing the weight without help from the structured groove of the machine.

Another word of caution: The Olympic Weightlifting Committee eliminated the military press from Olympic competition some years ago because of the danger of lower back injury from improper backbend during the lift. A tremendous amount of pressure is exerted on the lower back during this lift unless you stand straight (as the original name suggests you should). Always wear a weightlifting belt when you do this lift, and make sure it's tight before you start. It will give you some extra support in the lumbar area of the spine.

Some of the overhead press stations in multistation machines are used in a standing position; some are used in a seated position. Given the peculiarities of particular machines, you may find it more natural to sit than to stand. Further, most of the machines are not adjustable in terms of height, so an adjustable stool may be what is needed to make up for the lack of flexibility in machine design.

Nautilus combines its overhead

SEATED PRESS: NAUTILUS DOUBLE SHOULDER MACHINE

press machine with a lateral deltoid apparatus, thus giving the front and side deltoids a full workout at one station. Dynacam's Model 435 Vertical Shoulder and 434 Lateral Shoulder machines give separately essentially the same exercise as the Nautilus Double Shoulder machine. The bars on Dynacam's vertical shoulder machine are a little closer together than those on the Nautilus. The position of the shoulders for the lateral exercise is about the same on both machines.

In addition to the various pressing machines, there are other ways to work the triceps. All of the multistation machines feature pulley systems. One of the favorite triceps movements is the pulley pushdown, which simulates the movement of the old French press exercise. Grasp the bar that is usually used for latissimus work. Use a grip in which the hands are close together, with the palms down. Push in a straight line down towards the floor. When you've reached the bottom of the lift, allow the bar to return slowly to the starting position. Don't let the muscles relax, but instead keep the tension on them throughout the lift. Don't use too much weight at first or you'll injure your elbows.

Another way to do triceps pushdowns is to stand facing away from the machine and, if the pulley bar is sufficiently high, reach back and above, grasp it, and pull it down in front of your face. Again, the triceps should be made to do all the work as the arms straighten out. If there is not enough "travel" designed into the cable system, you can tie a towel

TRICEPS EXTENSION PUSHDOWN: UNIVERSAL OVERHEAD PULLEY STATION (STARTING POSITION)

TRICEPS EXTENSION PUSHDOWN (FINAL POSITION)

to the bar or to the end of the cable, and do the same motion by grasping the towel.

Another variation is to stand an incline bench up near the machine, facing away from the machine. Lie back on the incline bench and grasp the bar or towel as described above. The movement is the same, with the hands ending up in front of you and with the elbows straight.

For the Dynacam Vertical Shoulder and the vertical portion of the Nautilus Double Shoulder machines, you should sit back in the seat (which is tilted back at a shallow angle) and reach up and to the front to grasp the bars that stick out from the front of the machine. Then push upwards until the two bars are high enough so that the elbows are straight.

You can vary the angle at which you work the triceps and shoulders by grasping the bars, either back towards the machine (to intensify the shoulder work), or as far from the machine as possible (which lessens the shoulder intensity but doesn't change the triceps workout a great deal). Some will find it much easier to make the movement if the bars are grasped as far toward the ends as possible.

The seats on both of these machines are adjustable for height. Inevitably, people seek the easiest path, even when they're exercising. Many people adjust the seat in the lowest possible position, so that the lift will be easier to do. When the seat is in the lowest position, unless you are 7 feet tall, you will never bring the bars down close enough to the shoulders to give yourself a good workout. Try it both ways, and you'll see the difference. Further, many people fall into the trap of trying to lift more than they are really able to lift in good form. This leads them to cheat in the lift by putting the seat too low.

When you grasp the bars toward the ends, you are approximating the military press. When you grasp them back toward the machine, you are approximating the behind-the-neck press. In either case, the machine moves in a straight line, instead of the slight arc that you would traverse if you were using free weights. You can compensate for this by leaning slightly forward as you complete the lift. Resist the temptation to reach down to the floor with your feet and push. This action takes the pressure off the arms and shoulders, and deprives them of the benefit of the lift. If you can't do the movement without pushing with your feet, put the pin in a higher position and drop the weight.

The third type of machine used for pressing is the Dynacam floor-type bench press No. 107 and the Paramount multipress model 3250, mentioned above in the section on bench pressing. These machines can also be used for overhead presses by sitting on the bench instead of lying on it, and by putting the bar hooks on a higher set of pegs than you would use for the bench press. The machines are especially good for simulating the seated press behind the neck. The long bar allows the needed wide grip, and the safety feature of the bar hooks is a handy thing to have when there's nobody in the gym to spot you.

The word of caution about lower back injuries applies to the use of all of the machines, whether you are standing or sitting. In fact, some people are more apt to injure themselves in the seated position than in the standing position, for no other reason than the overconfidence they feel sitting "in" a machine. Even if you strap yourself in (as in the Nautilus

TRICEPS EXTENSION: NAUTILUS TRICEP MACHINE

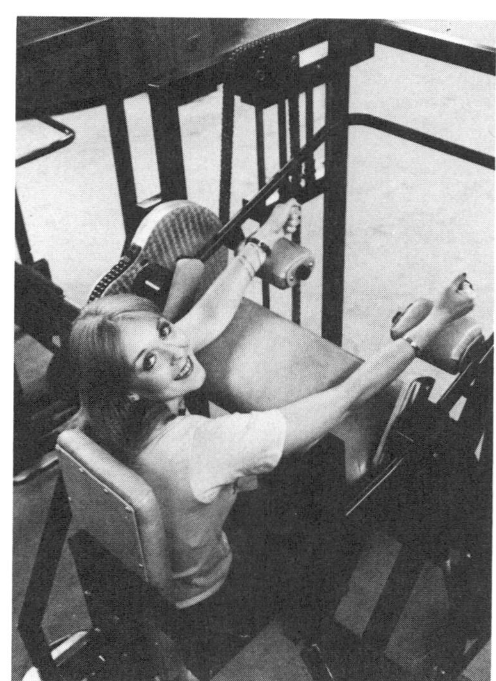

Double Shoulder machine), you'll still bend your back to a certain extent. Try to keep the back slightly arched and in a strong position, but don't let it bend excessively to the point that undue pressure is brought to bear against the lumbar vertebrae and discs.

The motion of the French curl and the triceps pushdown is also approximated by two Nautilus triceps machines, in the Dynacam No. 311 DC and in the Paramount model 3590 triceps machine.

The older-type Nautilus triceps machine is combined with a biceps-curling machine that we'll talk about later. Both the old and new Nautilus triceps machines use padded bars, as do the Dynacam and Paramount machines. To use them, sit in the seat facing the pads, place your forearms against the pads with the elbows bent, and push away from your body while keeping the elbow stationary. If you can't use the machine by sitting in it, you might try standing behind it and doing the movement with the counterbalance bar.

Each of the machines has a slightly different seating angle, as well as a slightly different position for the pads. Try them all, and see which one fits you the best. Another example of the difference between the machines: The older model Nautilus machine is a far better fit for Ralph than the new one. Neither of the other two fit Ralph's arm and shoulder structure.

TRICEPS EXTENSION: NAUTILUS TRICEP MACHINE, USING COUNTERBALANCE BAR FOR MOVEMENT (STARTING POSITION)

TRICEPS EXTENSION (FINAL POSITION)

Nautilus' New Triceps Machine

Nautilus' third generation triceps machine is just now getting into the better clubs around the country. It's far superior to anything they've yet produced. The machine is narrower, and isolates the triceps thoroughly. It's easier on the elbows, and can be used with both arms at once or alternating. Make sure that the seat is not too high, or you'll miss some of the effect of the machine's action. The hands rest on pads, just like they do on the older machines, but here there are guides for the hands as well as the elbows. Once you discover this machine, you'll probably give up pulley pushdowns altogether.

With all of the machines, the trick is to isolate the triceps and let them do all the work. To do this, the elbow must not be allowed to shift as you push the pads away. Since the padded bar is attached by cable or chain to an eccentric cam and then to a set of plates (or, with the older Nautilus, to a bar that holds barbell plates), it is easily possible to put on more weight than you can handle with good form. As in all movements that simulate the French curl or the pushdown, these machines will shape and tone but will not give you great bulk like the compound exercises that allow the use of greater poundages.

ARM MACHINES: BICEPS

Dynacam and Paramount both manufacture biceps-curling machines so similar in feel and structure that a single description will suffice for the operation of both. The machines incorporate a version of the "Scott bench" or "preacher stand," so that the elbows rest against a padded slant board while you are doing the exercise. The slanted board (which was used with free weights by Larry Scott, hence, "Scott bench"; and which looks like a podium, hence "preacher stand") is positioned so that you can lean against it while your arms lie across the front.

A curved bar, reminiscent of the old curling bars, is fastened to a rectangular structure, which is in turn fastened to a cable that runs through a pulley to the stack of pin-loaded

CURL: PARAMOUNT CURLING MACHINE (courtesy, Chicago Health Club)

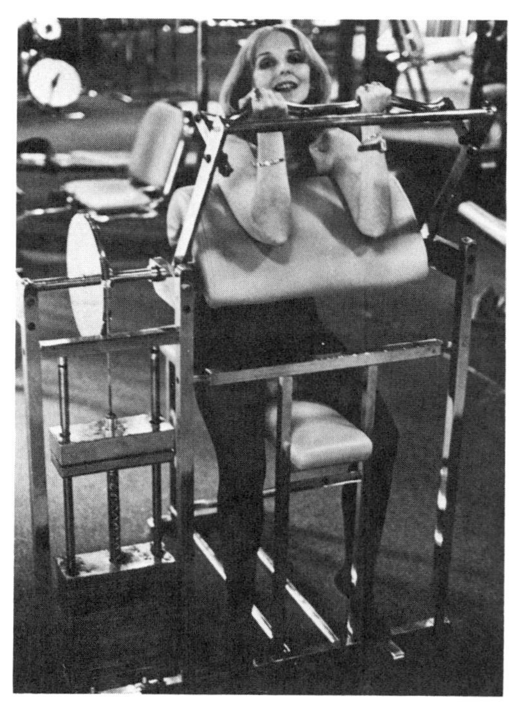

plates. A narrow bench provides a place to sit. If you have a short torso, you may find it too low. Neither machine is adjustable for height.

A cautionary note: Once when we were in Houston, we visited a new health club that had opened only a few weeks earlier. The person who set up the workout room didn't really know anything about the biomechanics of machine exercise but had, fortunately, bought a line of the best that Dynacam had to offer. The club was beautiful, and the machines were right out of *Star Wars*.

Ralph tried out the curling machine and promptly hit himself in the mouth with the curved bar. The manager himself had tightened the bar at the ends, not knowing that it was supposed to pivot at each end where it was fastened to the rest of the machine. He had also tightened it in such a way that the middle portion of the bar, which Dynacam carefully designed so that it would not be in the way, was pointed up so that it was impossible to do a full contraction of the biceps without hitting yourself in the mouth.

Amusingly enough, the Dynacam catalog shows somebody using the machine with the bar in exactly the same position. We've always wondered if the male model made it through the photo session without injury. The moral of the story is: You can't always be sure that the person running the club knows anything about the machines simply because he's running the club. Check for yourself. That's one of the things this book is for.

Nautilus has at least three curling machines. The oldest model is a combination curling and triceps machine.

With this machine, you sit on a bench with your arms resting on a slanted, cushioned board like the "Scott bench" or "preacher stand" mentioned above. A cambered curling bar is attached to pivoting metal arms, which in turn are attached to an eccentric cam and counterbalance weight. A chain runs from the cam through a pulley, down to a swinging metal arm that is equipped with a peg on which barbell plates can be placed.

Grip the cambered bar with the hands, palms facing towards you, elbows resting against the board. Pull the bar up in an arc toward the chin. Be sure that you go through the complete range of motion. Then slowly let the bar back down, while keeping tension against the weight all the way down.

The newer version of this machine uses a stack of pin-loaded plates, a similar seating position, but a horizontal board on which to rest the elbows. It has no bar but instead features pads against which the inner wrists are placed. The movement is much the same: an arc, with the hands ending near the head, then back down. However, without the bar to grip, the feel of the machine is entirely different, so it may take some getting used to.

The lever system used in the pad machine is several inches shorter than that found in the older machine. The result is that you do not feel that you have the "leverage" you need when making the lift. Of course, this is intentional on Nautilus' part and is a touted design feature. You'll have to try the machines yourself and decide which one suits you best. For Ralph, the older machine matches his own lever system better than the new one and always gives him a better workout. Our good friend, Walter Aymen of Judge's Club in Houston, Texas, swears by the newer model. Walter is incredibly strong and did it all on Nautilus machines. Again, you have to try for yourself.

CURL: NAUTILUS BICEPS MACHINE

Nautilus' New Biceps Machine

Nautilus' third generation biceps machine simulates dumbbell training. Sit in the seat and lay your arms across the horizontal pad. Bring the handles up one at a time, alternating from one arm to the other. Be sure that the seat is low enough to give you a full range of motion. Don't let the elbows slip when you bring the weight up. Work for maximum isolation of the biceps and you won't believe the pump you'll get.

Other Ways to Work the Biceps

Many people use bench press station handles for curling exercises. While some machine salesmen recommend it, we don't. It's not what the station was designed for, and in this case it is nearly impossible to get into a position that enables you to work the biceps without putting undue strain on some other part of the body.

Low pulley stations are popular for biceps work. To use them, sit on the floor in front of the pulley bar, grasp it with the palms facing you, rest your elbows against your knees, and do the curling motion in strict form. You'll find that you won't be able to use much weight because of the instability of the arms in such a position. Concentrate on form, multiple sets, and high reps. This is more of a finishing and polishing exercise than it is a muscle or strength builder.

CURL: PARAMOUNT BENCH PRESS STATION

You can also work the biceps with overhead pulleys. Lie on the floor under the pulley bar, reach up and grasp it with both hands, and bring it down toward the chest. Grip the bar with the palms facing you, and concentrate on letting the biceps do the work. You won't be able to use much weight on this one either, so try for strict form and intensity.

FOREARM MACHINES

Most bodybuilders work forearms with wrist curling movements, usually holding a barbell or dumbbell. The exercise is done with the palms facing upwards (to work the inner forearm) or facing downwards (to work the top or outer forearm). The forearms rest along the top of the thighs during the workout. You should be seated on a bench so that the forearms are parallel to the floor.

The old-time wrist rollers described earlier in this chapter have their machine counterparts. Several of the major manufacturers have bars that substitute for the wrist roller. Tension or resistance is provided either by friction or by a rope or cable which is attached to plates. Whatever the particular configuration, the movement is the same. The hands grip the bar, and the wrists bend backward and forward.

When using the wrist roller, you actually roll a rope or cable around the bar, thus lifting the weight. With the seated wrist curls (with a barbell or dumbbell), there is no winding motion, but the hands are pulled backward and forward, bending at the wrist.

Low pulleys can be used for wrist work as well as the biceps workout described above. Instead of pulling the bar up in an arc as you would for biceps curls, make the bend at the wrists (with the palms facing downward or toward you). There is only a small range of motion in these wrist movements. Concentrate on isolating the forearm muscles as you do the movements.

Several manufacturers have little "grip-building" machines, which also work the forearms. They are usually about 2 feet high, are pin-loaded, and feature a crossbar on

WRIST CURL: PARAMOUNT LOW PULLEY STATION

WRIST EXTENSION: PARAMOUNT LOW PULLEY STATION

which to rest the palm of the hand, and a finger bar to curl the fingers around and lift toward the crossbar. You can strengthen your grip tremendously with these machines. For a thorough forearm workout, you should use a variety of machines and free weights. The greater the variety, the more well-rounded your development.

MACHINES FOR LEG DEVELOPMENT

Nobody questions the importance of leg development. The legs have the biggest muscles in the body, and they carry us wherever we go. If they're strong, we glide along. If they're weak, each step drags. Many uninformed people think that weight-trained legs are slow and clumsy. Nothing could be farther from the truth. Weight training develops the fast twitch muscle cells, which gives them the explosive power needed to jump, sprint, lift a heavy weight, or come off the line in a football game. In fact, many runners have found that long-distance running to the exclusion of strength training has put them in condition to be unable to jump or move with great speed. Obviously, a combination of strength and endurance training would be best for most people, especially those who want neither the bulging legs of the bodybuilder nor the stringy limbs of the long-distance runner.

The leg is made up of many muscles. Each has its function in enabling us to run, jog, leap, slide, skip, dance, or to step forward, sideways, backwards. The adductors pull the leg toward the body's centerline, and the abductors pull it away. The quadriceps, the four muscles of the front, inner, and outer thigh, pull the lower leg forward and straighten the leg. The leg biceps pull the lower leg back, bending it at the knee.

Squatting, leg press, and leg extension movements develop the quadriceps. Leg curls develop the leg biceps. Any movement away from the body will develop the abductors, while any movement toward the body's centerline will develop the adductors.

Some of the machines we are about to describe are for compound leg work. That is, they work several leg muscles in combination at the same time. Others isolate specific muscles or muscle groups, in order to heighten specific muscular development.

Let's start with the upper leg machines.

UPPER LEG OR THIGH MACHINES

Quadriceps Machines

The machines and the movements described below work the quadriceps muscles of the front and outer thigh. They also work the calf and leg biceps muscles to a certain degree. If you go through a good workout, the next morning there'll be no doubt which muscles were worked and which ones were not!

Squatting with Free Weights

Although a power rack is not really a machine, it is a device that adds safety to the regular squat. Let's explain first what the squat is; then we'll show how the power rack is an improvement on completely free weight squats.

The squat is, at the same time, the most popular and the most detested exercise in the weight trainer's repertoire. It is difficult to do when you first start training, but it becomes easier the more you do it. While this is true for any weight training exercise, it is more impressive in the case of the squat, since you use more weight than in almost any other exercise.

Perform the squat as follows:

1. Use a squat rack to hold the barbell until you get ready to lift it. When you begin to use high poundages, you won't be able to lift the thing off the floor and onto your shoulders anyway.

2. Step under the bar, position yourself so that it rests on the trapezius muscles (not the neck!), just below the nape of the neck.

3. Grip the bar firmly with both hands, using a medium-wide grip (each hand should be about 1½ feet from the shoulders).

4. Arch the back, so that your lower back will not be in a weak configuration. The head should be up, with

QUARTER SQUATS: OLYMPIC BARBELL

the eyes to the front. Also, bunch the muscles in the upper back, not only to support the bar but to strengthen the column of muscles along the spine.

5. Get somebody to watch you, to see if you are keeping the spine vertical. If you have a curvature, especially to the side, you may need to do remedial work on one side (with side exercises, etc.) to build enough strength to be able to stand straight. We can't overemphasize the importance of keeping your spine in perfect vertical alignment during this lift. You want a solid column, not a wavy line. Otherwise, injuries may result.

6. Make sure that you are in the center of the bar, and not to either side of center. If you are not in the center, you will get a nasty surprise when you lift the bar off the rack and feel the imbalance. That's when you'll pull your lower back and your latissimus muscles.

7. Get both of your feet aligned with the bar before you lift. The feet should be about shoulder-width apart.

8. Lift up, make sure you are steady on your feet, and then step back away from the rack. Keep the back arched at all times, head up, eyes front.

9. For quarter-squats, bend the legs at the knees and go about one-fourth the way down to the floor. Then

HALF SQUATS: OLYMPIC BARBELL

straighten the legs and return to a standing position.

10. For half-squats, do the same thing, only go down halfway.

11. For parallel squats, go down until the tops of your thighs are parallel to the floor.

12. For full squats or deep knee bends, go all the way down until the backs of your thighs touch the backs of your calves. Then return to a standing position.

13. When you do the number of repetitions you want to do, carefully step back toward the squat rack, get under it until the barbell is over the troughs of the rack, sit it down in the troughs, make sure that both ends are firmly set, then bend down and step away.

That's the basic squat with a barbell and a regular set of squat racks. You should buy a lifting belt to wear when you do squats. It's a heavy-duty leather belt that will give your lower back extra support during the lift.

Now that you know how to do the squat, here are the variations.

PARALLEL SQUATS: OLYMPIC BARBELL

Squatting with a Power Rack

Power racks look like a diagram of a box. They are invariably built of steel pipe or angle iron, and usually stand 7 or 8 feet high. The vertical pipes have holes in them, through which you can slide sturdy metal rods (usually 1½-inch steel pipe). The barbell rests either on these rods or on brackets that are also adjustable for height.

To set the power rack up, place the brackets or troughs so that the barbell can rest on them at a height that will enable you to get under it without too much backbending. Then set the lower set of rods at a height below which you don't want to go.

Step into the power rack (between the vertical posts or pipes), and lift the barbell off the same way you would when using plain squat racks. Instead of stepping backwards, just lift the bar off the brackets or troughs, and do the squat. The bottom rods should be positioned so that the bar almost touches them at the bottommost point of travel.

Do whatever number of repetitions you want to do within the context of your workout. If you can't make the last rep, simply lower the bar until it rests on the bottom rods.

What's the purpose of the power rack? It enables you to use maximum poundages without having to worry about dropping the weight, or not getting up with the weight once you're in the downmost position of the exercise.

Also, by judicious placing of the rods, you can start the lift at any point in the range of motion that the squat encompasses—all with minimized danger to the lifter.

Squatting With the Moore Leg Blaster

The Moore Leg Blaster is a new device that enables you to do squatting movements while stabilizing your body (and the weight) by using your hands. The Leg Blaster consists of a heavily padded double U-shaped apparatus which fits over the shoulders. Weight is attached to vertical rods on the sides. This arrangement leaves the arms free to grip a horizontal bar for balance. Squats are then done in the regular manner, with variations depending on the placement of the feet relative to the horizontal bar. The horizontal bar could be a ballet bar, or it could be any handy object that can be gripped while doing the movement. Be sure that it is firmly attached, whatever it is, and that it is strong enough to hold up under the pull of your hands.

Ira Hurley of the Unique Training Device Company has a small metal bench that is sometimes used in conjunction with the Moore Leg Blaster. It consists of a metal stand with padded pieces against which the backs of the lower legs are placed. There is also a piece under which you can hook the feet. This small stand immobilizes the lower leg so that the quadriceps can be further isolated during the squatting movement. In a sense, it is the reverse of the leg-extension movement. In that movement, the upper leg is stationary

WIDE-STANCE ADDUCTION SQUATS: OLYMPIC BARBELL AND POWER RACK (STARTING POSITION)

WIDE-STANCE ADDUCTION SQUATS (FINAL POSITION)

while the lower leg moves. In this exercise, the upper leg moves while the lower leg is stationary.

CONCENTRATED SQUATS: MOORE LEG BLASTER AND UNIQUE TRAINING DEVICE COMPANY RACK

Squatting with the Rader Magic Circle

Peary Rader, who, with his wife Mabel, has published *Iron Man* magazine for many years, is one of the iron world's most respected persons. Completely democratic in editorial policy, Rader's *Iron Man* is the best source of weight-training lore in existence. We've never met the Raders, but people who know them have verified what we guessed from reading their magazine: Amidst all the hoopla and hyperbole of modern bodybuilding, the Raders are, refreshingly, just plain folks.

Peary Rader's Magic Circle is the kind of invention you would expect from just plain folks. It is so utterly sensible, simple, and effective, it is difficult to understand why it's not standard equipment in every gym in the country. Here's how it works.

The Magic Circle is a circle of metal, made out of heavyweight flat stock, bent in a circle about 4 feet in diameter. Attached to the circle of metal are four heavy-duty chains that in turn are attached to large metal rings. The rings are held to heavy cloth straps by leather connectors. The straps are quite wide and fit over the shoulders. A link holds the two front rings together. Another link holds the two back rings together.

To the sides, there are vertical rods on which you can pile a considerable number of barbell plates. The whole thing rests on a couple of sawhorses.

To use the Magic Circle, simply step between the sawhorses, get under the straps, and stand up. Keep the back arched the same way you would for the regular squat. But remember, you won't be holding the weight on the backs of your shoulders. You will have the weight distributed over the tops of your shoulders by the heavy cloth straps.

Step away from the sawhorses and

squat away. If you can't make it up from that last rep, just sit down on the floor and take the load off your shoulders! The circle is large enough in diameter so that you shouldn't get into any trouble. The device will hold over 1,200 pounds of weight. Take a look at a copy of *Iron Man* sometime. There is Mr. Rader, looking comfortable as he can be, standing in the middle of the Magic Circle, with 425 pounds.

Squatting with the Paramount and Universal Squatting Machines

For over a decade, machine builders have tried to lure people away from squatting to a variety of leg press machines. It ain't the same, and the bodybuilders know it. Several new squatting machines are currently available. Two are Universal's Centurion and the Paramount squatting machine, which feature pin-loaded plates for easy weight changing, sturdy construction, and a comfortable body position. The Paramount machine is similar to Universal's, so the description of how to use one will work for the other.

Place the pin in position for the desired weight, step back and stand up until the padded arms that extend from the machine are over your shoulders. Keep the back straight or slightly arched as in the regular squat. Lift upwards, straightening the legs as you rise. If you are not very tall, you may have to stand on a sturdy box in order to get a full range of motion out of these machines. Some are adjustable for individual height, and some are not.

Both machines have a common feature: When you do the squat, the arms that rest on your shoulders pivot at a point in the machine. That means that you are being pitched slightly forward as you do the lift. Be sure to stand a little closer to the machine than usual, so that your body is actually slanting backward. Thus, as you rise, you'll be better able to keep the spine in a strong position.

One thing to bear in mind about all of the squat helpers and squat machines: The less machinery, the more you will be able to approximate your own individual range of motion and the more you will be able to simulate the kind of osteopathic alignment that comes from having to balance the weight as well as lift it. It is no trivial matter to hold a heavy weight on your shoulders. If you have trouble with your back, it will surface with this lift.

Further, if you are weak in the stabilizing muscles that keep you erect, the problem will be compounded the more weight you use. Some people would do well to work on the stabilizing muscles before they try to do squats. Some powerlifting champions practice their balance and strengthen the stabilizing muscles in their backs and sides on a little teeter-totter device called a "kinesthetic primer board." Some of the more advanced do squats with considerable weight while balancing on the board! If you think that's easy, you should try it sometime.

Squatting with the Dynacam and Paramount Floor-Type Bench Press Machines

Earlier, we described Dynacam's and Paramount's floor-type bench press machines. These machines can also be used for squatting. Simply place the bar high enough on the vertical tracks to step under; then position the bar on your shoulders as you would do with free weights. Keep the back arched, and lift the bar off the pegs. Do the squat in the regular way. When you finish the exercise, rotate the bar and hang the hooks on the pegs. Then simply step away from the bar.

SQUAT: KINESTHETIC PRIMER BOARD

Squatting with Hack Machines

Paramount and Dynacam both manufacture hack squat machines. Both machines are combination hack squat and calf raise exercisers. They are both pin-loaded, with about 200 pounds of weight for each of the two exercises. We'll cover the calf raise portion of the machines in the section on calf exercise machines.

The two machines are so similar that one description will work for both. The hack squat station consists of a pair of runners, slanted at a shallow angle, with a padded board that runs up and down tracks mounted in the runners. There is a footboard, which is also slanted and is almost perpendicular to the upright board. To use the machine, set the pin for the amount of weight you want to use, climb onto the machine, lean back against the upright board, bend the knees, drop down and grasp the handles that stick out from either side of the board, and lift by straightening the legs.

Your hands must stay tightly gripped to the handles. Friction will keep your back from sliding on the board. The machine works the quadriceps, chiefly, especially the area at the bottom of the thigh next to the knee. If you have any knee problems, this lift will let you know it. Also, you will have a tendency to bend forward as you grip the handles. Don't bend

SQUAT: PARAMOUNT FLOOR-TYPE PRESS MACHINE (courtesy, Chicago Health Club)

HACK SQUAT: PARAMOUNT HACK SQUAT MACHINE

your back! Instead, bend the knees until you are low enough to keep the back flexed and slightly arched as you would in an ordinary knee bend or squat.

Most people bend at the waist and stretch their arms down to the handles so that they can avoid bending at the knees. That way, you can handle more weight and impress the guys around the gym. You won't impress anybody who knows anything about hack squats, however, because it's the kind of thing that novices do to get their poundages up to respectable levels.

Use a light weight at first, and add weight judiciously. These machines put terrific pressure on the knees and, if the form is bad, pressure on the lower back. This is not a design flaw. Both machines are superbly designed and built. It's the result of the bad form that most people use when doing hack squats.

Leg Press Machines

Leg press machines come in a variety of forms. Nautilus makes a leg press in combination with a leg-extension machine. In it, you sit leaning backwards at a shallow angle, with the feet on large pads at about eye level.

The knees are bent at about a 90-degree angle.

To use the machine, set the pins for the desired weight, climb onto the seat, place the feet on the pads, and push forward with your legs. Don't lock the knees at the outermost position, or you might suffer injury. Keep the tension constant all the way through the lift. Push slowly out, and then slowly let the weight back down.

You may find it uncomfortable to handle a lot of weight on the Nautilus leg press machine. The seat isn't all that well padded, and in Ralph's case, a lot of pressure is generated in the small of the back where he has an old injury. This is not the machine's fault but an irregularity in Ralph's spine. However, it means that pressure is being generated as you push the legs forward. The pressure is centered at the base of the spine where it joins to the pelvic bones. If you have injuries in this area, as Ralph does, be careful.

The leg press stations on the Dynacam, Paramount, and Universal multistation machines are much the same in design. They all feature a small seat, reminiscent of a Piper Supercub cockpit, with footpads or pedals to push against. All are pin-loaded for easy weight changes, and some have pin-loaded position changes for the seats so that you can position yourself closer or farther away from the foot pedals. The closer you are to the pedals, the more your

LEG PRESS: NAUTILUS COMPOUND LEG MACHINE

LEG PRESS: PARAMOUNT LEG PRESS STATION

knees are bent and the harder it is to do the lift. The farther away from the foot pedals you are, the easier it is to do the movement. It's analogous to the full squat and the quarter-squat in terms of relative difficulty.

Dynacam also makes a floor-type leg press machine, in which you lie on your back with your feet pointing toward the ceiling. The back pad is angled so that you can get a full range of motion. The plates are pin-loaded, but there is also provision for the addition of barbell plates on pegs on the horizontal bar that is pushed against with the feet. There is a smaller model that is not pin-loaded but is rigged with barbell plates exclusively.

Paramount makes what they call a "seated hips and buttocks press," which is a leg press in which you lie with the back in a bow, feet up at or above eye level, knees bent. The feet rest on a padded metal plate, which is fastened to a rectangular frame, which in turn is attached to a curved lever, a cable, and a pulley. The machine is pin-loaded.

While Paramount cites the curved backrest as a deliberate design feature, we should point out that, although braced, the back when bowed is in its weakest structural configuration. Electromyographs of muscle tension in a bowed back indicate that little muscular activity in the back muscles is possible in this position.

Some people swear by the machine. Others swear *at* it. Try it and see if it works for you.

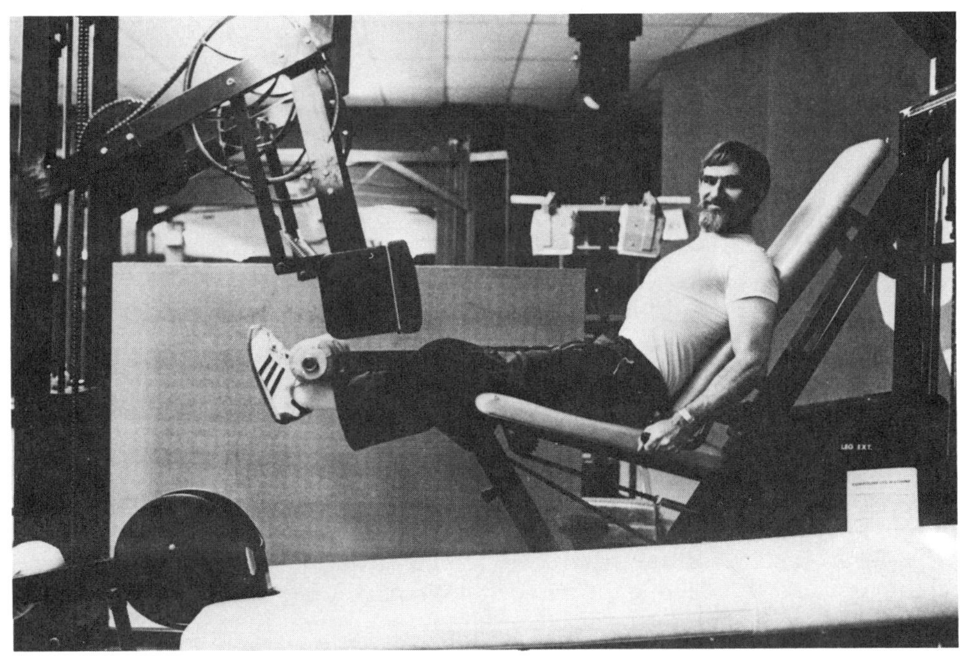

LEG EXTENSION: NAUTILUS COMPOUND LEG MACHINE

LEG EXTENSION: PARAMOUNT LEG EXTENSION STATION

Leg Extension Machines

Nautilus, Dynacam, Paramount, and Universal all make leg extension machines. These devices immobilize the upper leg, while allowing the lower leg to move upward in an arc. Since the movement is precisely the same in all the machines, they are all similar in design. They differ in the distance between the pivot point of the lever and the padded bar under which you place the feet.

Consequently, some machines are more comfortable for people with long lower legs, while some are better for people with shorter lower legs. The lever systems differ from machine to machine, so while the movement is the same, the way the machine allows you to make the movement differs. The Nautilus leg extension is too long for Ralph's legs. The Universal machine pivots in a way that doesn't match Ralph's own lever system. Dynacam is comfortable for him but doesn't give him a thorough workout. The Paramount leg extension fits Ralph as if it were tailor-made for him. These differences are not design flaws. It's just a matter of matching the lever system and the consequent range of motion of the machine with your own particular lever system and range of motion.

With all of the machines, the lift is done the same way. Sit in the seat that's provided. Loop the feet under the padded bar near the floor. Pivot at the knees and straighten the legs out until the knees are locked. Then slowly bend the knees and let the padded bar back down to the starting position. Plates in all the machines are pin-loaded. Some use cables, while Nautilus uses chains. Some are free-standing, while others are attached to multistation machines. Shop around and try them all.

The Unique Training Device Company has a device called the D.A.R.D., which consists of a plate holder, a couple of parallel bars with rubber cushions, and a pin to hold the plates on. With this device, you can simulate any of the leg extension movements. Simply sit in a chair or on the edge of a bench, slip your toes between the padded bars, and lift the device by straightening the legs. It's quick, easy, simple, and it works. You can put on as much weight as you could ever possibly handle. What's more, it's small enough to take with you on trips or vacations. With the D.A.R.D., there's no excuse not to do your leg work when you're out of town.

Leg Biceps Machines

The D.A.R.D. can also be used for leg biceps work. Lie prone on a bench, slip your feet between the padded bars, this time keeping the pressure on the heels instead of the toes. The legs begin the motion straight and end bent at the knee.

Dynacam, Nautilus, Universal, and Paramount manufacture leg curling machines. They all have benches on which you can either sit or lie on your stomach. From the sitting position, you can perform the leg extension by slipping the feet under a low padded bar. To do the leg curl, lie on your stomach and slip your heels under a high padded bar. Some of the machines are pin-loaded; others use

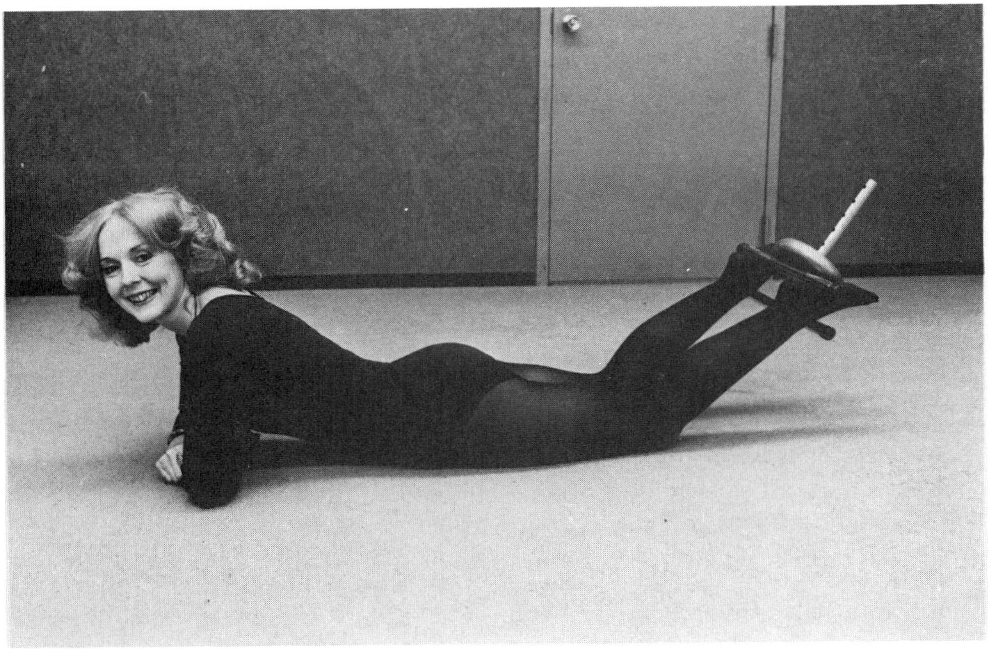

LEG CURL: D.A.R.D. DEVICE

LEG CURL: NAUTILUS LEG CURL MACHINE

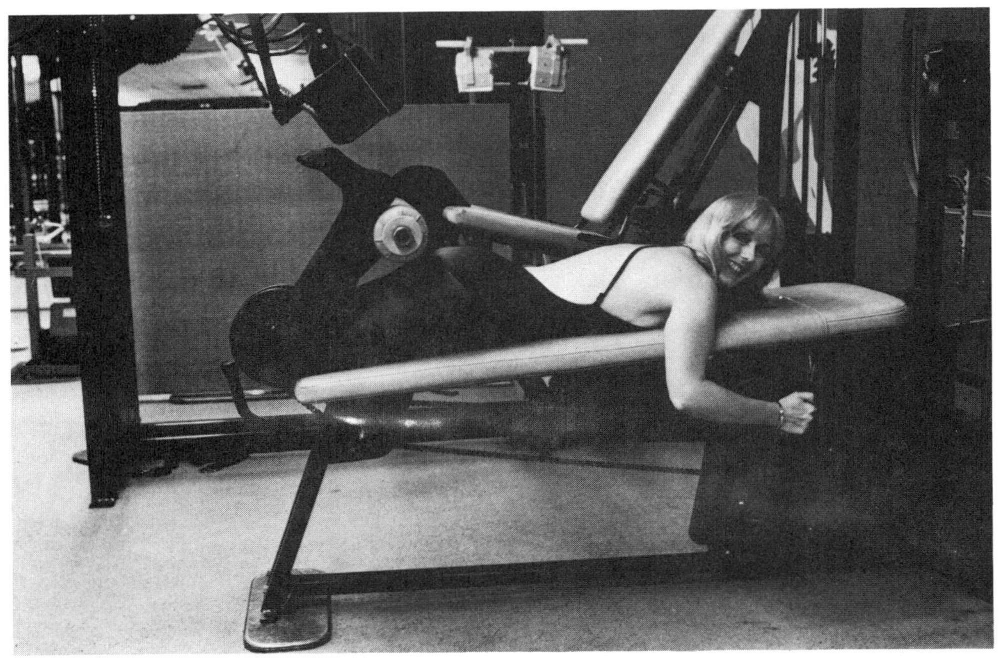

barbell plates mounted on small, protruding bars.

Paramount offers a standup leg curling machine, which is part of their multistation gym machine. This is the same multistation gym that has the leg extension station that fits Ralph so well. The standup leg curl station features pads against which the front of the legs are placed and padded bars against which the heels are placed. There is a bar for hand gripping, and the plates are pin-loaded. Set the weight with the pin, stand erect with the front of the legs against the pads, and lift one leg at a time, bending the leg at the knee. The foot will thus travel in an arc behind you.

LEG CURL: PARAMOUNT LEG CURL STATION

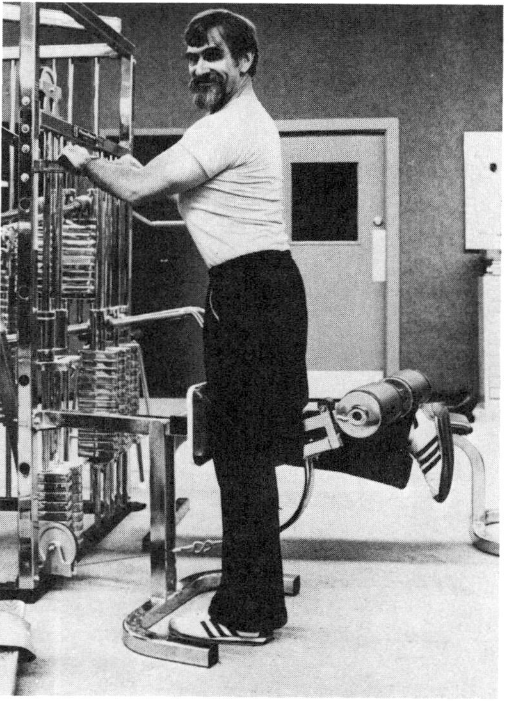

Try to touch your buttocks with your foot. You won't be able to, but that's the movement you're after.

You don't need much weight with any of these leg curl machines. They exert a lot of pressure on the knees, since the upper leg is immobilized. Be careful, especially if you've never used one of the leg extensions or leg curls before. When you use the leg curl machines in which you lie prone, don't bend your back from side to side. Also, don't allow the buttocks to rise up off the bench. Instead, keep the movement smooth, and use just enough weight to fatigue the muscles without sacrificing form.

When you use the Paramount standup leg curl machine, stand erect. Don't lean from side to side trying to get up more weight than you need. Keep the back slightly arched, hold onto the bar in front of you, and bring the leg up slowly. "Ballistic" or explosively rapid movements will serve only to increase the danger of serious injury to the knees and ankles. Go slowly, and add weight in small increments.

Inner and Outer Thigh Adductor and Abductor Machines

The inner thigh muscles are called "adductors," meaning that they pull the leg towards the body's center line. The outer thigh muscles are called "abductors," meaning that they pull the leg away from the center line. Paramount and Dynacam both make machines to work these muscles.

Dynacam makes both a single and a double version of the machine. The double model has a station at both ends. Both work on the same principle. They have two sets of pads between which your knees are placed as you sit on the edge of the bench. The pads are vertical and have adjustments for different sizes. Your knees are bent, and your feet are placed on little stirrups during the exercise.

A knob adjusts the amount of resistance to sideways motions. Adjust it for your individual adductor and abductor strength, and then move your legs from side to side, pivoting at the hip joint. Go easy on this one at first. These muscles are almost always neglected, and you could pull something if you're not careful.

Paramount's machine is dissimilar only in minor details. The action of the machine is precisely the same, with an adjustment wheel instead of a knob, square ends on the bench instead of rounded, etc. They're both chromed, well upholstered, and are solid pieces of equipment.

Adduction and abduction movements can be done with ankle weights or iron shoes. Strap the weights to your ankles or feet and you're ready to go.

For abduction movements, you can either stand erect or lie on your side on the floor. If you stand erect, lift the leg (knee locked) out to the side. Don't worry about not being able to lift the leg very high. The hip joint allows for only about 15 degrees of movement in this direction anyway.

LATERAL LEG RAISE: ANKLE WEIGHTS

ADDUCTION LEG RAISE: ANKLE WEIGHTS

ADDUCTION SQUATS: BARBELL

If you do the movement on the floor, be sure that you move the leg in a vertical plane while lying on the side. Don't allow yourself to roll back on the buttocks. If you do that, you'll work the lower abdominals instead of the leg abductors.

Adduction, or movements toward the body's centerline, are a little more complicated. While lying on your side, try to lift the leg that is against the floor toward the ceiling. You have to move the top leg out of the way while keeping your balance.

Another way to work the adductors is simply to use a wide stance in the full squat. Use a light weight, place the feet a little more than shoulder-width apart, point the toes outwards, and do slow, full squats. Don't bounce at the bottom of the movement. If you've never done this one before, your adductors will let you know where they are right away!

Calf Machines

The calf muscles are probably the most difficult to develop. The tissue is dense, and, because the calves propel us through every step we take all our lives, they are usually developed for endurance. That means that the slow-twitch muscle cells are developed in greater proportion than the fast-twitch cells, with the result that the calves are not terribly strong and not very large.

Few people develop their calves properly. Most people don't even try. Look around the beach someday at all the skinny calves. It's commonplace to find young bodybuilders with superb upper body development, moderate leg development, and no calf development at all.

In the old days, people developed their calves by doing calf raises with a heavy barbell on their shoulders. These movements are also called "heel raises" and (erroneously) "toe raises." To do them, all you have to do is raise your heels while standing on the balls of your feet. You work the calf muscles (hence, the name "calf raises"), and you stand on your toes (hence, "toe raises"). It's the heel you raise and lower. To stretch the muscles and also get a full range of motion in the exercise, it helps to stand with the toes on a raised block. That way, you can lower the heel to a point below the level of the toes. When you go up, be sure to go all the way up, achieving a full contraction of the calf muscles at the top of the lift.

When you do calf raises with a heavy barbell, you run the same risk of lower back injury that you run while doing the squat. The barbell is held in the same position for both lifts. Machine manufacturers have tried a variety of ways to get around this problem. Some have been successful, some haven't.

Whatever the specific machine design, there are two basic types of calf raises: seated and standing. Because the knee is bent during seated calf raises, the lower calf muscle, or soleus, is developed more than the upper calf muscle, or gastrocnemius. The standing calf raise emphasizes development of the upper calf muscle.

Dynacam and Paramount both make a combination hack squat and calf raise machine. The machines are similar enough to need only one description as far as their use is concerned. Both have a calf raise station which consists of a raised block (Paramount's block is higher), padded shoulder blocks that are attached to swinging metal arms (Dynacam's padding is thicker), and a stack of pin-loaded plates.

Both machines use a central shaft that attaches to plates at the bottom end and to the swinging arms at the top. A pin goes into the shaft to position the height of the shoulder pads. Another pin goes into the plates for weight selection.

To use the machines, set the plate pin for the desired weight, set the shaft pin for the desired shoulder pad height (set it low enough so that you don't lose the pressure on your shoulders when you are in the down-

CALF RAISE: DYNACAM CALF MACHINE

CALF RAISE: NAUTILUS MULTI-EXERCISE MACHINE

most position with your heels). Put the balls of your feet on the block, with the toes slightly over the edge. Dip down and position your shoulders under the pads. Arch the back as you would do in the squat so that you will have a strong foundation for the exercise, and then rise up on your toes, lifting the heels as high as you can go. If you do the exercise correctly and with the right amount of weight, you should feel a burning sensation after about eight to ten repetitions.

Make sure that the block is securely fastened to the machine. It has a tendency to work loose with heavy use, and you can snap your ankle if you slip off with a lot of weight on your shoulders.

Also, you'll find that the stack of plates is inadequate for any really serious calf work. Consequently, people tend to load up the top of the shaft with barbell plates. Eventually, this will bend the shaft and make the exercise difficult to do. Some gyms prohibit such plate loading; others encourage it. If there isn't enough weight in the stack to give you a good workout, ask about using extra plates.

Nautilus has tried to get around the back-strain problem by using a lifting harness instead of shoulder pads and swinging arms. The Nautilus calf raise machine also uses pin-loaded plates and features three different levels of steps on which your toes are placed, to assure you of all the calf work you could possibly want.

The harness is a wide cloth strap that loops around the pelvic girdle and fastens with a hook and chain to a small swinging arm. This arrangement takes the load off the shoulders and lower back, and places it on the top of the pelvic bones, distributed by the wide strap over the complete circle around the hips.

One word of caution: Wear substantial warmup clothes or a sweat suit when using the Nautilus calf machine. If you work with high poundages, the edge of the strap tends to cut into the skin. If your workout suit is not thick enough, put a towel around your waist before you start the lift.

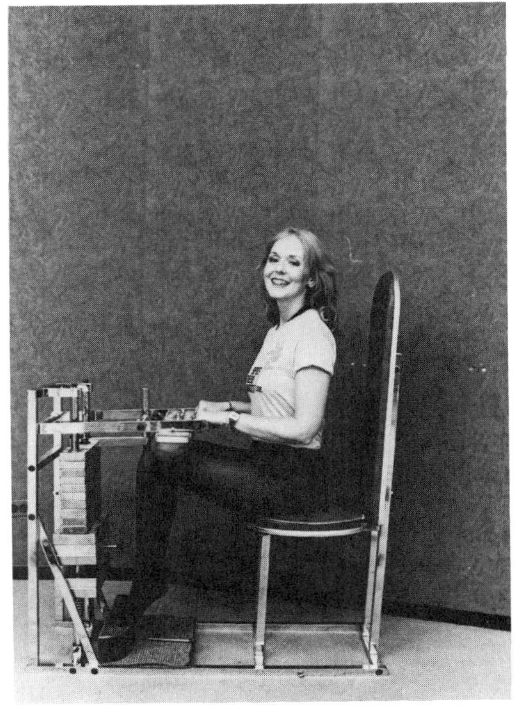

SEATED CALF RAISE: DYNACAM SEATED CALF RAISE MACHINE

Dynacam also makes a seated calf machine, which has a heavily padded bar that runs across the tops of your knees. Sit in the chair that is built into the machine, lean against the backrest, place the knees under the padded bar, put the balls of your feet on top of the wooden block, and raise your heels. The machine is pin-loaded for easy weight selection. The only problem is the lack of weight. The Dynacam catalog shows only fifteen plates on the seated calf raise machine, which is three less than the standing model. When you use the seated machine, you're raising only the weight of the plates, but when you use the standing machine you are lifting both the weight of the plates and your own upper body weight.

The common solution, of course, is to pile barbell plates on top of the machine, with the resultant damage that such overloading causes. Additional plates can be added by the manufacturers. It would seem logical to order more weight from the factory than to risk damage to the machine through overloading. It costs more in the short run but saves money in the long run. It also saves frayed nerves and injuries from equipment that is falling apart through no fault of the manufacturer.

CALF RAISE: PARAMOUNT LEG PRESS STATION

All of the multistation machines have a leg press station which can double as a calf raise station. Push the pedals out as far as you can, lock the knees, and then push farther with the toes.

Obviously, this is not a good method for doing calf raises. First, you should never lock your knees when doing leg presses. The danger of injury to the knee is considerable. Second, if you try to push the pedals farther out by using the toes or the ball of your foot, you will place even greater strain on the knee joint. This is because the foot is levering in an arc that tends to raise the top of the lower limb. Since the hips are immobilized and the knee is locked, it is the knee joint that gets the force of the lever action. That's why Nautilus warns against locking the knees when doing leg presses. Doing calf raises with a leg press machine only compounds the likelihood of injury.

The same holds for leg press machines in which you lie horizontally while pushing upwards with the feet. With these machines, the sciatic nerves are already taut, given the angle of the hips and the legs. To lock the knees and push farther with the toes places more strain on the whole system of levers that begins with the bones of the toes and ends with the hip joints.

There is also a wide variety of dreadful calf-exercise machines, some of which should not be allowed in any reputable gym. We won't re-

BOB GAJDA COACHES VALERIE ON THE OSCILLATING BALANCE BEAM

view them here, but you'll see them when you go out to tour the health clubs. Here's what to look for. If it's a standing calf exerciser, check out the shoulder pads. One of the major manufacturers makes a standing machine with padding only a quarter of an inch thick. Since the weight rests not only on the trapezius muscles but across the collarbones as well, there is no way that you can comfortably do calf raises with the machine.

If it's a seated machine, check the thickness of the padding on the bar that rests across the tops of the knees. One such machine, which is gaining in popularity lately, has pads that are nothing more than lightweight foam rubber under cheap vinyl covering. Every day the guys get up from the machine with white spots on the tops of their knees where the circulation has been cut off during the exercise. Remember, if you are going to develop your calves, you need to *increase* the circulation to the calves, not cut it off. This particular machine also has a peculiar lever system in which the weight moves a distance of more than triple the distance traveled by the heels when the lift is made. The result is a momentum built into the design of the machine which makes slow, measured raises impossible to perform. Also, there are no pins or collars to keep the plates from sliding off, and the gym resounds occasionally with clanging plates and cursing members.

ADDITIONAL MACHINES AND SPECIAL EQUIPMENT

In addition to the Tension Bands described on pp. 38 and 39 and the kinesthetic primer board described on page 116, the Sports Fitness Institute also uses a balance-beam exercise sequence as part of athletic training programs. The beam is a narrow (4-inch) wooden beam that rests on the floor. If the floor is covered with a carpet, all the better, since it will make it even more difficult to walk on the beam. The balance beam is much narrower than the ones that Nadia Comaneci uses in the Olympics. Its edges are rounded, and it'll slip right out from under you if you don't watch out.

The first step is to learn to stand on the beam without wobbling. Then you learn to walk forward, then backward. Next, you must learn to stand on one foot, then hop from one foot to the other. Finally, you learn to hop and switch foot positions in the process, then hop from one beam to another that is about five feet away.

The purpose of all this is to accomplish two things: to work the stabilizing muscles that give us symmetrical performance; and to achieve what is called "structural integrity," which is another way of talking about strengthening, aligning, and coordinating all of the bodily components of athletic performance.

Some excellent machines are available only in large cities or in the state in which they are manufactured. Furthermore, there are over 200 firms presently manufacturing weight-training machines, ranging from small benches to complex double-pulley crossover pectoral machines. It is impossible to list all of these machines; in fact, it is impossible even to keep up with them. Tiny companies wink in and out of existence overnight.

Consequently, we've limited ourselves to the major manufacturers. (Consult the list at the end of the book.) Almost any gym or health club will have machines made by the firms we've listed. The odds are that no matter where you live in the United States, you will find Paramount, Dynacam, Universal, or Nautilus equipment.

You may also run across equipment made by Mini-Gym, a relatively new company which has designed a line of machines around a new concept in weight training: isokinetics.

The isokinetic machines are similar to other machines in the sense that no matter what kind of resistance is employed in the machine, a press is still a press and a squat is still a squat. However, it is in the concept of the resistance itself that Mini-Gym has made its breakthrough.

Most machines use pin-loaded plates for resistance. Some use friction clamps, and some use barbell plates hung on pegs. Mini-Gym uses a patented "black box" that provides a resistance slightly lower than whatever pressure is applied to the machine. This is called "accommodating resistance." It means that you are operating at almost peak effort throughout the range of motion, not through the action of a complicated system of levers, counterbalances, eccentric cams, pulleys, cables, etc., but through a device that accommodates itself to the amount of effort you put into any particular movement so that the resistance is always just under what would be required to stop the movement altogether.

Further, the device controls the speed at which the movement is made. It inhibits acceleration through the movement, thus preventing the cheating motions that we usually achieve by ballistically tossing the weight up with the strongest, most rapid motion at the beginning of the lift.

The result is a resistance that is consistently accommodating itself to the amount of effort you are able to exert throughout the entire range of motion of any specific exercise, and a resistance that controls acceleration so that the movement is done in strict form.

Further, you can control the resistance by twisting a dial on the black box. If you want to train for speed as well as strength, you can do the movements quickly (but with controlled acceleration through the movement). If you want to train for slow, steady strength, you can do that, too.

Since most sports movements are made with considerable speed, the Mini-Gym equipment has become very popular with coaches and trainers. Among the pieces of equipment currently available are:

1. The "Leaper," which consists of shoulder-padded lever arms and which enables you to simulate the leaping motions you would perform in a basketball game.
2. Forearm and hand "Shivers," which enable you to simulate the forearm- and hand-pushing movements usually done in football scrimmage.
3. Swim benches, which simulate the motions of swimming.
4. Tennis-simulation machines.
5. Mobile rehabilitation units for physical therapy.
6. Floor-type press machines.

LEG EXERCISE: MINI-GYM LEAPER (Andy Dumpis)

DELTOID AND QUADRICEP EXERCISE: MINI-GYM SHIVER

SEATED PRESS: MINI-GYM FLOOR-TYPE PRESS MACHINE

In addition to these machines, Mini-Gym also makes devices for bench presses, leg raises, rowing, sit-ups, latissimus exercises, leg kicks, dips, leg presses, pectoral development, incline bench presses, lat and shoulder exercises, triceps extensions, hamstring strengtheners, and many other specific exercises.

All of the machines incorporate the unique isokinetic resistance device instead of stacks of plates. If you have the chance, give them a try. You'll be surprised at the difference in feel between Mini-Gym and the regular machines. Ideally, you should use them all: free weights, regular isotonic machines, and isokinetic machines in your total workout program. Remember: Exercise is specific. The more well rounded the program, the more well rounded you'll be.

Hydra-Gym

Of all the new machines on the market, one of the most fascinating both in design and concept is the Hydra-Gym line, manufactured by Jerry Brentham's Hydra-Gym Athletics in Belton, Texas. These machines are isokinetic (the speed of the exercise movements is controlled by the resistance), but they do not use noisy friction clutches, black boxes, cables, oily chains, or heavy plates.

Instead, they use hydraulic cylinders, similar in concept and operation to the shock absorbers found on fine automobiles. They are not auto shock absorbers, or course, but are precision designed to be commensurate in resistance with the forces that human muscles are able to exert.

The cylinders do the same thing for muscular movements that shock absorbers do for cars: they resist movement when a force is applied to them. The faster the force is applied, the harder they resist. The slower the force is applied, the less they resist. If you want to really work those muscles out, do all the movements as fast as you can. If you want an easy workout, just slow down.

As you may have guessed by now, these machines accomodate themselves automatically to the strength of the person using them. That's why they're becoming so popular with physical and corrective therapists in the treatment of injuries. Further, they are marvelous machines for endurance work (high reps, with over two minutes at each machine), which

HIP EXERCISE: HYDRA-GYM POWER RUNNER MACHINE

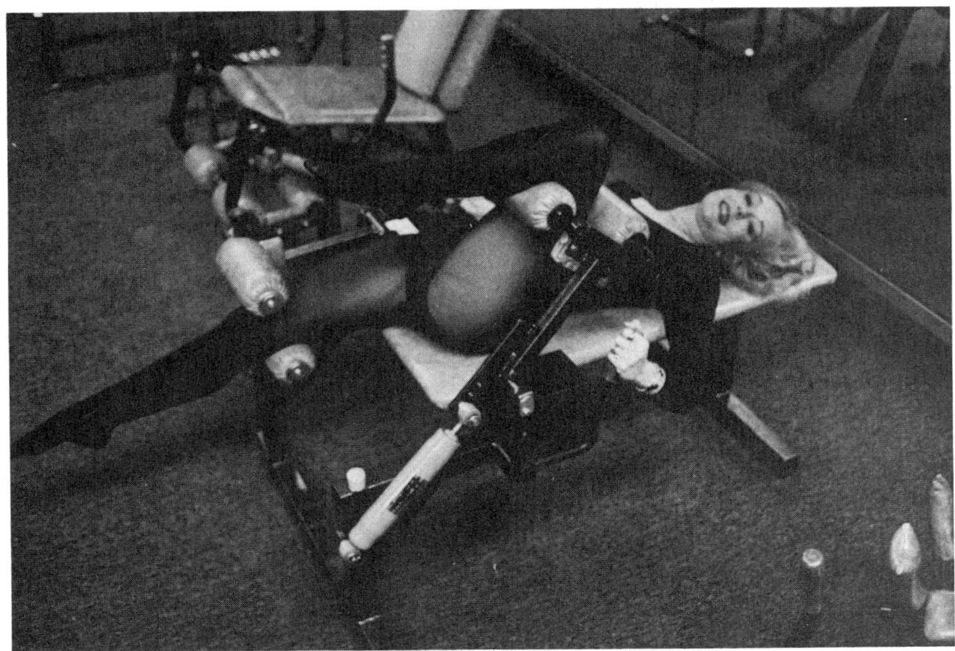

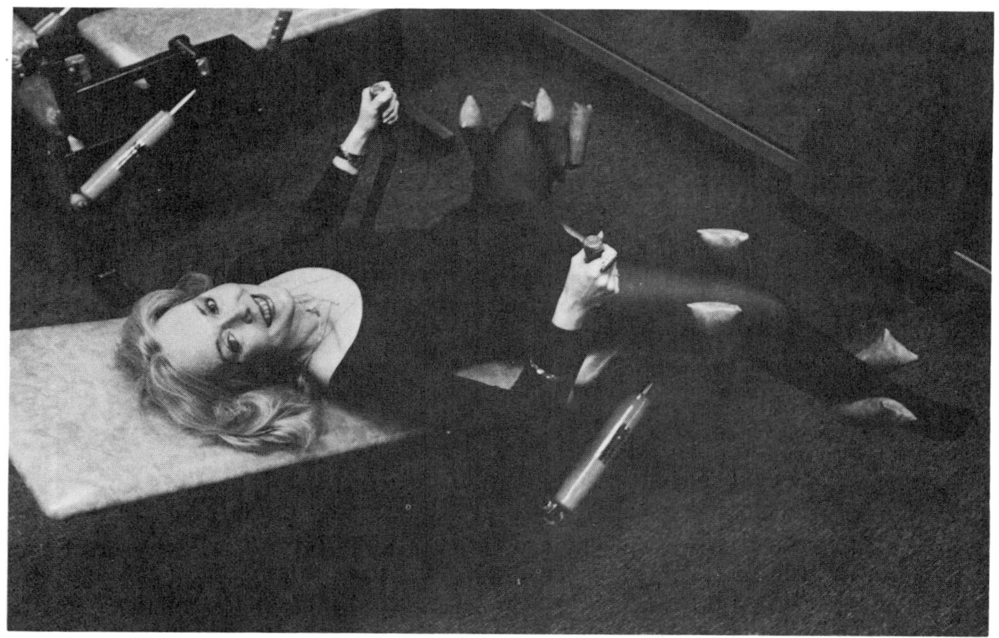

ABDUCTION AND ADDUCTION EXERCISE: HYDRA-GYM AB/AD HIP MACHINE

makes them ideal for everything from fat burning to cardiovascular conditioning.

And the neatest thing about using hydraulic cylinders for resistance is that they're clean, completely silent (no clanking or whirring), light in weight (you don't have to worry about stress loads on the floor), and the maintenance is minimal. The machines themselves are relatively small in size, and can be moved around by one person with no difficulty. Consequently, Hydra-Gym machines are ideal not only for health clubs and gymnasiums, but for office buildings, condominiums, apartment buildings, and private residences. You can put

CURL: HYDRA-GYM BILATERAL ARM CURL MACHINE

in four or five machines for what some people spend for a deluxe hi-fi set. All things considered, Hydra-Gym comes pretty close to the ideal in isokinetic exercise machine design.

See the index of manufacturers in the back of the book for the address.

In the next chapter, we'll familiarize you with the language of weight training, and we'll show you what's going on inside when you do exercises. Then we'll give you a cross-referenced compendium of exercises that will enable you to put together any kind of program you want, no matter what your needs are. By the time you finish the chapter, you will be able to walk into any health club and feel right at home.

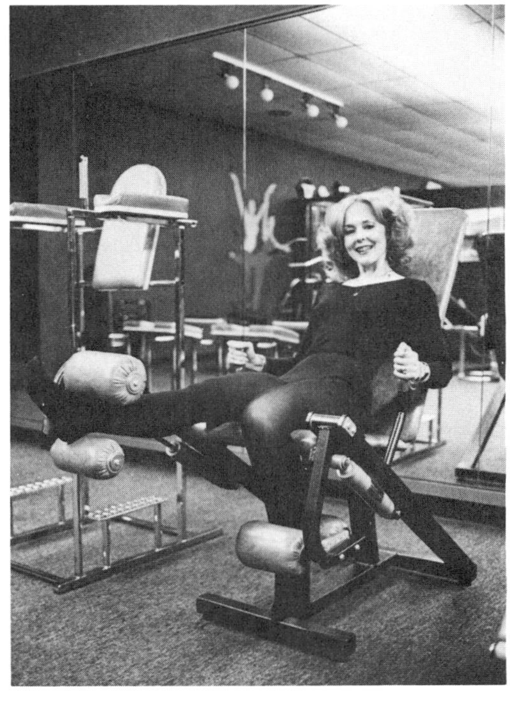

LEG EXTENSION AND LEG CURL: HYDRA-GYM DOUBLE KNEE MACHINE

4

PUTTING ALL THE EQUIPMENT TO WORK FOR YOU

Section One: Getting to Know The Territory

A. THE LANGUAGE OF WEIGHT TRAINING: HOW TO KNOW WHAT THEY'RE TALKING ABOUT DOWN AT THE GYM

Before you start on your program, you'll need to know a few terms that weight trainers, bodybuilders—and people who talk and write about exercise with weights—often use. Like any other field in sports, working with weights has its own special vocabulary, and it's helpful to be able to follow all the shoptalk about sets, reps, burns, split days, pumping, flushing, and PHA training. So let's get our terminology straight, as they say in school:

REPETITIONS

Repetitions ("reps" for short) are specific exercise movements. A completed movement that you would do to a count of "1" or "2" is one *repetition.* If you're doing situps on a slant board and do five full situps to the count of "1-2-3-4-5," you have done five *repetitions* of the situp.

SETS

Sets are specific exercises done for a given number of reps. In the example above, you would have done one *set* of situps with five reps in the set. If you wanted to do three sets of twenty reps, you would do twenty situps, rest for a few seconds, then do twenty more, rest again, and then do the last twenty—hence, three sets of twenty reps each. By breaking up your repetitions in this way, you can often do more repetitions than by not dividing the work into sets. Few people can do sixty situps without pausing for rest, but three sets of twenty reps each is easier to do.

SUPERSETS

Supersets represent a way of working the same or related muscle groups by using different exercises for the same or related body parts. For example, if you want to do supersets for the biceps/triceps area, you might do a set of French curls, followed without rest by a set of machine curls. Another school of thought about supersetting—still controversial in many body-building and weight-training circles—is that supersets can, and should, work *opposing* muscle groups.

FORCED REPS

Forced reps are a good way to help break through sticking points in terms of either weight or reps. Let's say that you can do six reps of the bench press using a weight of two hundred pounds. But six reps is all that you can do; you can't possibly manage a seventh. Then one way to break through this barrier is to have a spotter (a friend or workout partner who stands behind you to catch the weight should it prove to be too heavy). The spotter will give you just enough help so that you can squeeze out a seventh, eighth, even ninth and tenth rep. After several sessions of these forced reps, you'll be strong enough to handle the extra reps by yourself and will have increased your set from six to ten reps.

BURNS

Burns are slow partial movements done at the end of an exercise—the last few inches on the leg extension, say, or the last slow turn to the supinating curl. Incidentally, there's also controversy over this term. Some bodybuilders and weight trainers say that the burns should be done slowly; others say to do them fast.

THE SPLIT SYSTEM

The *split system* refers to a system of working one area of the body during one workout, another area for the next. A common split system is to work the lower body one day and upper body on alternate days. Most bodybuilders, coaches, and training experts, however, advise beginners to do a well-rounded, general conditioning routine each workout and save the split system until they have been training intensively for six months to a year. The system's chief advantage: It allows a person to train upper and lower body on alternating days, so that arm muscles can recover on leg days and vice versa. It also reduces the total number of exercises per workout, yet allows the entire body to get a thorough workout several times a week.

GIANT SETS

Giant sets is a term used in both of two senses: either a "giant set" of many reps—twenty, thirty, or even more—literally, as many reps as you can do; or for three to four exercises for a particular body part done without rest in between, thus composing a "giant set" for a body area. For example, ten leg extensions followed by ten half-squats followed by ten leg curls and ten leg presses, with no rest at all in between, is a *giant set* for the legs.

CIRCUIT TRAINING

Circuit training, popular in many gyms and health clubs, is an effective way of using the machines to achieve aerobic training effect. Participants are asked to go from machine to machine, doing ten to twelve reps per machine or to spend fifteen to thirty seconds per machine, all without resting. Typically, the coach or instructor will take members through six to ten machines before stopping to take a resting pulse-rate reading. Many clubs and spas use circuit training alone, or as an end to an exercise class—and it certainly gives the lie to the notion that weight training is not aerobic exercise.

NEGATIVE RESISTANCE MOVEMENTS

Negative resistance movements involve doing forced reps on exercise machines, using another body part to get the maximum amount of weight up, then resisting the weight and doing the movement in strict form on the way down. The Nautilus bench press machine lends itself particularly well to negative resistance movements. Here the trainer pushes the machine to the "up" position with his/her feet and arms, then drops the feet and brings the weight slowly back with the arms, resisting the weight all the way back down. Obviously, you can handle more weight with this method, so it's a good way to help break out of a sticking point and learn to handle heavier poundages. It really involves a form of "cheating" (see the definition below) so that you throw the weight up ballistically—get it up any way you can—then do the "down" movement in strict form, resisting the weight all the way down.

PARTIAL MOVEMENTS

Partial movements are exactly what you might expect—movements which are only partially completed in order to work out a certain body part or muscle more intensely. For example, if you want to shape and sculpt the bottom third of the thigh—the part right above the knee—you can do partial movements with a leg extension machine. These are really "quarter leg extensions," which move the padded bar only a few inches, in contrast to the full range of motion which might move the bar a foot or more from "down" to "up" positions. Usually, partial movements are undertaken for the purpose of sculpting or shaping, or otherwise more intensely working, a certain body part that the full movement of the exercise works less intensely.

CHEATING MOVEMENTS

Cheating isn't just the topic of innumerable country-western love lyrics; it's also the name for a popular bodybuilding and weight-training technique which we've referred to earlier. Cheating movements are movements in which you use the principles of negative resistance to handle all the weight you can handle. For example, you may "throw" the bar up over your head in clean-and-jerk style in a "cheating" military press, then use strict form and resist the weight as you bring it down slowly and perfectly. You should "cheat" sparingly, but it's often a good way to help break through a sticking phase and enable you to handle more weight than ordinarily.

PUMPS

The *pump* is the tight, swollen feeling you get in a muscle that you've just trained to the point of exhaustion. While bodybuilders have waxed lyrical over the pump—one noted former star has declared it's even better than sex—the pump is really a rather simple physical phenomenon. Pumping is caused by the congestion of fluid and blood in a particular body area, caused by repeated stress on a certain muscle. *Flushing,* on the other hand, refers to the blood flowing through the muscle instead of remaining there, as in the pump. The ultimate in flushing action is Bob Gajda's Peripheral Heart Action training (PHA), based on the principle that the best way to promote strength, stamina, power, and increased muscle size is to keep the blood pouring through the muscle instead of congesting in one area, as with the pump.

MAXIMUM EFFORT

Finally, when you hear trainers or coaches talk about *maximum effort* workouts (or days), they simply mean times when you handle all the weight you can handle, using negative resistance, cheating, or whatever—any way to get the weight up and do as many reps as possible, until the muscle is worked to the point of exhaustion. It's not a workout technique to use every day, but it *is* a useful way to break out of a training rut and force yourself to move on to higher poundages and/or more reps.

B. WHAT MAKES THE MUSCLES WORK: A FEW REMARKS ABOUT WHAT'S GOING ON INSIDE

The word "muscle," as Dr. Gabe Mirkin reminds us in *The Sportsmedicine Book,* comes from the Latin word for mouse. The metaphor is descriptive, if imperfect. Like a mouse, a muscle has a rounded body and a tail (the tendon). Unlike the mouse, the tendon is fastened to a bone instead of a mousetrap.

Each muscle is made up of millions of individual cells or fibers, called "myones." When stimulated by the nervous system, these fibers contract. When they contract, they shorten in length. Since the muscle itself is nothing more than the aggregate of all these fibers, when they shorten individually, it shortens collectively.

If a large percentage of the individual fibers shorten at a given time, the muscle exerts a strong pull on the bones to which it is attached. If a small percentage of the individual fibers shorten at a given instant, the muscle exerts a weaker pull on the bones to which it is attached.

Each muscle "arises" from a relatively stationary bone or bones, and "inserts" into a relatively movable bone. When the muscle contracts, something has to give, and it's usually the movable bone. If it all sounds very mechanical, that's because it is.

As we've said earlier, each bone is held into place next to its neighboring bone by ligaments. The parts of the bones that interface with each other are called "articular surfaces." The area where two or more articular surfaces meet—along with the ligaments that hold the bones together, the articular capsule that surrounds it, and the tendons that move over it or nearby—is called a "joint."

The human skeleton is a systematic collection of bones, each related to nearby bones through the joints and each moved by contracting muscles that are attached to them by tendons. Muscles not only cause the bones to move, they stabilize and strengthen the joints as well. Further, for every major muscle there are usually a number of smaller muscles that either aid the large muscle directly or stabilize the area so that the bigger muscle can do its work more efficiently.

Muscles move when the nervous system makes them move. The individual fibers are stimulated by nerve fibers, through a complex electrochemical process called "synapse." Synapse occurs when "neurotransmitter" chemicals at the nerve endings are set in motion by electrical impulses from other nerve cells. These neurotransmitter chemicals travel from the nerve fibers into receptors in the muscle fibers. That's when the muscle fiber contracts. The muscle fiber relaxes when the neurotransmitter chemicals are recycled back into the adjacent nerve fiber, where they await the next impulse.

All of us know people who are "naturally strong." Physiologically, this means that in any given muscle contraction, more fibers are capable of contracting than would be present in an ordinary person's muscle. Muscle fibers either contract or they do not. There is no middle ground. Consequently, when we lift ten pounds, it means that more fibers are contracting than would contract if we were lifting five pounds. The naturally strong person has a better "neurotransmitter" capability than the "naturally weak" person.

Many factors go into the contraction of muscle fibers. There must be a nerve impulse, there must be sufficient neurotransmitter chemicals to make the trip, and there must be functional muscle fibers complete with working receptors to receive the signal. Whether or not a person is naturally strong depends to a large extent on heredity. If your parents were both strong, the chances are that you will be, too.

If your parents were relatively weak, it doesn't mean that you can't be strong. Maybe they never trained for strength, or perhaps they suffered from some illness that debilitated them. You won't really know until you try it yourself.

Diet, mental attitude, tension or lack of tension, alcohol, drugs, tobacco, and hundreds of other things affect the ability of muscles to contract. Everybody has good days and bad days at the gym. Tension alone is enough to bring the poundages down. Loss of sleep will do the same thing. The human body is not merely an aggregate of parts. As the great American philosopher Charles Hartshorne once said, we are all compound individuals. We aren't merely machines, no matter how instructive it is to think of the body in terms of biomechanics. We are organic wholes, of which mind and body can be thought of as points along a continuum. Consequently, we aren't really trying to be mysterious when we say that strength is as much mental as it is physical. We mean it on the cellular level. The fibers don't contract with peak efficiency unless the total organism is working properly.

Muscle contraction makes certain demands on the body, and the body must have time to recover from these demands if progress is to be made. Intensive exercise depletes the potassium reserves. Perspiring, something that always accompanies vigorous exercise, depletes the sodium reserves. Protein is required for increases in muscle size. Fats are required for energy. Long chain carbohydrates (preferable to simple sugars) stabilize and support the body's ability to sustain the effort of workouts.

Further, depending on the individual, specific shortages will occur. Many bodybuilders must supplement their iron intake. Others seem to need little salt but always need more potassium. The best way to find out your own tendencies is to have an examination made of your deficiencies before beginning a workout program and then have another series run after you have really gotten down to business. Most people find it enough to maintain a balanced diet, accompanied by common mineral supplements and multiple vitamins.

Whatever your personal genetic composition, muscle fibers come in two types, red and white. The red fibers are oxygen burners, and they contract more slowly than the white ones. Consequently, they are called the "slow twitch" fibers, while the white ones are called the "fast twitch" fibers. The white fibers don't make as great an oxygen demand as the red ones, and this has led many people to cite exercises that work the red fibers as superior for cardiovascular conditioning.

If we are speaking strictly of cardiovascular conditioning, this is probably true. We say "probably" because the whole subject is a matter of current dispute among physiologists. It is true that each red fiber uses more oxygen than each white fiber for x amount of work done. On the other hand, *all* muscle fibers, red or white, use oxygen in the recovery phase of contraction, so the amount of work you do determines the amount of oxygen you burn.

Further, "strength training," as it is called, while not a premier cardiovascular conditioner, does something that cardiovascular conditioning exercises do not do: It conditions the individual muscles to react under a load, to gain in strength, and to maintain individual muscle tone. Strength training will also assure you of being able to act quickly with explosive movements when necessary. Far from the popular notions about weightlifters, most of them are lightning-fast in their movements as a result of concentration on white-fiber development.

One of the liabilities of training for strength or power alone is that you will lose your ability to sustain movements over a long period of time. In short, you will lose your endurance. On the other hand, people who train only the red fibers lose their strength. Long-distance runners, for example, are sometimes incapable of jumping over a two-foot-high barrier. While they can run for miles and for hours, some couldn't leap across a ditch if their lives depended on it.

The conclusion should be obvious. There is no single kind of exercise that will give you everything you want or need. The best program would combine strength and endurance exercises in a total-development approach. Work on both kinds of fibers. Work for endurance as well as strength. Work on stamina as well as power. Treat your body like the complex system it is, and it will reward you by doing what you want it to do.

And while you're at it, don't forget to develop skills. Nothing is more pathetic than the runner who can do nothing but run or the weightlifter who can do nothing but lift barbells. Not only pathetic, but boring, too. Once you've got the system going, learn to use it. If you've never been very good at recreational sports, you may find that you will now be able to enjoy them as much as the next person.

So what's going on inside is a vastly complex set of events, each of which is related to the other. If you're burning fat, then the thermodynamics of muscle contraction will assure you of losing some of it. Work requires energy. We store energy in the form of fat. If we demand more energy than we are taking in, in the form of food, we'll tap the fat reserves. If we have circulation problems, the increased circulatory activity sparked by exercise will enable you to reach fat reserves that have heretofore resisted diets. If you have fluid retention in the soft tissues, the increased circulation and the attendant dilation of the vessels will help you to bring your fluid problem into line.

And remember: Because of the changes in the body that exercise causes, you'll continue to burn calories for hours after you've stopped working out. There isn't a more efficient way to lose weight. And considering the fact that if you lose weight by diet alone, at least 50 percent of what you lose is lean muscle tissue; all other things being equal, a good diet *plus* exercise is the safest way to lose weight.

Progressive resistance exercise is the most efficient of all the exercises, both in helping you to lose unwanted fat and to gain muscle strength, size, power, and stamina. The theory is simple: Start exercising with a certain amount of weight, and then add weight periodically through the weeks and months you work out. You will gradually increase your strength, power, and stamina, depending on the specific ways you train. We'll explain this in the section on exercise programs.

The key is to add weight. For men, this will mean corresponding increases in muscle size. For women, there will be little appreciable increase in muscle size (due to the absence of high levels of male hormones, which are necessary for muscle growth), but there will be a tremendous improvement in muscle tone, shapeliness, and general strength.

Sometimes you'll add only a couple of pounds. Sometimes you'll add ten or fifteen. The secret is to keep adding. It all started with Milo in ancient Greece. Every day he lifted a calf. By the time the calf grew into a full-sized cow, he had developed the strength to lift the cow.

It really works. And it's a straight road to greater and greater improvement.

Section Two: The Major and Minor Skeletal Muscles

In this section, we'll identify the major and minor skeletal muscles so that you'll know which muscle does what when you make movements with your body. While it's not necessary for you to know the names of all the muscles to get a good workout, you should try to learn them anyway. The more you understand how your body works, the more progress you'll make.

Here's a case in point. We have an acquaintance at a local health club who recently complained that he was frustrated with his gluteus (hip) development. When asked what he was doing for it, he said that he did multiple sets of leg extensions.

We were astonished at this, since leg extensions don't work the gluteus muscles. As it turned out, he had misread a sentence in an article in one of the muscle magazines and had been slaving away for months. His quadriceps (thigh muscles) were responding beautifully, since they are the muscles that the leg extension works.

Had our friend known anything about muscular anatomy, he could have saved himself a lot of time and effort. This is especially true in his case, since he had stopped doing full squats in order to have time for the leg extensions. Full squats *do* work the hip muscles, probably better than any other exercise.

It would be merely an amusing anecdote if this sort of thing weren't so common. Even the professional bodybuilders sometimes reveal an incredible ignorance of the functions of particular muscles. In their case, their genes assured progress in spite of poor training methods.

There are other reasons for learning about the muscles. Knowing the names of the muscles and being aware of what they do makes you more aware of the body as a whole and what it can do. During the years that we've been writing body-shaping and fitness books, we've come across literally hundreds of people who have no idea of what their bodies can do, what they look like, or what they should look like if they're healthy.

We've seen people who could not perform simple movements such as shoulder shrugs because they could not conceive of the shrug as an exercise movement! To them, the shrug signifies helplessness: It's a gesture that Woody Allen uses when he's playing Alvie Singer. A close friend of ours simply could not do the shrug as an exercise until we played a semantic trick on her: We gave her a light barbell and told her to give us some body language about the place where she worked. The shrug happened, as we thought it would, and for the first time in her life she realized that simple movements were caused by muscular contractions of specific muscles. She knew this, of course, but not consciously, not specifically. For her, the realization was like finally making the right connection in an electronic circuit.

Look at some of the back issues of *Vogue* and *Bazaar, Cosmopolitan* or *Glamour*. Look all the way back to the sixties. You'll find that models with no muscle tone at all, no calf development, and emaciated legs were being presented as icons for the ideal female shape. Women all over America crash-dieted so that their legs could look like little poles. What they didn't know was that if they lost weight without exercising, they lost at least as much muscle tissue as fatty tissue.

Of course, the models had done the same thing, with the result that they become parodies of the healthy, vital, agile female shape.

They couldn't get away with it now. The look currently is more natural. By natural, we mean that models such as Cheryl Tiegs display the long, lean, willowy curves that come from exercise and an active life. The new standard shows those fine lines of muscle separation that delineate the new, active woman.

Take a look at the drawings of the female figure on page 148. The one on the left was based on a photo of a model from the early seventies. She was lean enough to be a professional model, to get her photograph reprinted in magazines all over the country.

Look also at the drawing on the right. It was based on the first drawing and done with a knowledge of what the muscles looked like under the layer of fat. By knowing what the muscles looked like, it was possible to project the appearance of the lean woman who lived under the layer of fat. To put it another way, by knowing the shape of the muscles, we were able to chip away the fat and sculpt the girl who was hidden underneath.

To be able to do this, you have to know:

(a) Which muscles are where
(b) Which exercises work those muscles
(c) How to do the exercises

If you don't know what and where the muscles are, you can't do a good job of shaping your body. Can you imagine Michelangelo carving statues without a solid knowledge of muscular anatomy?

Take a look at the anatomy charts. We've simplified them into the major and minor muscle groups that you need to know to achieve your goal during your workout. We've used a male figure simply because the muscles are larger and therefore more easily seen. We've also drawn the figure of a well-muscled man, instead of the undeveloped man usually seen in anatomy textbooks. This is intentional and for good reason. If you've ever had occasion to scan through a medical anatomy book, you probably found no charts depicting people with significant muscular development. That's because the average doctor sees a lot of average people over the years, and the people who write and illustrate medical textbooks want to depict familiar body types.

If you are a weight-training enthusiast, you've probably been frustrated in your attempts to identify the muscles from medical anatomy charts, because what you see seems so remote from the way Arnold Schwarzenegger, Frank Zane, Chris Dickerson, and all the muscle stars look, there aren't many points of comparison.

The standard wall chart found in bookstores all over the country is a case in point. It's better than most in showing good muscular development, but you really have to stretch your imagination to see how the trapezius could be developed into the mountains that Mike Mentzer has on his shoulders. The disparity between, say, Pete Grymkowsky's (the

THE EFFECTS OF BODYSCULPTURE ON THE FEMALE FIGURE: SAME BONE STRUCTURE, SAME MUSCULATURE, NEW GIRL

current manager of the famous Gold's Gym in L.A.) deltoids and triceps and the ones shown on the chart is enough to send you away looking for another chart.

Consequently, the chart in this book is anatomically correct but is based on an idealized version of what intermediate weight trainers look like. It's not the massive musculature of champion bodybuilder Mike Mentzer, but it is the kind of musculature you would find in a man who has worked out diligently and scientifically for a couple of years. We've emphasized leg development in the chart as a gentle reminder that you should work the legs as much as the upper body, especially as a beginner.

We've also paid a lot of attention to torso development, since this is an area that is usually neglected by beginning weight trainers. Unfortunately, the hold that bench pressing has on the popular imagination is great enough to cause most beginners to spend most of their time on that exercise alone. Don't do it. Go through the programs we've outlined, and work all the muscles with equal intensity.

Now, let's take a trip down through the muscles, beginning with the neck and ending with the feet. If it sounds a little dry, hang in there. You really need to get acquainted with your body.

We'll follow the numbering system on the charts and the identification list. Before we start, there are a few terms you should learn, here numbered for the sake of clarity:

1. *Tendons* are the cords that connect muscles to bones.
2. *Ligaments* connect bones to bones and in some cases support organs.
3. *Fascia* refers to the connective or soft tissue that envelops muscles and organs throughout the body.
4. Muscles "arise" from one bone and "insert" into another bone or into surrounding tissue. Muscles "arise" from a bone that is usually stationary and insert in a bone that usually moves. An example would be the arm biceps, which arises from the *scapula,* or shoulder blade (which is relatively stationary), and inserts into the *radius,* one of the bones of the forearm.
5. All muscles have multiple functions. In most cases, we've given the chief functions of each muscle cited.
6. The muscles cited are the ones most commonly spoken of in exercise literature. They are the ones you'll need to know when you have conversations in the gym. If you learn the information given in this section, you'll be able to hold your own with almost anybody you'll ever run into at the local health spa.
7. Finally, here's a short list of the major bones we'll be referring to in this section:

(a) Vertebrae: the sections of the spine.
(b) Scapula: the shoulder bone or shoulder blade
(c) Ribs: those bands of bones that hold your chest together
(d) Clavicle: the collarbone
(e) Humerus: the bone of the upper arm
(f) Radius: one of the bones of the forearm
(g) Ulna: the other forearm bone
(h) Pelvis, hip, ischium, ilium, symphysis pubis: various areas of the pelvic or hip bones
(i) Femur: the thigh or upper leg bone
(j) Tibia: one of the bones of the lower leg
(k) Fibula: the other lower leg bone

From time to time, we'll give both the official name and the popular name for both the bones and the muscles, so you can learn not only the official language but the lingo that's spoken around the gym. Thus, the Ilial Crest is also the top of the hips, and the latissimus dorsi are simply the lats.

Ready? Here we go.

Key for Skeletal Muscles, Front View

1. TRAPEZIUS (page 152)
2. LATERAL DELTOID (page 152)
3. ANTERIOR DELTOID (page 152)
4. PECTORALIS MAJOR (page 152)
5. LATERAL HEAD OF THE TRICEPS (page 153)
6. SERRATUS ANTERIOR (page 153)
7. BICEPS BRACHII (page 153)
8. MEDIAL HEAD OF THE TRICEPS (page 153)
9. BRACHIALIS (page 153)
10. BRACHIORADIALIS (page 154)
11. RECTUS ABDOMINIS (under the sheath of rectus) (page 154)
12. EXTERNAL OBLIQUE (page 154)
13. FLEXORS FOR THE FINGERS AND WRIST (page 154)
14. GLUTEUS MEDIUS (page 155)
15. ILIACUS (page 155)
16. PSOAS MAJOR (page 156)
17. PECTINEUS (page 156)
18. ADDUCTOR LONGUS (page 156)
19. GRACILIS (page 156)
20. ADDUCTOR MAGNUS (page 156)
21. TENSOR FASCIAE LATAE (page 156)
22. SARTORIUS (page 157)
23. RECTUS FEMORIS (page 157)
24. VASTUS LATERALIS (page 157)
25. VASTUS MEDIALIS (page 157)
26. PERONEUS LONGUS (page 158)
27. GASTROCNEMIUS (page 158)
28. TIBIALIS ANTERIOR (OR ANTICUS) (page 158)
29. EXTENSOR DIGITORUM LONGUS (page 158)
30. EXTENSOR HALLUCIS LONGUS (page 159)
31. SOLEUS (page 159)

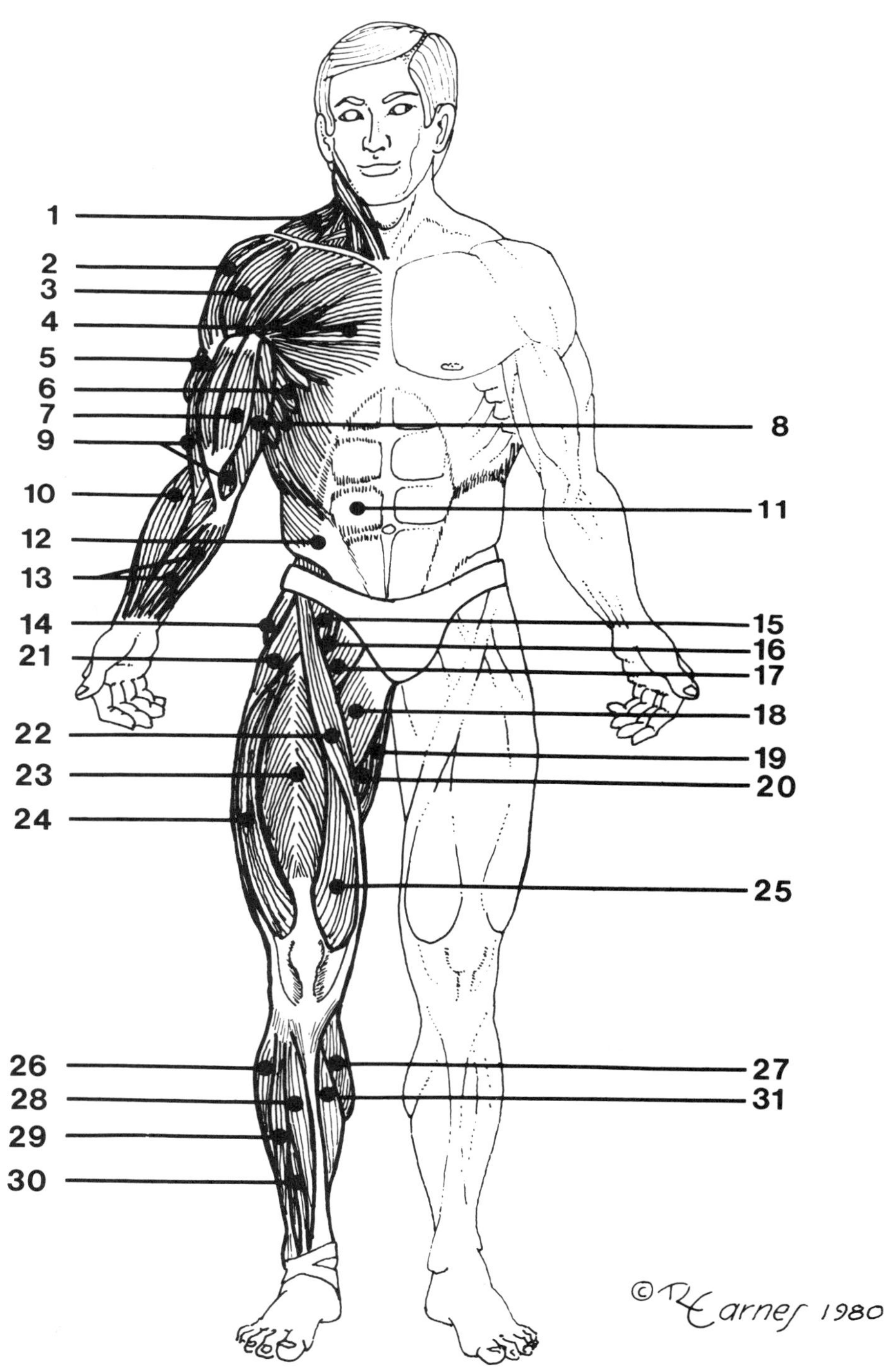

HUMAN MUSCULAR ANATOMY, FRONT VIEW

THE MAJOR AND MINOR SKELETAL MUSCLES

A. FRONT VIEW

1. Trapezius

These are the muscles that form the top of the body between the shoulders and the neck. They arise at the base of the skull behind the *sternomastoid* or neck muscles, and from the vertebrae of the spine. They insert into the shoulder blades and the collarbones. They extend laterally and downward to the small of the back. They are used in shrugging movements, assist in rotating the shoulder blades, and pull the head backward. When you bunch the muscles of the upper back, you are contracting the *trapezius*.

2. Lateral Deltoids

These muscles form the sides of the shoulders and, if properly developed, give you that w-i-d-e look. They and the *posterior* and *anterior deltoids* join in a common tendon that inserts into the *humerus* or upper arm bone. The *anterior deltoid* arises from the *clavicle* or collarbone, the *lateral deltoid* arises from the outer tip of the *scapula* or shoulder blade, and the *posterior deltoid* arises from the spine of the *scapula*. The *anterior, posterior* and *lateral deltoids* pull the arm outward and upwards to the side in an arc; the *anterior deltoid* pulls and rotates the arm to the front; and the *posterior deltoid* rotates and pulls the arm to the back. Working together, they stabilize the shoulder joint.

3. Anterior Deltoid

See description in (2) above.

4. Pectoralis Major

These are the chest muscles that give men depth to their torso and women support for the bust. They arise alongside the *anterior deltoid* from the collarbone and from the *sternum* or breastbone in the center, and fan out along the ribs. As you can see from the chart, the fibers are oriented in the direction of the arm just under the *anterior deltoid,* where the pectorals insert by a flat tendon to the front of the upper arm bone. The *pectoralis minor* muscles are not shown on the chart and are located beneath and toward the sides of the *pectoralis major.* The "pecs" assist the *anterior deltoids* in moving the arms to the front. They also move the whole shoulder structure to the front. Try to flex them without moving the arms, and you'll see what we mean.

5. Lateral Head of the Triceps

The *triceps* is a three-headed muscle (hence the name) and is located on the back of the upper arm. The lateral head arises from the outside back of the upper arm bone and joins the long head and the short head in a common tendon, which in turn inserts into a small knob called the *olecranon,* located at the top end of the *ulna,* one of the bones of the forearm. The medial or deep head arises from the upper arm bone in the back and to the inside. The long or scapular head arises from the shoulder blade or *scapula.* The action of the triceps is to extend the arm: If your arm is bent at the elbow, it is the *triceps* that straightens it out.

6. Serratus Anterior

These muscles are sometimes called the *serratus magnus,* and they form the fanlike ridges on the torso at the sides just in front of the *latissimus dorsi* muscles. They arise from the ribs and insert into the shoulder blades. They assist other muscles in pulling the shoulder blades to the front and downward, and they also help rotate the shoulder blades.

7. Biceps Brachii

The *biceps* has two heads and is probably the most popular muscle with beginning bodybuilders. Some biceps have a high peak (Arnold Schwarzenegger's, for example) and others are long and full-bodied (Sergio Oliva's). The short head of the *biceps* arises from a small knob called the *coracoid process,* which is located on the front of the shoulder blade or *scapula* near the end of the upper arm bone. The other head arises nearby from another part of the *scapula,* called the *glenoid cavity.* Both heads join in a common tendon that fastens or inserts to the *radius,* one of the bones of the forearm. The *biceps* causes the arm to bend at the elbow and also assists in rotating the forearm in a movement called *supination.* To supinate the forearm means to rotate it from a position in which the palm is away from you to a position where the palm is facing you. The opposite of *supination* is *pronation,* in which you begin with the palm facing you and rotate the forearm until the palm is away from you.

8. Medial (or Deep) Head of the Triceps

See the description in (5) above.

9. Brachialis

This muscle runs down the outside of the upper arm, arising from the upper end of the *humerus* or upper arm bone and inserting into the *ulna,* one of the bones of the forearm. At its lower end, it runs under the *biceps,* and it assists the *biceps* in bending the arm at the elbow by bringing the forearm up. It also stabilizes the elbow and thus is important for any sport that involves bending or rotating at the elbow joint. It brings the forearm up whether the hand is pronated or supinated.

10. Brachioradialis

This muscle is sometimes called the *supinator longus,* so don't worry if you run across the other terminology. It is the most prominent muscle along the outside top of the forearm and extends from its origin on the *humerus* all the way down to the *radius,* one of the bones of the forearm. The *brachioradialis* assists as a forearm flexor. There is dispute among many researchers about whether or not a key function of the *brachioradialis* is to rotate the forearm in a supinating motion.

11. Rectus Abdominis

These are the famous "abs" that everybody wants and that are hard to get. They insert into the top to the fifth, sixth, and seventh ribs and arise from the *symphysis pubis,* that small area of the hip bone above the pubic area. The abs are divided into two flat lengths, each broken up by divisions (usually three above the navel and one below it). The entire muscle is covered by a sheath. Unfortunately, it is this area where both men and women collect fatty tissue between the sheath that covers the abs and the skin that covers the sheath. The function of the *rectus abdominis* is to shorten the distance between the *symphysis pubis* and the fifth, sixth, and seventh ribs. This is done when you arch your body forward. Think for a moment, and you'll see why situps are only partially effective for developing the abdominals. It's only in the forward arching motion that the abs are used. The rest of the situp is done by other muscles. The abs also assist in rotating the trunk to either side and can flex in a line on either side.

12. External Oblique

As its name implies, these muscles are located at the sides and front of the body, bordered by the abdominals to the front, the pectorals to the top, the *serratus anterior* and *latissimus dorsi* to the sides, and insert into an area of the pelvis called the *crest of ilium.* The *external obliques* arise from the ribs by means of eight fleshy interleavings, comprising a complex origin. Suffice it to say that the *external obliques* help in torso-twisting motions and motions that involve returning to an erect position when you are leaning to the side. For men, the *external obliques* are especially worrisome: They collect fat like mad, and they also respond to exercise with rapid development. Unfortunately, when developed they often merely push the fat farther out, making the waist look worse than it did before you started exercising.

13. Flexors For the Fingers and Wrist

This complex set of muscles enables you to flex the fingers, make a fist, and perform the thousands of complicated movements that are made when the fingers are bent at the joints. The extensors for the fingers are located on the other side of the forearm. While most people develop these muscles all at once, by moving all the fingers at the same time (as in wrist rolls, squeezing motions with a rubber ball, etc.), they should also be developed individually in order to ensure maximum strength and coordination. Turn your palms up and wiggle your fingers. The cords you see at your wrist are the tendons for the flexors. Turn your hand palm down and straighten your fingers. The cords you see on top of your hand are the tendons for the extensors.

obliques. These are the infamous "love handles," which are the hardest fat for any man to lose. This happens because the fat collects not on the "belly" of any of these muscles, but at the edges where circulation is at a minimum. As you grow older, these muscles are used less and less, and the fat begins to pile up. The key here is that the fat has found a crevice, a niche, an out-of-the-way place where not much is going on. The best way to control this particular area of fat accumulation is by diet, twisting motions, and movements that take the leg away from the centerline of the body (these are called *abduction* movements, as opposed to *adduction* movements, which move the leg back towards the body's centerline).

14. Gluteus Medius

These muscles are barely visible from the front, and run from the back and sides of the pelvic bone area called the *ilium* down to that portion of the thigh bone called the *greater trochanter,* which is a raised area of bone to the side of the thigh bone a few inches from where it makes a joint with the hip bones. The *gluteus minimus* is not shown on the chart, but it is located beneath the *gluteus medius.* Both of these muscles are used chiefly to lift the leg out to the side when it is straight, to rotate the thigh medially, and to support the body when you are standing on one foot. Most men pack fat right up on top of the *gluteus medius,* along the *external*

15. Iliacus

These muscles arise from the upper portion of the *ilium* and from the *sacrum,* to insert at the *femur* or thigh bone along the area called the *lesser trochanter,* which is on the inside of the *femur,* near the hip joint. These muscles bring the thigh up in front of you, bend the small of the back and the pelvis forward, help you to remain standing erect, and help you when you sit up from a reclining position. They come into play during running when you bring the leg to the front, they help you do situps, and they help you to arch your back. They join with the *psoas* muscles in a common tendon and are often called the iliopsoas muscle.

16. Psoas Major

This muscle is barely visible beneath and between the *iliacus* and the *pectineus.* See (15) above for functions.

17. Pectineus

The *pectineus* is one of five muscles that connects the *femur* or thigh bone of each leg to the hip-bone portion of the pelvic girdle. The *pectineus* arises from the pubic area above and to the front of the hip joint, and inserts at the other end to the area of the *lesser trochanter* mentioned in (15) above. The other four muscles are the *adductor longus,* the *adductor brevis,* the *adductor magnus,* and the *gracilis.* The *pectineus* and the *adductors* pull the leg inward toward the body's centerline. They also help in rotating the leg medially. The *pectineus* and the *adductor brevis* and *longus* help bring the leg up toward the pelvis, and they also help to bring the leg forward in activities such as running or walking. These muscles flex the leg against the hip. The *gracilis* helps rotate the thigh inward.

18. Adductor Longus

These muscles arise from a small area at the front of the pubic bone and insert along the back of the *femur* between the *vastus medialis* and the *adductor magnus.* See (17) above for the functions.

19. Gracilis

The *gracilis* runs along the innermost area of the thigh, from its origin on the underside of the pubic bone to its insertion at the upper and inner surface of the shaft of the *tibia,* one of the bones of the lower leg. In addition to bringing the thigh toward the body's centerline, it also helps the *sartorius* muscle in rotating the thigh inward, and it helps to keep the body erect when standing.

20. Adductor Magnus

This muscle arises along what is called the "ramus" of the pubic bone and the *ischium,* which is the lower edge of the hip bone. It inserts along almost the entire length of the back of the *femur.* See (17) above for its functions.

21. Tensor Fascia Latae

This is a small muscle that leads into a long fascial band that runs down the side of the thigh. It arises along the front part of the outer rim of the *crest of ilium* (which is the top ridge of the pelvic bone), as well as other places along the pelvic bones and the fascia that surrounds the muscles in that area. It inserts into the *fascia lata* along the side of the thigh, which then inserts at the *tibia,* one of the bones of the lower leg. This muscle flexes the thigh, steadies the pelvis when you are standing, gives support to the knee joint when the leg is straight, and stabilizes the *femur* at its junction with the *tibia.* It is an important inward rotator of the thigh.

22. Sartorius

This is the longest muscle of the body. It runs across the front of the thigh from the outside to the inside, arising from the *ilium* or top part of the pelvic bone and continuing down to an insertion at the upper and inner surface of the *tibia*'s shaft. The *sartorius* has many functions, among which are to flex the thigh against the pelvis, to rotate the thigh outward, to help rotate the thigh inward when the knee is bent, and to flex the pelvis upon the thigh when the leg is straight. It also assists in rotating pelvic movements.

23. Rectus Femoris

This muscle is among the four called the "quadriceps." They are the largest muscles in the body and run along the front of the thigh between the *vastus lateralis* and the *vastus medialis* muscles. The *rectus femoris* arises by two tendons, one from the lower front of the *ilium* and the other from a groove above the hip joint or *acetabulum*. The two heads join in a common tendon to insert into the *patella* or kneecap. The patellic ligament then connects it to the front of the *tibia*, one of the bones of the lower leg. The *rectus femoris*, the *vastus lateralis*, the *vastus intermedius* (which is hidden from view under the *rectus femoris*), and the *vastus medialis* extend the lower leg, and they all join in the common tendon that connects to the *patella*. The *rectus femoris*, because of its origin in the pelvis, helps other muscles in stabilizing the leg and the pelvis. It flexes the thigh upon the pelvis when the pelvis is stationary and conversely flexes the pelvis upon the thigh when the legs are stationary. This means that it contracts both during leg raises (when the body is stationary) and in situps (when the legs are stationary).

24. Vastus Lateralis

This muscle runs along the outside front of the thigh, between the *rectus femoris* and the *tensor fascia latae*. It arises from the front upper portion of the *femur* and inserts along the outer border of the *patella* or kneecap. See (23) above for its functions.

25. Vastus Medialis

This muscle arises from the back of the *femur* and comes around to insert along the inside edge of the *patella* or kneecap. You should note that of the three muscles that converge on the *patella*, only one, the *rectus femoris*, is attached to the hip bones. The other two are connected to the *femur* itself. This means that the *vastus medialis* and the *vastus lateralis* are primarily used to extend the lower leg, while the *rectus femoris* helps both to extend the lower leg and to stabilize the thigh with the pelvis. The *vastus medialis* is also important along with the *vastus lateralis* in providing stability to the knee in potential sideways motions. The *vastus medialis* comes strongly into play during the last 15 degrees of the range of motion involved in straightening the leg at the knee.

26. Peroneus Longus

This muscle arises from two places, the lateral condyle of the *tibia* and the upper, outer surface of the *fibula,* both of which are bones of the lower leg and, after a long and circuitous route, inserts underneath the foot at one of the bones of the big toe. Its job, along with the *peroneus brevis* (which lies right next to it), is to flex the foot in a movement called "plantar flexion." You do plantar flexion when you do calf raises. The *peroneus longus* also helps to pronate the foot, as it everts the sole of the foot to the outside in a rotational motion.

27. Gastrocnemius

These are the showy muscles of the calf and probably the most neglected among beginning bodybuilders. They are usually dense and hard to develop. They arise by separate tendons from the condyles of the *femur.* They unite with the *soleus* in the *Achilles tendon* (so named after the mythical hero of the Trojan war, who was wounded by an arrow in the heel). The *Achilles tendon* then connects to the lower part of the back surface of the heel bone. Both the *gastrocnemius* and the *soleus* flex the foot at the ankle joint, raising the foot up onto its ball.

When you do calf exercises, you will find that standing raises seem to work the *gastrocnemius* more than the *soleus,* and that the situation is reversed when you do seated raises. The difference is the knee position: When the leg is straight, you tend to work the *gastrocnemius,* and when it's bent at the knee, you tend to work the *soleus.*

28. Tibialis Anterior (or Anticus)

The *tibialis anterior* is one of four muscles of what is called the *anterior tibiofibular region.* The other three are the *extensor hallucis longus,* the *extensor digitorum longus,* and the *peroneus tertius.* All of these muscles stabilize the foot at the ankle when you are standing. The *tibialis anterior* assists in supinating or inverting the foot (rotating the bottom of the foot inward), and the *peroneus tertius* assists in pronating or everting the foot (rotating the bottom of the foot outward). The *tibialis anterior* arises from the upper and outer area of the *tibia,* and inserts after a circuitous path underneath and to the inner side of one of the bones of the big toe. The *tibialis anterior* is of major importance in *dorsiflexion:* pulling the foot back.

29. Extensor Digitorum Longus

This muscle arises along the upper front side of the *fibula* and the lateral condyle of the *tibia,* and travels down the front of the lower leg to connect to the four smaller toes. See (28) above for its functions. It is important for toe extension, dorsiflexsion, and eversion.

30. Extensor Hallucis Longus

This muscle is located between the *extensor digitorum longus* and the *tibialis anterior.* It arises from the front middle portion of the *fibula* and inserts into the base of one of the bones of the big toe. See (28) above for its functions. It is especially important in the extension of the big toe, and assists in dorsiflexion and inversion.

31. Soleus

The *soleus* arises from the back of the upper portion of the *fibula,* from the *tibia,* and from the *interosseous* membrane. It shares the *Achilles tendon* in common with the *gastrocnemius.* See (27) above for its functions.

Key For Skeletal Muscles, Back View

1. TRAPEZIUS (page 152)
2. LATERAL DELTOID (page 152)
3. POSTERIOR DELTOID (page 162)
4. TERES MAJOR (page 162)
5. RHOMBOIDEUS MAJOR (page 162)
6. LATERAL HEAD OF THE TRICEPS (page 153)
7. LONG HEAD OF THE TRICEPS (page 153)
8. LATISSIMUS DORSI (page 163)
9. BRACHIALIS (page 153)
10. MEDIAL HEAD OF THE TRICEPS (page 153)
11. BRACHIORADIALIS (page 154)
12. EXTENSOR CARPI RADIALIS LONGUS (page 163)
13. FLEXOR CARPI ULNARIS (page 164)
14. EXTENSOR DIGITORUM COMMUNIS (page 164)
15. ERECTOR SPINAE (page 164)
16. EXTENSOR CARPI RADIALIS BREVIS (page 164)
17. EXTENSOR CARPI ULNARIS (page 165)
18. GLUTEUS MEDIUS (page 165)
19. ABDUCTOR POLLICIS LONGUS AND EXTENSOR POLLICIS BREVIS (page 165)
20. TENSOR FASCIAE LATAE (page 156)
21. GLUTEUS MAXIMUS (page 165)
22. ILIOTIBIAL BAND (page 165)
23. GRACILIS (page 156)
24. ADDUCTOR MAGNUS (page 156)
25. BICEPS FEMORIS (page 166)
26. SEMITENDINOSUS (page 166)
27. SEMIMEMBRANOSUS (page 166)
28. VASTUS LATERALIS (page 157)
29. SHORT HEAD OF THE BICEPS FEMORIS (page 166)
30. GASTROCNEMIUS (page 158)
31. SOLEUS (page 159)
32. PERONEUS LONGUS (page 158)
33. FLEXOR HALLUCIS LONGUS (page 167)
34. FLEXOR DIGITORUM LONGUS (page 167)

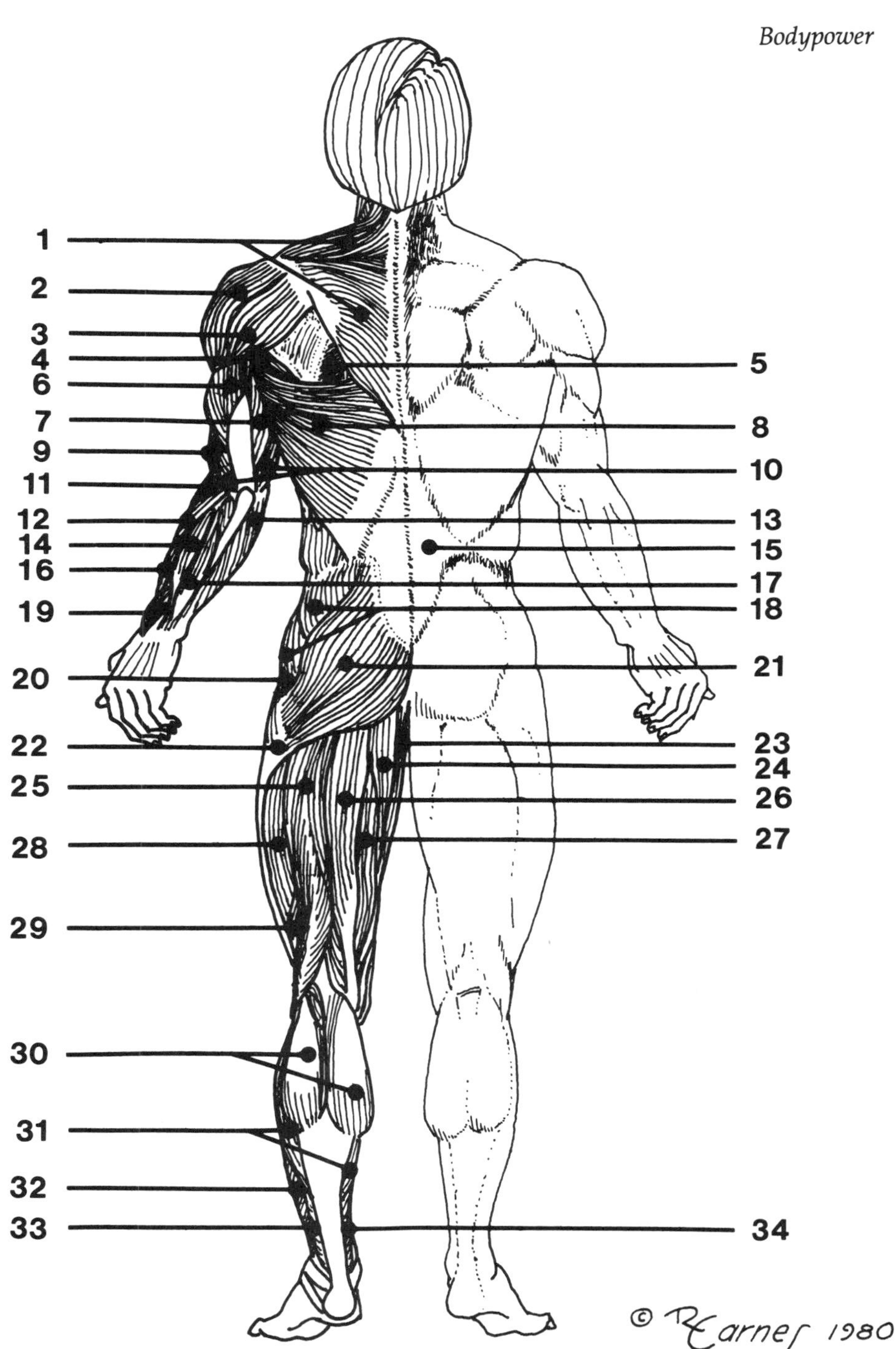

HUMAN MUSCULAR ANATOMY, BACK VIEW

THE MAJOR AND MINOR SKELETAL MUSCLES

B. BACK VIEW

1. Trapezius

See section (A), number (1), for description.

2. Lateral Deltoid

See section (A), number (2), for description.

3. Posterior Deltoid

The *posterior deltoid* is the third of the deltoid muscles, and forms the back "cap" that makes up the shoulders. It arises from the lower lip and the back border of the *scapula* or shoulder blade, and joins with the *anterior* and *lateral deltoid* in a common tendon that inserts in a small area in the middle and outer side of the *humerus* or upper arm bone. The *posterior deltoid* helps lift the upper arm out to the side, and when you are bent forward at the waist, it helps lift the arms upward or backward in rowing motions. It assists in outward rotation.

4. Teres Major

The *teres major* is one of four muscles in what is called the posterior scapular region. The other three are the *supraspinatus*, the *infraspinatus*, and the *teres minor*, which are not shown on the chart. The *teres major* arises from the *scapula* or shoulder blade and inserts at the inner upper portion of the *humerus*. It assists the *latissimus dorsi* muscles in pulling the *humerus* downward and backward (as in performing pulldowns behind the neck with a pulley apparatus). When the arm is stationary, it assists the *trapezius* and the lats in drawing the torso forward. The *supraspinatus* helps the deltoids lift the arm to the side, while the *infraspinatus* and the *teres minor* rotate the upper arm bone outward. All of these muscles are important in stabilizing and protecting the shoulder joint. The *infraspinatus* is located between the *teres major* and the *rhomboideus major* on the chart but is not labeled because it is under a fascial sheath and is thus not directly visible. The *supraspinatus* is also not visible on the chart, lying under the *trapezius* and the *posterior deltoid*. The *teres minor* likewise is not visible on the chart but lies beneath the *posterior deltoid*.

5. Rhomboideus Major

This is one of three muscles found in the second layer of the muscles of the trunk. It is visible as a small triangle between the *trapezius* and the *latissimus dorsi*. The other muscles are the *levator scapulae*, located underneath the *trapezius* at the back of the neck;

and the *rhomboideus minor*, which lies underneath the *trapezius* farther down the back between the shoulders. The *rhomboideus major* arises from four or five of the *dorsal vertebrae* or spinal bones and inserts into a tendinous arch at the edge of the *scapula* or shoulder blade. The *rhomboideus major*'s chief function is to rotate and change the lower angle of the shoulder blades. It and the other muscles in this group are all involved in supportive and rotational actions relative to the shoulder blades, moving the *scapula* upward and inward in conjunction with other muscles of the upper back.

6. Lateral Head of the Triceps

See section (A), number (5), above for description.

7. Long Head of the Triceps

See section (A), number (5), above for description.

8. Latissimus Dorsi

This is one of the most popular muscles with bodybuilders. Nobody has ever complained about having "lats" that were too wide. These are the muscles that spread like a fan from the waist and give you that "V" look that marks you as a bodybuilder or weightlifter. The lats arise from a number of places: from the six lower thoracic vertebrae, the posterior layer of the lumbar fascia, the sacrum, the three or four lower ribs, and from the external edge of the *ilium* or pelvic bones. From this broad base, it runs upward and narrows on each side to insert into the *humerus*, above the insertion of the *pectoralis major*. The lower part of the tendon merges with the *teres major*. The lats draw the *humerus* backward and inward, with an inward rotation, and downward. If the body is stationary, the lats move the arms downward. If the arms are stationary, as they would be between two parallel bars, the lats will move the body upward. They extend and hyperextend the shoulder joint. The lats are also the "rowing" muscles.

9. Brachialis

See section (A), number (9), for description.

10. Medial Head of the Triceps

See section (A), number 5, above for description.

11. Brachioradialis

See section (A), number (10), above for description.

12. Extensor Carpi Radialis Longus

This muscle, along with the *extensor carpi radialis brevis* and the *brachioradialis*, forms the *radial region*. The two extensors arise from a ridge on the side of the *humerus*. The *extensor carpi radialis longus* inserts into a bone of the index finger on the radial side. The other extensor inserts in similar fashion into a bone of the middle finger. These muscles extend the hand or straighten the wrist.

13. Flexor Carpi Ulnaris

Working in opposition to the hand extensors are the flexors, whose job it is to bend the wrist downward so that the palm moves toward the forearm. The *flexor carpi ulnaris* is one of four muscles that form the *anterior radio-ulnar region.* The *flexor carpi ulnaris* has two heads, and arises from the medial epicondyle of the *humerus* and from the *ulna.* It then inserts at the bones of the little finger.

14. Extensor Digitorum Communis

Located with three others in the *posterior radio-ulnar region,* this muscle arises from the lateral epicondyle of the *humerus,* then fans out into multiple tendons, which insert into the bones of the four fingers. In addition to extending the fingers, this muscle also helps to stabilize the wrist.

15. Erector Spinae

Erector spinae is the name given to a large group of muscles which comprise the fourth layer of muscles in the lower and middle back. It is popular to call the outermost muscles of the lower back the *erector spinae,* but this is at best only partially correct. On some charts, the area indicated will be called the *sacrospinalis.* The *erector spinae,* the "erectors of the spine," have many origins and as many insertions. They run from the *sacrum,* or lower and back portion of the pelvic bones, all the way to the middle and upper back, inserting into various ribs and common tendons along the way. The purposes of the *erector spinae* are as varied as their origins and insertions: to hold and maintain the body in an erect position; to bend the trunk backward, as in the exercise called "spinal hyperextensions"; to help related muscles to steady the neck and head; to counterbalance the action of the abdominals and the external obliques, thus providing a solid foundation for holding heavy weights on the shoulders, etc.; and to assist related muscles in providing twisting motions for the trunk of the body. They align the spine from all angles, and proper development of this muscle group is absolutely necessary for such exercises as the squat and the military press.

16. Extensor Carpi Radialis Brevis

This muscle, one of the three forming the *radial region* (see number (12), directly above), arises from the lateral epicondyle of the *humerus* and inserts into one of the bones of the middle finger on the radial side.

17. Extensor Carpi Ulnaris

This muscle, one of the *posterior radio-ulnar region* extensors cited in number (14), directly above, arises from the lateral epicondyle of the *humerus* and inserts into one of the bones of the little finger. Like the other extensors, it straightens the wrist.

18. Gluteus Medius

See section (A), number 14, above for description.

19. Abductor Pollicis Longus and Extensor Pollicis Brevis

These muscles form the deep layer of the *posterior radio-ulnar region,* along with the *extensor pollicis longus,* the *supinator brevis,* and the *extensor indicis*. They lie side by side (with the *extensor pollicis brevis* closest to the hand). The *abductor pollicis longus* (sometimes called the *extensor ossis metacarpi pollicis:* if your only source is the classic edition of *Gray's Anatomy,* don't be confused by the terminology) arises from the back and outer shaft of the *ulna,* and inserts into the base of one of the bones of the thumb. The *extensor pollicis brevis* arises from the back of the *radius* and *ulna,* and inserts into one of the bones of the thumb. The *abductor pollicis longus* moves the thumb outward and backward, while the *extensor pollicis brevis* extends the thumb.

20. Tensor Fasciae Latae

See section (A), number (21), above for description.

21. Gluteus Maximus

This is the largest of the gluteus muscles and forms the back of the buttocks from top to bottom. It merges with the *gluteus medius* and the *fascia lata* at the top and sides. It and the *gluteus medius* are among nine muscles that form the *gluteal region*. The *gluteus maximus* arises from several places: the curved upper line of the *ilium* or pelvic bone, the lower and back part of the *sacrum* (another portion of the pelvic bones), the side of the coccyx (our vestigial tail), the band arising from the *erector spinae,* the *sacro-tuberous ligament,* and the fascia that covers the *gluteus medius.* It inserts into the *fascia lata* and into a line running from the *greater trochanter* to the *linea aspera* along the femur or thigh bone near the hip joint. The functions of the *gluteus maximus* are many: to extend the *femur,* to bring the thigh in line with the rest of the body, to support the pelvis and the torso as its weight rests on the *femur,* to keep the standing body erect, to return the body to an erect position after it has bent at the waist, to lift the *femur* out and to rotate it, and to assist the other gluteal muscles in similar functions.

22. Iliotibial Band

This is not a muscle but is the thick, strong band that connects the *tensor fasciae latae* down the side of the leg to the *tibia*. It is often confused with the *vastus lateralis* and occupies enough space on the chart to warrant identification.

23. Gracilis

See section (A), number (19), above for description.

24. Adductor Magnus

See section (A), number (20), above for description.

25. Biceps Femoris

This is the biceps muscle of the thigh, corresponding in function to the biceps of the arm: It flexes the lower leg the same way that the arm biceps flexes the forearm. The *biceps femoris* has two heads, a long one and a short one. The long head arises from the *ischium,* or lower back portion of the pelvic bone, in a tendon common with the *semitendinosus* muscle. The short head arises from the *linea aspera* of the pelvic bone, almost at one of the *gluteus maximus's* points of insertion. They both join in a common tendon that inserts into the outer side of the top of the *fibula,* one of the bones in the lower leg. A small slip joins the tendon to the *tibia*. The tendon divides into two parts, which encompass the fibular collateral ligament of the knee joint. The *biceps femoris*'s companions, the *semitendinosus* and the *semimembranosus,* share functions. They flex the lower leg when bending it at the knee joint, and they rotate the thigh outward *(biceps)* and inward *(semitendinosus).* They stabilize the pelvis at the joint with the femur, and they pull the trunk of the body backward. As anybody who has ever tried has discovered, these muscles, called collectively the *hamstrings,* also limit the amount to which the body is able to bend forward.

26. Semitendinosus

This muscle shares an origin common with the *biceps femoris*. It inserts into the *tibia* after forming a tendon that begins halfway down the thigh. See (25) immediately above for a description of its functions.

27. Semimembranosus

This muscle arises from the *ischium* and inserts into the back part of the inside of the *tibia*. It lies to the inside of the *biceps femoris,* which in turn lies to the inside of the *semitendinosus.* See (25) immediately above for a description of its functions.

28. Vastus Lateralis

See section (A), number 24, for description.

29. Short Head of the Biceps Femoris

See (25) immediately above for description.

30. Gastrocnemius

See section (A), number (27), above for description.

31. Soleus

See section (A), number (31), above for description.

32. Peroneus Longus

See section (A), number (26), above for description.

33. Flexor Hallucis Longus

This muscle, with the *popliteus,* the *flexor digitorum longus,* and the *tibialis posterior,* form the deep layer of the *posterior tibio-fibular region.* The *flexor hallucis longus* arises from the lower portion of the back surface of the shaft of the *fibula,* as well as from various membranes and fascia. It inserts into the base of one of the bones of the big toe. It acts as a flexor for the big toe, providing opposing force to the *extensor hallucis longus.*

34. Flexor Digitorum Longus

This muscle arises from the back surface of the *tibia* and divides into four tendons to insert into the bones of the four lesser toes. It provides flexing movement for the toes and opposes the pull of the *extensor digitorum longus.*

That, in a rather large nutshell, is a description of the origins and functions of the major and minor muscle groups. As you should have guessed by now, the muscular system is far more complicated than the muscle magazines would have you believe. In addition to the muscles we've described above, there are many, many more whose functions complement, stabilize, and augment those described. Muscles constitute 40 percent of the body's weight. They are what make you move. You can't *do* without them.

If you want to go deeper into the study of muscles, the best bet is still *Gray's Anatomy,* which, through innumerable printings and revisions, has been the standard text for medical school anatomy classes for over a century. An excellent modern explication of muscular anatomy is Rasch and Burke's *Kinesiology and Applied Anatomy.* Published in Philadelphia by Lea and Febiger, it has gone through over five editions since 1959. While it's not as detailed as *Gray's,* it is much clearer in some places. Further, it uses photographs of bodybuilders and weight trainers to illustrate muscle groups. The drawings are excellent, and you'll recognize a few familiar illustrations from *Gray's.*

Now that you have begun to learn your muscular anatomy, let's go on to the exercises that work all those muscles. We'll arrange them by muscle groups so you can make use of the orientation you've just developed, and we'll give specific free-weight exercises and references to the appropriate machines for each muscle cited.

Section Three: The Exercises, Cross-Referenced by Muscle Groups, Free-Weight Exercises, and Appropriate Machines

In this section, we will give you a compendium of exercises with which you can develop any of the muscles described in the preceding section. Some of the exercises isolate particular muscles, while others work the muscles in groups. The former are usually called "isolation" or "concentration" exercises, while the latter are usually called "compound" exercises.

In each case, we'll follow this format:

1. We'll name the muscle and give the page number where it is described.
2. We'll list the appropriate exercises to develop that muscle.
3. We'll give a brief description of how to do the exercises with free weights (when applicable).
4. We'll list the appropriate machine to be used for the various exercises, with a page reference to the place in Chapter Three where the machine and its use is described.

We'll give you the appropriate number of sets and repetitions for each exercise in Chapter Five. Different programs call for different ways of training. There is no single "right" way to train in terms of the number of sets or the number of reps. Also, we wait until Chapter Five to discuss the amount of weight or resistance you should use in each exercise, since the amounts will vary according to the type of program you're on and the goals of that program.

Ready? Here are the exercises.

Index to the Exercises, Cross-Referenced by Muscle Groups, Free Weight Exercises, and Appropriate Machines

NECK (STERNO-MASTOID AND UPPER TRAPEZIUS) (page 152)

EXERCISES: NECK FLEX, NECK EXTENSION, LATERAL NECK MOVEMENT

A. Free Weights

Here you should use one of the neck harnesses described on pages 37-38. Sit on a bench, put the harness around your head, attach a barbell plate to the end of the rope that is attached to the harness, lean over, and move your head backward and forward. This will work the upper part of the *trapezius* where it inserts at the back of the skull. To work the *sternomastoid* in front and to the sides of the neck, lean to the side and move the head from side to side; then reverse the position of the harness, lean back, and move the head forward.

B. Machines

1. DYNACAM NECK DEVELOPER (page 68)

2. NAUTILUS NECK MACHINES (page 68)

TRAPEZIUS *(page 152)*

EXERCISES: SHOULDER SHRUG, UPRIGHT ROWING, BENTOVER ROWING, MACHINE ROWING

A. Free Weights

1. SHOULDER SHRUG You can use either a pair of dumbbells or a barbell for this exercise. If you use a barbell, stand erect, holding the barbell in front of you with the hands pronated (that means the palms should be facing down or toward your body). If you use dumbbells, hold them at your sides, with the palms facing your legs. Lift up in a shrugging movement, then back, then down. Make a circle with your shoulders.

SHOULDER SHRUG: BARBELL

2. UPRIGHT ROWING This one is best done with a barbell. Most people use one of the curling bars that are bent along the shaft. Hold the bar in front of you as you stand erect, hands pronated and close together. Keep the elbows high and lift the barbell until it is right under your chin. The traps are worked throughout the movement, but especially during the last few inches. To really work them, lift the bar a little past the chin. Be careful that you don't strain the muscles in your forearms.

3. BENTOVER ROWING We include this exercise *only* to advise you against doing it. The exercise is done with the back bent in a bow and thus in its weakest configuration. The number of serious injuries that result from this exercise is appalling. When you keep the arms out at a 90-degree angle to the body, the traps are worked. When the arms are kept close to the sides, the lats are worked. In both cases, the lower back is under severe strain. Don't do this one unless you are lying on a high bench that supports your torso. Don't risk getting hurt. Use the machines for this one.

B. Machines

1. NAUTILUS TRAPEZIUS (page 69)

2. NAUTILUS DELTOID (page 69)

3. DYNACAM DELTOID (page 70)

4. PARAMOUNT MULTIPRESS (page 70)

5. NAUTILUS UPPER BACK (page 71)

6. OTHER MACHINES THAT CAN BE USED FOR TRAPS DEVELOPMENT (a) DYNACAM BENCH PRESS (pages 70-71) **(b) NAUTILUS CALF RAISE** (pages 70-71) **(c) PARAMOUNT BENCH PRESS** (pages 70-71) **(d) UNIVERSAL BENCH PRESS** (pages 70-71) **(e) LOW PULLEY STATION** (pages 70, 78-79)

UPRIGHT ROWING

LATERAL DELTOIDS (page 152)

EXERCISES: LATERAL RAISE, MILITARY PRESS, PRESS BEHIND THE NECK, FORWARD RAISE, UPRIGHT ROWING

A. Free Weights

1. **LATERAL RAISE** Use two dumbbells for this one. There are two ways to do it: straight arm and bent arm. For both ways, begin either seated or standing, with the dumbbells in front of you, arms straight and relaxed. Move the arms up in an arc to the sides until the dumbbells are above the level of the shoulders. If you do the bent-arm version, bend the arms at the elbows as you bring the dumbbells up, finishing with the arms bent at right angles, elbows high, weights to the front, hands slightly higher than the elbows.

2. **MILITARY PRESS** Use a barbell for this one. Stand erect with the bar held across the top of the chest. The hands should be pronated. Now lift the barbell up and to the back so that it finishes its movement in line with the back of the head.

2. **PRESS BEHIND THE NECK** This one is similar to the military press, except that you begin it with the bar resting across the shoulders. The movement ends in the same place as the military press.

3. **FORWARD RAISE** You can use barbells or dumbbells for this one. Most people prefer a barbell because it's easier to keep in line. Stand erect, holding a bar in front of you, hands pronated, arms straight. Now lift the barbell in an arc until it is overhead. The hands should be placed about shoulder width apart.

4. **UPRIGHT ROWING** (page 172-73, 176)

LATERAL RAISE: DUMBBELLS

MILITARY PRESS (STARTING POSITION)

MILITARY PRESS (FINAL POSITION)

BEHIND-THE-NECK PRESS (STARTING POSITION)

FORWARD RAISE

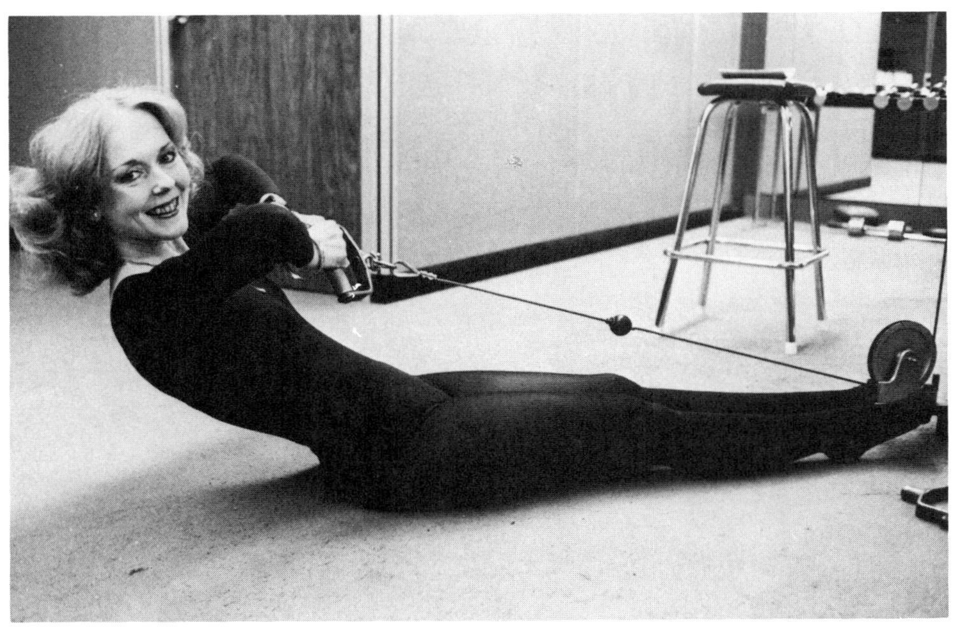

UPRIGHT ROWING: PARAMOUNT LOW PULLEY STATION

B. Machines

1. DYNACAM AND NAUTILUS SHOULDER (pp. 71-72)

2. Upright rowing can be done on any machine that has a low pulley station (pages 78-79). Sit on the floor or stand erect facing the machine, and do the same movement that is described on pages 172-73 above. The low pulley can also be used for shoulder shrugs.

POSTERIOR DELTOIDS (page 162)

EXERCISES: BENT-OVER RAISE, MACHINE APPLICATIONS

A. Free Weights

1. Like the bentover rowing exercises, this one puts a strain on the back. We recently saw a person at the gym doing this exercise with heavy dumbbells. He reinjured several disks in the lumbar-sacral region and wound up on the floor, unable to move. Fortunately, there was a doctor present, and the pressure was relieved quickly. In his case, the old injury was severe, and when he racked himself up the other night, the pressure was on the spinal cord itself. We shouldn't have to tell you how serious that could have been. When you do this one, do it lying facedown on a high or an incline bench. That way, the bench itself will give you the support you need. Hold the dumbbells downward with the arms straight, palms facing each other. Lift the dumbbells out to the side in an arc until they are even with the shoulders.

BENT OVER RAISE

B. Machines

1. NAUTILUS, DYNACAM, PARAMOUNT "PEC-DECKS" (pp. 73, 74).

2. Posterior deltoid exercises can also be done at low pulley stations. Brace one hand against the machine, bend over, and lift the arm out in an arc while grasping the pulley handle. Watch out for the cable: It'll come close to your eyes at the end of the movement. See pages 172-73 for a description of low pulley stations.

ANTERIOR DELTOIDS (page 152)

EXERCISES: FORWARD RAISE, MILITARY PRESS, PRESS BEHIND THE NECK

A. Free Weights

1. FORWARD RAISE (page 174)

2. MILITARY PRESS (page 174)

3. PRESS BEHIND THE NECK (page 174)

B. Machines

1. NAUTILUS BENCH PRESS AND PEC DECK (pp. 72-73)

2. DYNACAM SEATED BENCH PRESS (pp. 72-73)

3. DYNACAM, PARAMOUNT, UNIVERSAL BENCH-PRESS STATIONS (pp. 72-73)

4. DYNACAM FLOOR-TYPE PRESS (pp. 72-73)

5. PARAMOUNT MULTIPRESS (pp. 72-73)

6. DYNACAM, PARAMOUNT, NAUTILUS MILITARY PRESS (pp. 98–100)

PECTORALIS MAJOR *(page 152)*

EXERCISES: BENCH PRESS, FLYING EXERCISE, INCLINE AND DECLINE PRESS, STRAIGHT-ARM PULLOVER, BENT-ARM PULLOVER, PARALLEL DIP

A. Free Weights

1. **BENCH PRESS** This is the most popular of all exercises with the guys around the gym. You should never do the bench press without a spotter: somebody to get it back up when your arms and pecs get so tired they can't make that last repetition. You can do the bench press with a barbell or with dumbbells. Most people prefer a barbell. Lie on your back on a sturdy bench or bench-press rack; lift the barbell off the rack and bring it down to your chest. Don't bounce the bar off the chest, but make the movement smooth and without jerks. Then, without a pause, push the barbell up until the arms are straight. This is a compound exercise, and it works the anterior deltoid (during the first part of the movement up from the chest), the pectorals (during the initial movement off the chest and during the middle portion of the movement), and the triceps (toward the end of the movement).

2. **INCLINE BENCH PRESS** This one is done the same way as the bench press, except that you will be lying on a bench that is angled from the floor at about 60 degrees. You won't be able to handle as much weight on this one as on the regular bench press. It works the upper pectorals.

3. **FLYING EXERCISE (FLYES)** This one is done with two dumbbells, either on a flat bench (parallel to the floor) or on an incline bench. Start the movement with the arms extended toward the ceiling with a dumbbell in each hand. Let the arms down to the sides until they are roughly parallel to the floor. Be careful with this one. Your elbow joints are in a weak position, and you will put a lot of stress on the sternum.

4. **STRAIGHT-ARM PULLOVER** Lie on a bench on your back with your arms extended back past your head. You can do the movement with dumbbells or barbells. Bring the arms up in an arc until they are almost directly overhead. Keep the elbows slightly bent and the arms rotated slightly to the sides at the shoulders.

BENCH PRESS: POWERLIFTING BARBELL

5. BENT-ARM PULLOVER This is done the same way as the straight-arm pullover, except that the elbows are bent at almost 90 degrees.

6. DECLINE PRESS This is similar to the bench press, except that you lie on an incline bench with the head downward instead of upward. Get somebody to hold your feet so that you don't slip off. This works the lower pectorals.

7. PARALLEL BAR DIP You can also work the lower pectorals by doing dips between parallel bars. If you are really strong, you may want to suspend some barbell plates between your legs by a strap when you do this one.

INCLINE BENCH PRESS: POWERLIFTING BARBELL

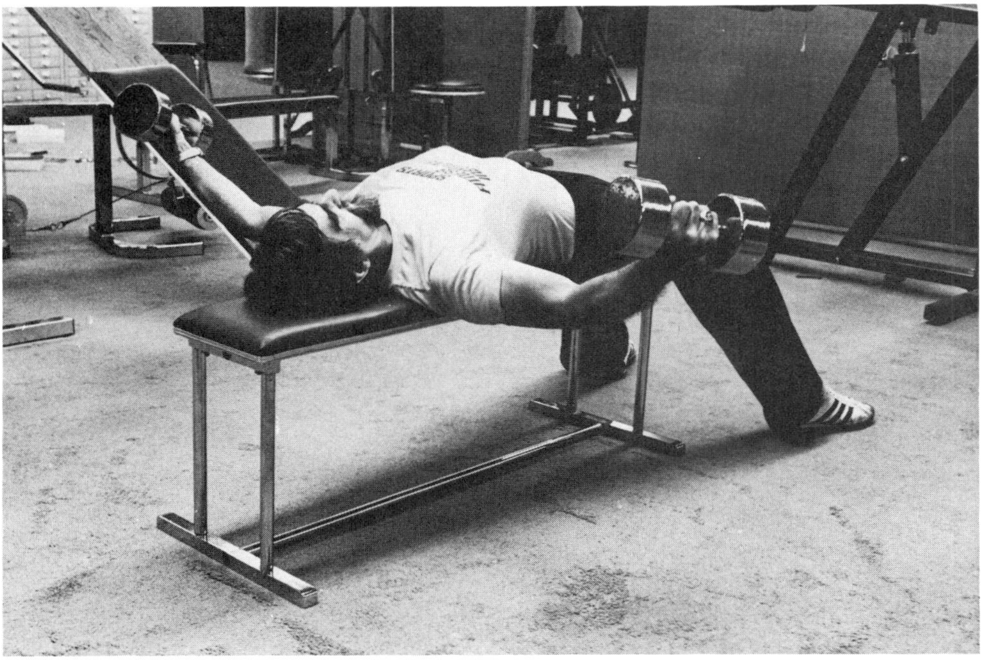

STRAIGHT-ARM FLYES

BENT-ARM FLYES

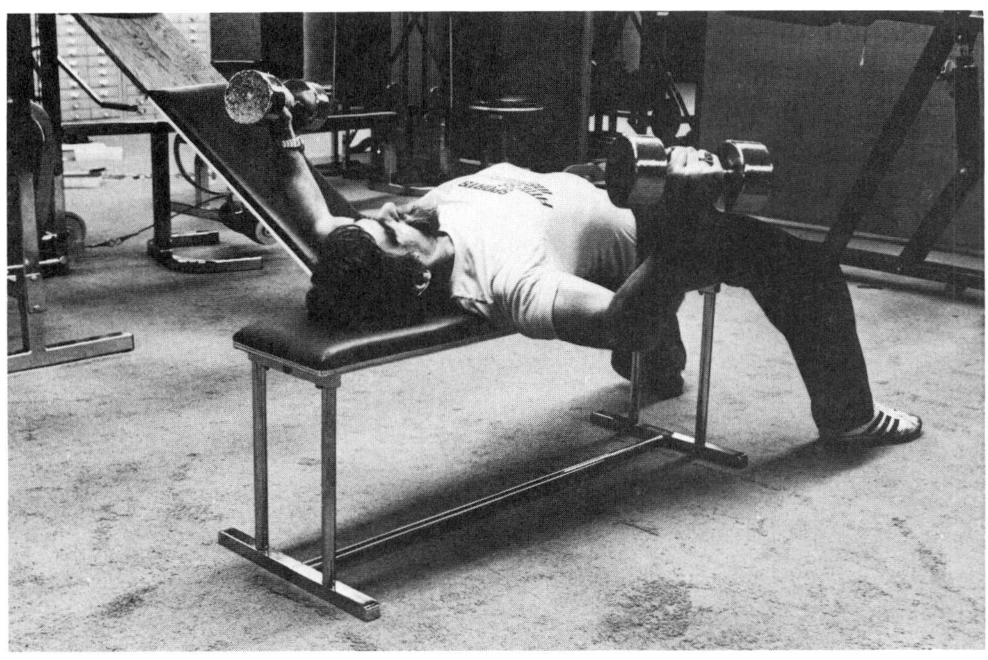

DECLINE BENCH PRESS: POWERLIFTING BARBELL

B. Machines

1. **DYNACAM, PARAMOUNT, UNIVERSAL MULTISTATION** (pp. 93-94)

2. **DYNACAM BENCH-PRESS MACHINE** (pp. 95-96)

3. **NAUTILUS CHEST MACHINE** (page 95)

4. **DYNACAM, PARAMOUNT FLOOR-TYPE PRESS MACHINES** (pp. 95-96)

5. **DYNACAM, PARAMOUNT "PEC DECKS"** (pp. 96-97)

6. **DYNACAM PRONE BUTTERFLY** (pp. 97-98)

7. **PULLOVER MACHINES** (pp. 74-75)

PARALLEL BAR DIP: PARAMOUNT PARALLEL BAR STATION

TERES MAJOR (page 162)

EXERCISES: BENTOVER ROWING, PULLEY PULLDOWN BEHIND THE NECK, LOW PULLEY WORK, PULLUP BEHIND THE NECK, PARALLEL PARTIAL

A. Free Weights

1. BENTOVER ROWING (page 173)

2. PULLUP BEHIND THE NECK (pp. 75-76) Grasp a chinning bar, palms pronated, and pull yourself up until your head is in front of the bar.

3. PARALLEL PARTIAL Hold yourself between two parallel bars as if you were going to do parallel bar dips. Instead of bending your arms at the elbows, keep them straight and lower your body until your shoulders are in a high shrug position. Then, using only the muscles around the back and shoulders, lift your body up until you are as high as you can go. If you have problems with your elbow joints, try resting the elbows on the bars or on the pads of a vertical leg-raise bench, and do the same movement described above. (pp. 75-76)

B. Machines

1. NAUTILUS UPPER BACK (page 74)

2. DYNACAM, PARAMOUNT "PEC DECKS" (pp. 96-97)

3. OVERHEAD PULLEY STATIONS ON MULTISTATION MACHINES, NAUTILUS PULLDOWN (pp. 76-78)

4. LOW PULLEY STATIONS (pp. 78-79)

5. BACK EXERCISES ON OTHER MACHINES (pp. 79-81)

PULLUP BEHIND THE NECK: NAUTILUS MULTI-EXERCISE MACHINE

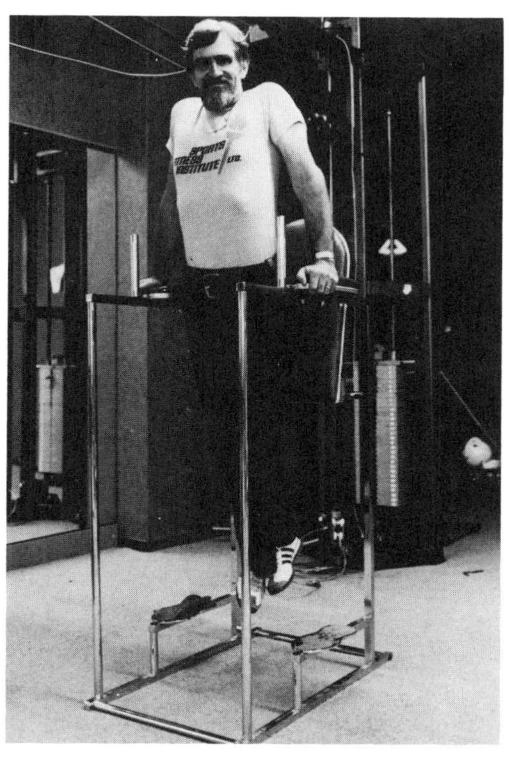

PARTIAL PARALLEL BAR DIPS: DYNACAM VERTICAL LEG RAISE APPARATUS (STARTING POSITION)

PARTIAL PARALLEL BAR DIPS (FINAL POSITION)

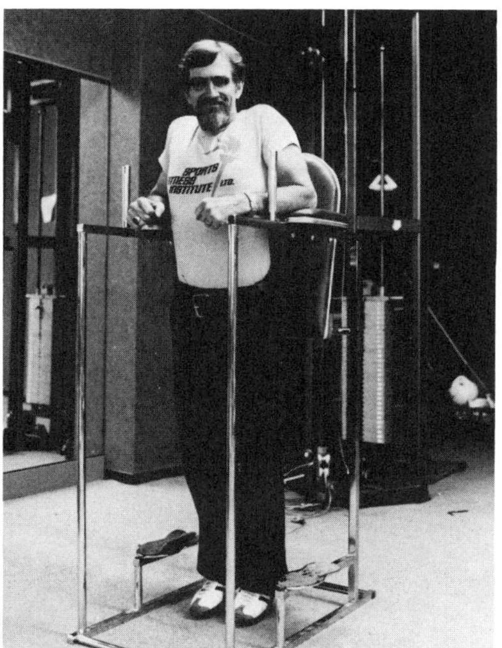

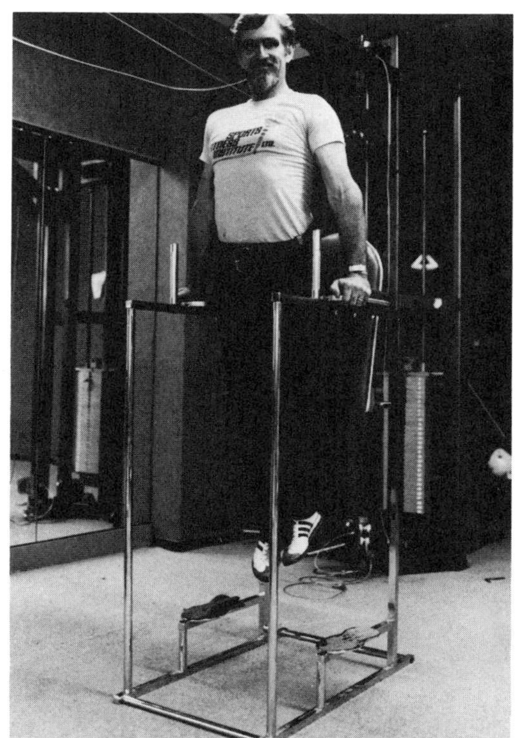

PARTIAL PARALLEL BAR DIPS ON ELBOWS (STARTING POSITION)

PARTIAL PARALLEL BAR DIPS ON ELBOWS (FINAL POSITION)

RHOMBOIDEUS MAJOR *(page 162)*

EXERCISES: BENTOVER ROWING, CHINS, PARALLEL PARTIALS, PULLUP BEHIND THE NECK, PULLEY PULLDOWN BEHIND THE NECK, POSTERIOR DELTOID MACHINES

A. Free Weights

1. **BENTOVER ROWING** (page 173)

2. **CHINS** (pp. 75-76)

3. **PARALLEL PARTIALS** (page 182)

4. **PULLUPS BEHIND THE NECK** (pp. 75-76)

B. Machines

1. **DYNACAM, PARAMOUNT "PEC DECKS"** (pp. 96-97)

2. **OVERHEAD PULLEY STATIONS ON MULTI-STATION MACHINES** (pp. 76-78)

3. **NAUTILUS UPPER BACK** (page 74)

TRICEPS *(page 153)*

EXERCISES: MILITARY PRESS, PRESS BEHIND THE NECK, BENCH PRESS, INCLINE PRESS, DECLINE PRESS, TRICEPS EXTENSION, PULLEY TRICEPS EXTENSION

A. Free Weights

1. **MILITARY PRESS** (page 174)

2. **PRESS BEHIND THE NECK** (page 174)

3. **BENCH PRESS** (page 178)

4. **INCLINE PRESS** (page 178)

5. **TRICEPS EXTENSION** You can use a barbell, a pair of dumbbells, or a single dumbbell for this one. You can lie on a bench or stand erect. Each way of doing the exercise works the muscles from a slightly different angle. The element common to all of them is keeping the upper arms stationary when you bend the elbow. This isolates the triceps and makes them do all the work. If you are lying on a bench, raise the arms toward the ceiling, holding a barbell or two dumbbells with the hands pronated.

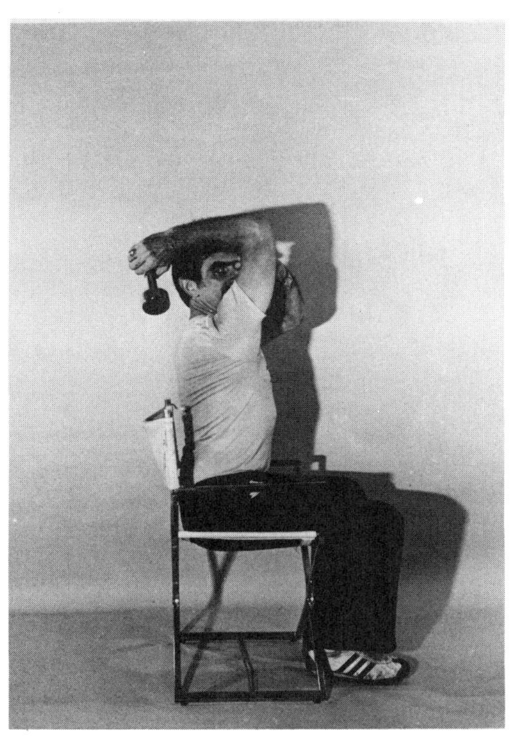

SEATED TRICEPS EXTENSION (STARTING POSITION)

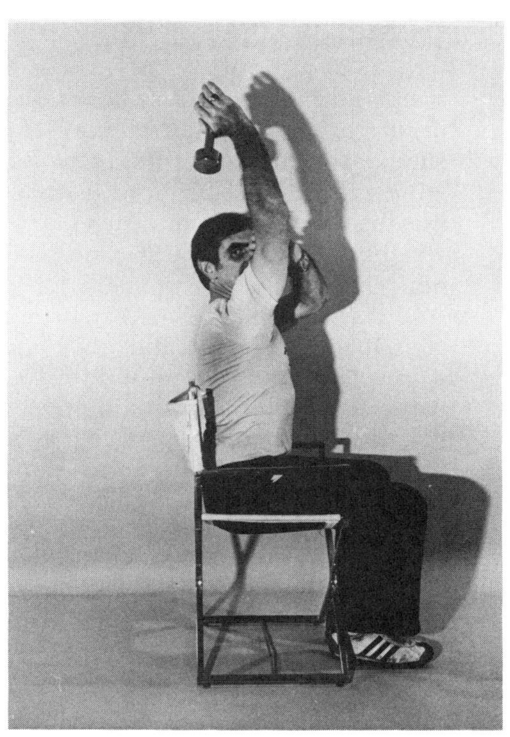

SEATED TRICEPS EXTENSION (FINAL POSITION)

SUPINE TRICEPS EXTENSION (STARTING POSITION)

SUPINE TRICEPS EXTENSION (FINAL POSITION)

Keep the upper arms stationary by flexing the muscles surrounding the shoulders. Now lower the barbell in an arc toward your head without moving the upper arms. Then lift the weight in an arc to the starting position.

Another way to do triceps extensions is as follows: Bend at the waist and support your upper body with one hand on a bench. Grasp a dumbbell in the other hand, palms facing your body. Place the upper arm along your side so that it is parallel to the floor. Then extend the arm until it is straight. Keep the elbow against the side while you do the movement.

If you are standing erect, point the upper arm at the ceiling, keep it stationary, and lift the arm up in an arc. Most people use a dumbbell for this one.

6. DECLINE PRESS (page 179)

7. PARALLEL BAR DIPS (page 179)

B. Machines

1. NAUTILUS AND DYNACAM SEATED PRESS (pp. 98, 99, 100, 101)

2. MULTISTATION MILITARY PRESS (pp. 98-100)

STANDING TRICEPS EXTENSION (STARTING POSITION)

STANDING TRICEPS EXTENSION (FINAL POSITION)

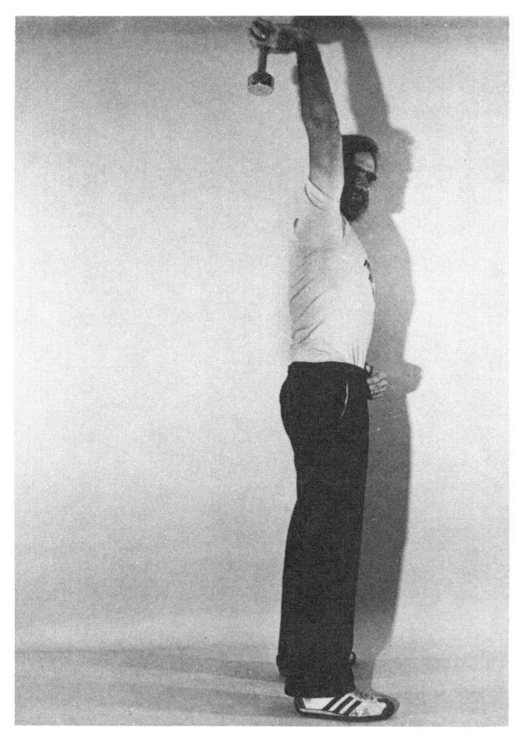

3. NAUTILUS, DYNACAM, AND PARMOUNT TRICEPS MACHINE (pp. 102-104)

4. FLOOR-TYPE PRESS MACHINES (pp. 72-73, 102-103)

5. PULLEY STATIONS AND PULLEY MACHINES (pp. 100-101)

6. NAUTILUS TRICEPS EXTENSION MACHINE (pp. 102, 104)

7. DYNACAM AND PARAMOUNT TRICEPS (page 103)

Note: For machine incline presses and decline presses, use an incline bench in conjunction with the floor-type press machines described on pp. 72-73, 102-103)

BICEPS BRACHII, BRACHIALIS (pp. 153-54)

EXERCISES: MILITARY CURL, DUMBBELL CURL, ALTERNATING CURL, SUPINATING CURL, CONCENTRATED CURL, MACHINE CURL, PULLEY CURL

A. Free Weights

1. MILITARY CURL Stand erect, holding a barbell or two dumbbells. Your hands should be supinated, grasping the bar about shoulder width apart. Keep the elbows firmly placed at the sides, and bring the forearms up in an arc until the bar is about 10 inches from your chest (don't let the bar "collapse" over to the top of the chest, because if you do you'll lose the tension on the biceps).

2. DUMBBELL CURL Same as above, but start with the arms at the sides. Don't lean to one side in order to help the weaker arm do the lift. This lift can also be done on an incline bench. Simply lie back and let the dumbbells dangle at the sides. Then lift them up while keeping the elbows in place.

3. ALTERNATING CURL This curl is also done with dumbbells. Bring one up at a time, alternating from one to the other. When one is on the way down, the other should be on the way up. This one can also be done on an incline bench.

4. SUPINATING CURL Begin this dumbbell exercise (a great favorite of Arnold Schwarzenegger's) with the hands fully pronated, and supinate them as you bring the dumbbells up. For half-supinations, begin with the palms facing your legs.

MILITARY CURL: BARBELL

MILITARY CURL: DUMBBELL

INCLINE BENCH DUMBBELL CURL

ALTERNATING DUMBBELL CURL

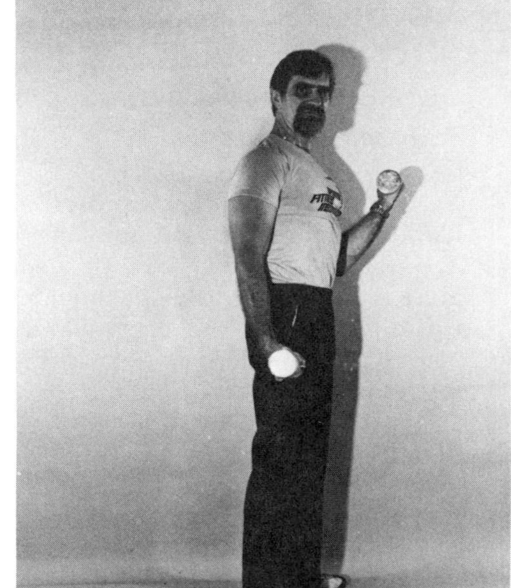

SUPINATING OR ZOTTMAN CURL (POSITION A)

SUPINATING OR ZOTTMAN CURL (POSITION B)

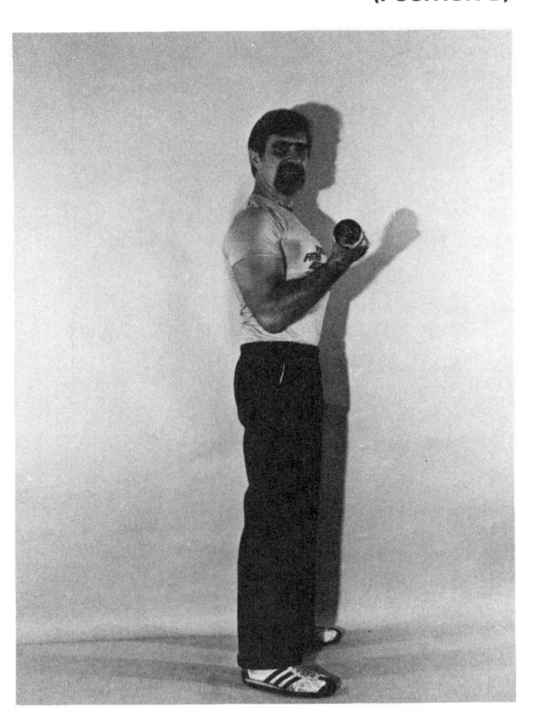

SUPINATING OR ZOTTMAN CURL (POSITION C)

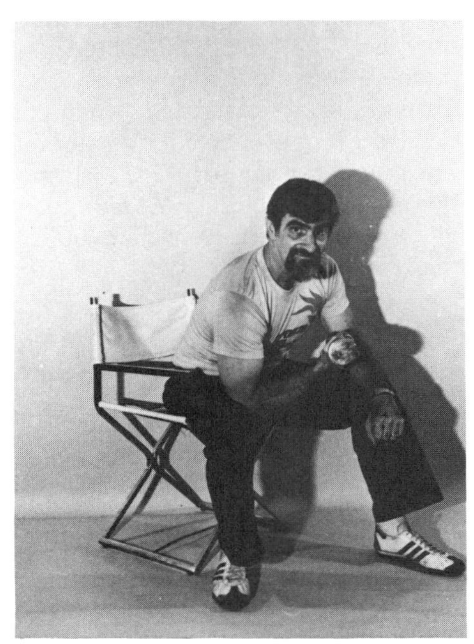

SEATED CONCENTRATED CURL

5. CONCENTRATED CURL The best way to do this is in a seated position, leaning forward, using one dumbbell at a time. Either prop the active arm on the inside of the leg, or let it hang free between your legs. Brace yourself with the free arm. From a fully extended position, bring the arm up in a curling arc.

6. CURL WITH A SCOTT BENCH OR PREACHER STAND The Scott Bench (named after Larry Scott) or preacher stand (so named because a Scott bench also looks like a podium or pulpit stand) is an adjunct to most curling machines. It started, however, as a separate piece of equipment or a type of rack that could be used with free weights. Some are attached to benches, and others are attached to floor stands. Make sure it's mounted securely, whatever the mounting may be. The bench is slanted and padded so you can lay your arms across it, palms supinated, when you do curls. It makes the elbows stationary so you can't cheat. While most of them slant at about a 45-degree angle, a few are vertical so that you can really isolate the biceps.

7. REVERSE CURL The only difference between a regular curl and a reverse curl is the hand position. With a reverse curl, the hands are pronated, thus putting the load on the *brachialis* more than on the biceps. You can do reverse curls with the machines, with the Scott benches, and with barbells or dumbbells.

REVERSE CURL (NOTE POSITION OF HANDS)

B. Machines

1. DYNACAM AND PARAMOUNT CURLING MACHINES (pp. 104-106)

2. NAUTILUS CURLING MACHINE: OLDER MODEL (page 105); **NEWER MODELS** (page 106)

3. LOW PULLEY STATIONS AS CURLING MACHINES (page 107)

4. BENCH PRESS STATIONS FOR CURLING (pp. 106-107)

FOREARMS: BRACHIORADIALIS (page 154) EXTENSOR CARPI RADIALIS LONGUS (page 163) FLEXOR CARPI ULNARIS (page 164) EXTENSOR DIGITORUM COMMUNIS (page 164) FLEXORS FOR THE WRIST AND FINGERS (pp. 154-55)

EXERCISES: WRIST CURL, WRIST EXTENSION, GRIP MACHINE FINGER CURL, TENSION-BAND EXERCISE, PRONATION/ SUPINATION

A. Free Weights

1. **WRIST CURL** This is usually done with a barbell. Sit on a bench with your knees together in front of you. Hold a barbell in your hands, with the hands supinated. Let the arms rest on your legs so that the wrists can bend over the tops of the knees. Let the bar down; then bring it back up, using only the action of the wrists.

2. **WRIST EXTENSION** Assume the same position as you would for the wrist curl, but this time pronate the hands. Make the same up-and-down motions.

WRIST CURL

B. Machines

1. **WRIST ROLLER** (pp. 107-108)

2. **LOW PULLEY APPLICATION** (page 107)

3. **GRIP MACHINES** (pp. 107-108)

4. TENSION BAND EXERCISE (pp. 38-39) The Tension Band can provide resistance for movements of the entire hand, or for each finger at a time. Since pronation and supination are rotational movements, the tension band is especially valuable; it can provide a resilient tension throughout the range of motion, regardless of the direction of rotation.

WRIST EXTENSION

LATISSIMUS DORSI *(page 163)*

EXERCISES: BENTOVER ROWING, ONE-ARM BENTOVER ROWING, PULLEY ROWING, LOW PULLEY ROWING, CHINNING

A. Free Weights

1. BENTOVER ROWING (page 173)

2. ONE-ARM BENTOVER ROWING Use a dumbbell for this one. Stand by a bench, and rest your free arm on it. Bend at the waist until your upper body is parallel to the floor. Grasp a dumbbell with one hand, and pull it up until your elbow is at your side. Do the pull with the lats, not with the biceps. Don't jerk the weight up, but try to feel the proper pull in the lats.

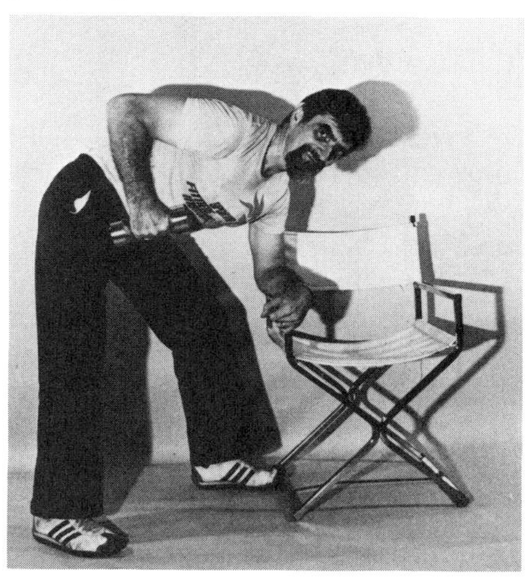

ONE-ARM BENTOVER ROWING

3. CHINNING AND PULLUPS (pp. 75-76) There are two ways to do this. Behind-the-neck pullups are described on (pp. 75-76). To do the regular chin, grasp a chinning bar with the palms either pronated or supinated, and pull yourself up until your chin is over the bar. Another way to work the lats is by pullups. Grasp the bar with the hands pronated, and pull yourself up until the bar is in a position behind the neck. Vary the width of your grip on the bar until you find the position that works the lats the most. Pullups will also work the *teres major* (page 162) and the *rhomboideus major*. (page 164)

4. PARALLEL BAR PARTIAL DIP (page 182)

Machines

1. OVERHEAD PULLEY WORK (pp. 76-78)

2. LOW PULLEY WORK (pp. 78-79)

3. LATISSIMUS EXERCISES ON OTHER MACHINES (pp. 79-81)

4. PULLOVER MACHINES (pp. 74-75)

SERRATUS ANTERIOR *(page 153)*

EXERCISES: STRAIGHT-ARM PULLOVER, BENT-ARM PULLOVER, TWIST WITH A BAR, PULLOVER MACHINE EXERCISES, OVERHEAD PULLEY WORK

Free Weights

1. STRAIGHT-ARM PULLOVER This exercise should be done with a barbell, preferably one of the bent-shaft curling bars, because the bend in the middle makes a good gripping place for the hands. Lie on your back on a bench, with the top of your head even with the end of the bench. Hold the bar with the hands pronated, with a grip about eight inches wide. Hold the bar at arm's length toward the ceiling. Take a deep breath, and let it down in an arc to a position where your arms are parallel to the floor (you'll actually go a little farther as you become more flexible). Let the breath out as you move the bar back to the starting position. Keep the arms straight at the elbows. You won't be able to use much weight on this one. It's more a chest expander than a muscle builder, but it does get the *serratus*.

2. BENT-ARM PULLOVER Do this the same way you do the straight-arm pullover, except this time bend the arms at the elbows. You'll be able to use more weight this way. When you get in the downmost position, let the arms rotate slightly

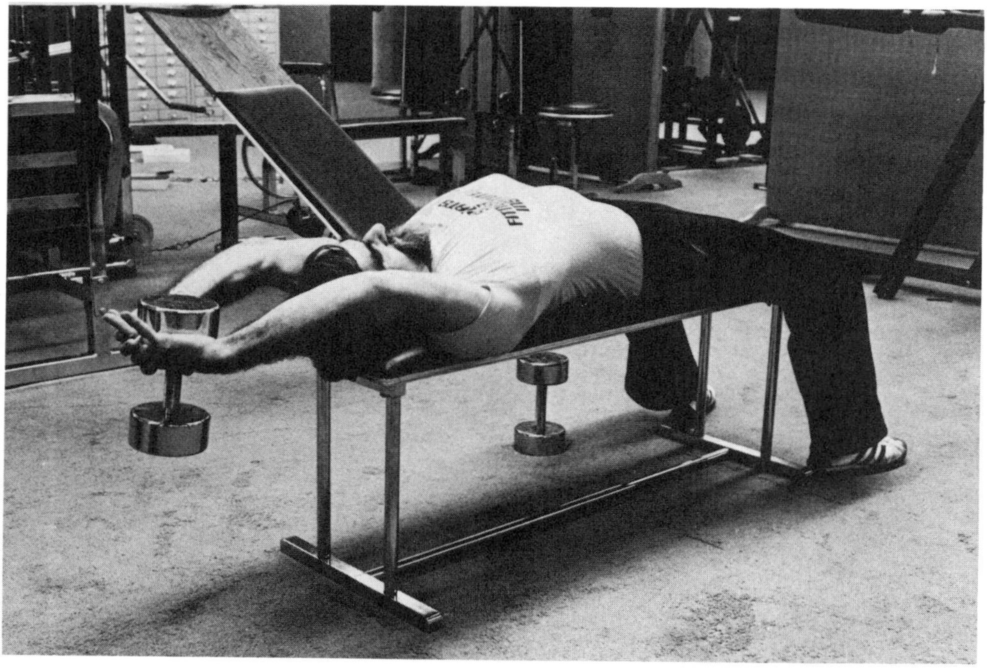

STRAIGHT-ARM PULLOVER

BENT-ARM PULLOVER

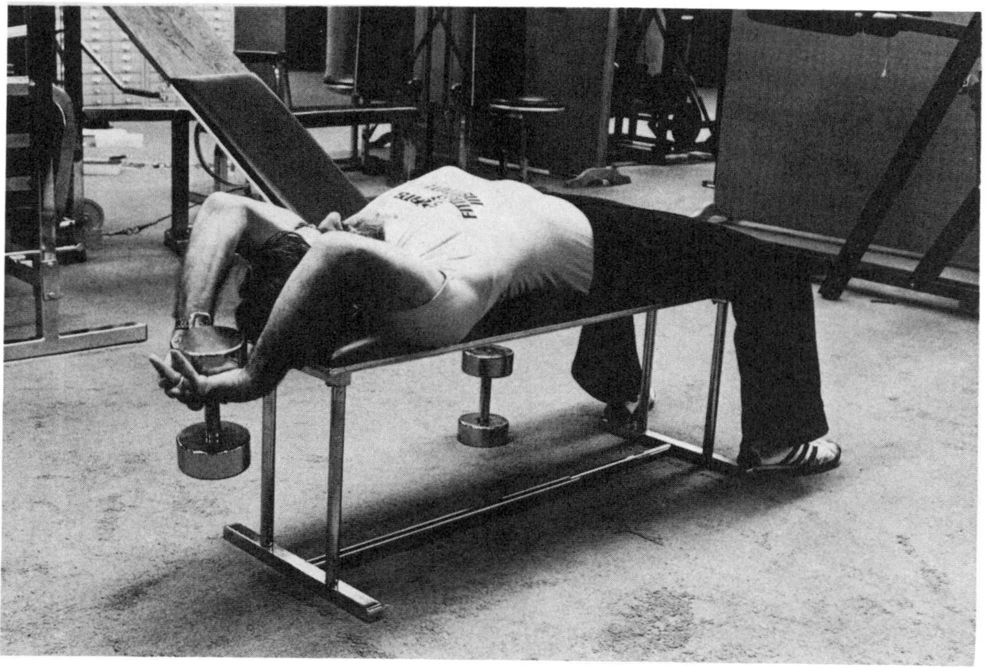

SEATED TWIST WITH A BAR

outward at the shoulder, and you'll get a better pull on the lats and the *serratus*.

3. TWIST WITH A BAR The best way to do a twist is in a seated position. This keeps the hip from rotating and thus centers the action on the torso. Hold a bar (either unweighted or with only five pounds on each end) and twist your body from side to side. Let the arms lie along the length of the bar.

Machines

1. PULLOVER MACHINE WORK (pp. 74-75)

2. OVERHEAD PULLEY WORK (pp. 76-78)

RECTUS ABDOMINIS *(page 154)*

EXERCISES: SITUP (KNEES STRAIGHT, KNEES BENT), CRUNCH OR BODY ROLL (KNEES STRAIGHT, KNEES BENT), SLANT BOARD SITUP AND CRUNCH, TWIST WITH A BAR, ROMAN CHAIR SITUP AND CRUNCH, VERTICAL AND SUPINE LEG RAISE, VARIABLE RESISTANCE ABDOMINAL WORK, SIDE/WAIST EXERCISE MACHINES, TWISTING MACHINES, MULTISTATION MACHINES

Free Weights

1. **SITUP (KNEES STRAIGHT, KNEES BENT)** If the knees are kept straight, most of the work will be done by the *psoas major* muscles. If the knees are bent and kept wide apart, the abdominals get most of the work. (pp. 84-89)

2. **CRUNCH OR BODY ROLL** (pp. 84-88. Also (1), immediately above)

3. **SLANT-BOARD SITUP AND CRUNCH** (pp. 84-88, and (1), immediately above.)

4. **TWIST WITH A BAR** This exercise works the abdominals as well as the *serratus*. (page 195)

5. **ROMAN CHAIR SITUP AND CRUNCH** (pp. 84-88)

6. **VERTICAL AND SUPINE LEG RAISES** (pp. 90-93)

Machines

1. **DYNACAM VARIABLE RESISTANCE ABDOMINAL MACHINE** (page 88)

2. **PARAMOUNT SIDE/WAIST EXERCISER** (pp. 88-89)

3. **PARAMOUNT, DYNACAM TWISTING MACHINES** (pp. 89-90, 91)

4. **MULTISTATION MACHINES FOR ABDOMINAL WORK** (page 93) Although side leans work the external obliques primarily, they also work the abdominals to a degree.

EXTERNAL OBLIQUES (page 154)

EXERCISES: TWISTS (STRAIGHT-BACK, SEATED, BENT-OVER); SIDE LEANS WITH A BARBELL, WITH DUMBBELLS; SIDE CRUNCHES ON A ROMAN CHAIR AND ON A SLANT BOARD

Free Weights

1. TWIST When you do a twist in a bentover position, make sure that you use very little weight. The back is in a weak configuration when you are bent forward at the waist, and serious injury can result if you become careless. (page 195)

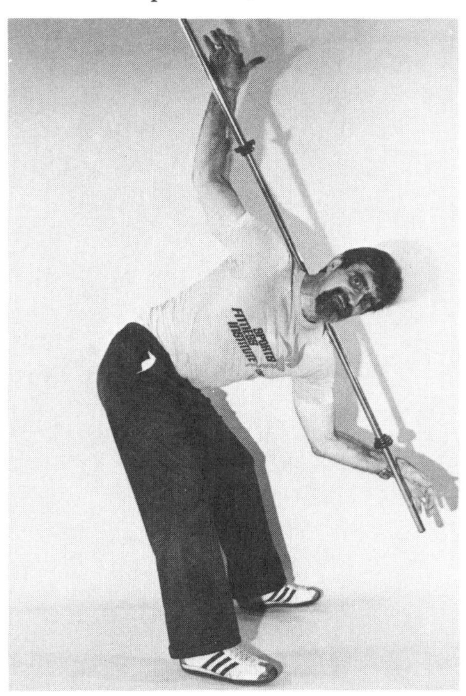

BENTOVER TWIST WITH A BAR

2. SIDE LEANS WITH A BARBELL, WITH A DUMBBELL If you do a side lean with a barbell, hold it across the shoulders and let your

SIDE LEAN WITH A BAR

arms lie along the length of the bar. Lean first to one side and then to the other. A dumbbell will give you a better workout. Hold one dumbbell in your hand and lean to the side. Don't hold a dumbbell in the other hand. It will just nullify the weight of the other dumbbell by balancing your body. This is a controversial exercise for men. Most men collect fat along the external obliques, and the fat is hard to get rid of. Also, the obliques respond to weight training very quickly. Consequently, they often grow rapidly and push the fat farther out instead of helping to burn it up.

SIDE LEAN WITH A DUMBBELL

Better to stick with twists and full squats. The twists will massage the sides, and the full squats will burn calories as well as work the *gluteus medius* muscles, which lie right below the obliques.

3. SIDE CRUNCH OR SIDE BODY ROLL ON A SLANT BOARD When using the slant board for a side crunch, lie on the side instead of on the back. (see page 84)

4. SIDE CRUNCH OR SIDE ROLL ON A ROMAN CHAIR Lie on the side instead of on the back. This means that you will have to hook your feet under the Roman chair bar with the side of your ankle against the underside of the padded bar. Your hips will be on the seat of the Roman chair. Don't bend at the waist too much. You have no support past the horizontal plane, and you can injure yourself if you're careless. (see pp. 86-88)

Machines

1. SIDE/WAIST EXERCISE MACHINES (page 88, 89)

2. TWISTING MACHINES (pp. 89-90, 91)

3. MULTISTATION SIDE LEANS (page 93)

ERECTOR SPINAE (page 164)

EXERCISES: STIFF-LEGGED DEAD WEIGHT LIFT, GOOD MORNING EXERCISE, DEAD WEIGHT LIFT, SPINAL HYPEREXTENSION, HIP AND BACK MACHINES, LOW PULLEY WORK

Free Weights

1. STIFF-LEGGED DEAD WEIGHT LIFT Like the bentover rowing motion, we put this one in so that we can tell you not to do it. The stiff-legged dead weight lift has been popular for years and years, and criticism of it is largely ignored. Let us give you a winning argument against doing the lift. First, it doesn't do that much for the *erector spinae* group. They begin to flex when you are fully erect, especially if you arch your back at the top of the lift. But most people never stand fully erect at the top of the lift. Second, the back is in its weakest configuration during 90 percent of this lift (see the discussion on pp. 81-84). Don't do the lift. Do spinal hyperextensions instead.

2. GOOD MORNING EXERCISE In this one, you hold the barbell across the shoulders instead of holding it in front of you as you would in the stiff-legged dead weight lift. Also, the knees are slightly bent. If you do this one, make sure that your back remains arched throughout the lift. Otherwise, you're right back into the old bent-back configuration, with all the danger that that entails.

3. DEAD WEIGHT LIFT This is one of the three lifts done at power-lifting meets. Stand in front of the barbell with your feet in a wide stance. Supinate one hand and pronate the other. Keep the back straight and arched, with the lower-back muscles contracted. Now bend only slightly and go down to the bar by bending the legs. Grasp the bar and stand erect. Obviously, you should never use heavy weights in this lift when you are just beginning. Don't let the back bow.

4. SPINAL HYPEREXTENSION This is the best way to develop the *erectors*. Most people don't do it because it isn't glamorous: It doesn't involve lifting h-e-a-v-y weights off the floor. Instead, you do it with the body alone (when you get really good at it, you can add weight and hold a plate on your back or a dumbbell clasped to your abdomen). (pp. 81-84)

Machines

1. DYNACAM AND NAUTILUS HIP AND BACK MACHINES (pp. 81-84)

STIFF-LEGGED DEAD WEIGHT LIFT (THE LIGHTNING BOLT POINTS TO THE MOST COMMON INJURY POINT)

GOOD MORNING EXERCISE

REGULAR DEAD WEIGHT LIFT (STARTING POSITION)

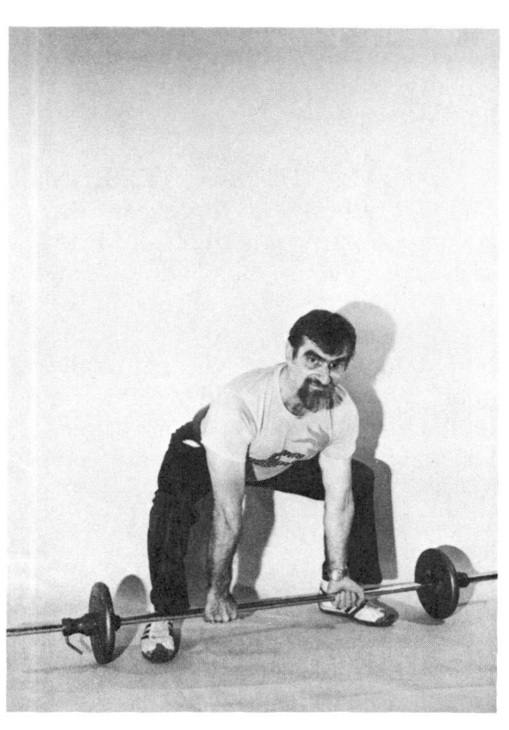

REGULAR DEAD WEIGHT LIFT (FINAL POSITION)

ILIACUS, PSOAS MAJOR (page 155, 156)

EXERCISES: FORWARD LEG RAISE, SUPINE LEG RAISE, VERTICAL LEG RAISE, STRAIGHT-LEG SITUPS (SLANT BOARD, ROMAN CHAIR), HIP AND BACK MACHINES, LEG-KICK MACHINES)

Free Weights

1. **FORWARD LEG RAISE** This leg raise is done while standing erect. If you want to add weight, put on a set of ankle weights or iron shoes. Do one leg at a time, of course. Bend the knee slightly as you bring the leg up. At first, you should bend the leg at the knee so that at the top of the lift the lower leg is perpendicular to the floor. You can extend the leg in the top position after you develop some strength in the lift. You don't need much weight. Keep the back straight while you're doing the exercise, and don't try to lift the leg too high.

2. **SUPINE LEG RAISE** This can be done either on a slant board (page 92) or on the floor. You can lift the legs one at a time or together. If you lift them together, you might need to put a small pad beneath your buttocks to ease the pressure on the lower back. Be careful with this one, especially if you lift the legs together. If you've got any lower-back problems, you'll find out about them here. Also, don't forget to bend the legs at the knees slightly when you bring the legs up.

3. **VERTICAL LEG RAISE** (pp. 90-91)

4. **STRAIGHT-LEG SITUPS (SLANT BOARD OR ROMAN CHAIR)** Do a regular situp, starting completely supine on the slant board or Roman chair, bringing yourself up

FORWARD LEG RAISE

until your upper body is almost erect (don't sit up all the way because it lets the tension off the muscles). Keep the legs straight at the knees. This way the bulk of the work will be thrown to the *iliacus* and *psoas*. (Also, see pp. 84-88)

5. ALTERNATING LEG RAISES Lie on your back either on the floor or on a slant board, either flat or on an incline, and bring the legs up one at a time instead of both at the same time. Do the movement in such a way that the legs pass each other when they are at about a 45-degree angle to the floor. This way, almost all of the work is done by the iliopsoas muscles, with only marginal involvement by the abdominals.

Machines

1. HIP AND BACK MACHINES (pp. 81-84)

2. DYNACAM LEG-KICK MACHINE (page 84)

GLUTEUS MAXIMUS *(page 165)*

EXERCISES: HIP EXTENSIONS WITH ANKLE WEIGHTS OR IRON SHOES, FULL SQUAT, PARTIAL SQUAT, HIP AND BACK MACHINES, LEG PRESS, LEG-KICK MACHINE

Free Weights

1. HIP EXTENSION WITH ANKLE WEIGHTS OR IRON SHOES Stand erect or lie facedown and lift the leg directly to the back. You won't be able to lift it more than a few inches, because we haven't evolved far enough from being four-legged to acquire much range of motion to the rear in an erect position. Don't swing the leg; lift it slowly and steadily. Add weight by putting on iron shoes or ankle weights.

2. FULL SQUAT (pp. 110-118, 126)

3. PARTIAL SQUAT When you do the squat, get down into the lowest position of the full squat and come up only about a foot. This will work the glutes terrifically. You'll know it the next morning. Don't bounce; make the movements slowly and steadily.

Machines

1. DYNACAM AND NAUTILUS HIP AND BACK MACHINES (pp. 81-84)

HIP EXTENSION: ANKLE WEIGHTS

2. PARAMOUNT, DYNACAM FLOOR-TYPE PRESS MACHINES (page 117)

3. NAUTILUS, DYNACAM, PARAMOUNT, UNIVERSAL LEG-PRESS MACHINES (pp. 81-84)

4. LEG-KICK MACHINES (page 84) Work the glutes by doing hip extensions as described above, but with the kick machine cable and weights supplying the resistance instead of iron shoes or ankle weights.

GLUTEUS MEDIUS, MINIMUS; (page 155) TENSOR FASCIAE LATAE (page 156)

EXERCISES: LATERAL RAISES WITH ANKLE WEIGHTS OR IRON SHOES, LEG KICK MACHINES, ABDUCTOR/ADDUCTOR MACHINES

Free Weights

1. LATERAL LEG RAISE WITH ANKLE WEIGHTS OR IRON SHOES This exercise can be done either standing erect or lying on the side. The motion should be exactly to the side. Bring the leg up in an arc as far as it will go (it won't go far). If you can bring your leg up higher than knee level, you're probably cheating in the movement. To develop the muscles, add resistance with ankle weights or iron shoes. You'll probably be surprised at how weak you are in this lift unless you've been doing a lot of side thrust kicks in your karate class. (see also page 126) For the tensor fasciae latae, bring the thigh up towards the chest.

Machines

1. DYNACAM LEG KICK MACHINE (page 84)

2. DYNACAM, PARAMOUNT ADDUCTOR/ABDUCTOR MACHINE (page 124)

ADDUCTORS:
ADDUCTOR LONGUS (page 156)
ADDUCTOR BREVIS (page 156)
ADDUCTOR MAGNUS (page 156)
PECTINEUS (page 156)
GRACILIS (page 156)

EXERCISES: IRON-SHOE AND ANKLE-WEIGHT MOVEMENTS, ADDUCTION SQUAT, ADDUCTOR/ABDUCTION MACHINE, LEG KICK MACHINE

Free Weights

1. IRON SHOE AND ANKLE-WEIGHT MOVEMENTS (pp. 125-126)

2. ADDUCTION SQUAT (pp. 110-118, 126) This is a wide-stance squat.

Machines

1. DYNACAM, PARAMOUNT ADDUCTOR/ABDUCTOR MACHINE (page 124)

2. DYNACAM LEG KICK MACHINE (page 84)

SARTORIUS (page 157)

EXERCISES: FRONT LEG RAISE WITH ANKLE WEIGHTS OR IRON SHOES, LEG KICK MACHINES

Free Weights

1. FORWARD OR FRONT LEG RAISE WITH ANKLE WEIGHTS OR IRON SHOES (page 201)

Machines

1. DYNACAM LEG KICK MACHINE (page 84) The *sartorius* is also a rotator. Fasten the leg kick machine collar around your ankle, and lie down beside the machine on your stomach with your leg bent at the knee. The ankle to which the collar is attached should be the one away from the machine. Now rotate the leg at the hip, keeping the knee bent so that the ankle swings away from the machine. This works the *sartorius* only if the knee remains bent. You won't need much weight.

QUADRICEPS: RECTUS FEMORIS, VASTUS INTERMEDIUS (page 157) VASTUS LATERALIS (page 157) VASTUS MEDIALIS (page 157)

EXERCISES: SQUATS (FULL, PARALLEL, HALF, QUARTER), LEG EXTENSION WITH IRON SHOES OR ANKLE WEIGHTS, POWER RACK SQUAT, SPECIAL SQUAT DEVICES AND EQUIPMENT, SQUAT MACHINES, FLOOR-TYPE PRESS MACHINES FOR SQUATS, LEG PRESS MACHINES, LEG EXTENSION MACHINES AND DEVICES, PRIMER BOARD SQUAT, TENSION BAND EXERCISES

Free Weights

1. SQUATS (FULL, PARALLEL, HALF, QUARTER) (pp. 110-118, 126)

2. LEG EXTENSION WITH IRON SHOES OR ANKLE WEIGHTS For this one, sit on the edge of a bench with your lower legs dangling off the side. Attach ankle weights or put on a pair of iron shoes. If you use the iron shoes, you can fasten them together with a dumbbell bar, and you can also add a considerable amount of weight in the form of dumbbell plates. Keep the knees close together, and bring the legs up until they are no longer bent at the knee. This exercise works all of the quads, but it is especially effective during the first part of the movement on the *rectus* and the *vastus lateralis*, and in the last 15 degrees of the movement on the *vastus medialis*. If you have no definition in your leg, the leg extension will give it to you.

Machines

1. POWER RACKS (page 113)

2. DEVICES FOR INTENSIFYING THE SQUAT (a) THE MOORE LEG BLASTER AND HURLEY BENCH (pp. 113-115) **(b) THE RADER MAGIC CIRCLE** (pp. 115-116) **(c) THE KINESTHETIC PRIMER BOARD** (page 116)

3. UNIVERSAL CENTURION, PARAMOUNT SQUATTING MACHINES (page 116)

4. DYNACAM, PARAMOUNT FLOOR-TYPE PRESS MACHINES FOR SQUATS (page 117)

5. HACK SQUAT MACHINES (pp. 117-118)

6. LEG PRESS MACHINES (pp. 118-120)

7. LEG EXTENSION MACHINES (pp. 121-122)

LEG FLEXORS:
BICEPS FEMORIS *(page 166)*
SEMITENDINOSUS *(page 166)*
SEMIMEMBRANOSUS *(page 166)*

EXERCISES: SQUATS, LEG CURL WITH ANKLE WEIGHTS OR IRON SHOES, LEG CURL MACHINE, D.A.R.D. DEVICE

Free Weights

1. LEG CURL WITH ANKLE WEIGHTS OR IRON SHOES
Stand erect on one foot. Fasten an ankle weight or an iron shoe to the free foot. Keep the thigh perpendicular to

the floor, and bring the lower leg up until the heel is near to or touches the buttocks. (see also pp. 122-123)

STANDING LEG CURL: ANKLE WEIGHTS

Machines

1. DYNACAM LEG CURL MACHINE (pp. 122-124)

2. PARAMOUNT LEG CURL MACHINE (pp. 122-124)

3. DYNACAM, PARAMOUNT, UNIVERSAL RECLINING LEG CURL (pp. 122-124)

4. D.A.R.D. DEVICE (pp. 122-124)

PLANTAR AND TOE FLEXORS:

GASTROCNEMIUS:	*(page 158)*
SOLEUS	*(page 159)*
PERONEUS LONGUS	*(page 158)*
PERONEUS BREVIS	*(page 158)*
FLEXOR HALLUCIS LONGUS	*(page 167)*
FLEXOR DIGITORUM LONGUS	*(page 167)*

EXERCISES: CALF RAISE WITH BARBELL (STANDING AND SEATED), TENSION BAND EXERCISES FOR THE TOE FLEXORS

Free Weights

1. CALF RAISE WITH BARBELL (STANDING) Place a barbell across the shoulders just behind the neck. Rise up on the balls of the feet until your calf muscles are fully contracted. Then let yourself slowly back down. There are three foot positions for the calf raise: feet parallel; toes pointed out; and toes pointed inward. The first will develop the entire calf equally. The second will work the inner calf more than the outer. The last will work the outer calf more than the inner. Try it on one foot, and feel the two heads of the *gastrocnemius*; you'll see what we mean.

2. CALF RAISE WITH BARBELL (SEATED) Standing calf raises emphasize *gastrocnemius* development. Seated calf raises emphasize *soleus* development. You should do them both. To do seated raises, sit in a sturdy chair with both feet on the floor. Place a cushion across your knees, and place a barbell across the cushion. Now do the calf raises as described above.

2. TENSION BAND EXERCISES FOR TOE FLEXORS The Unique Tension Band, while applicable to any exercise movement, is particularly useful in exercises which do not lend themselves readily either to weights or machines. To work the toe flexors, loop the band around the underside of the toes, holding the band above them with one hand. Pull the band until it is taut, and move the toes downward against the resistance of the band. You can increase the tension by pulling back with your hand. Be sure that you isolate the movement so that you are moving only the toes and not the entire foot. (pp. 38-39)

Machines

1. DYNACAM, PARAMOUNT COMBINATION HACK AND CALF RAISE MACHINE (pp. 127-28)

2. NAUTILUS STANDING CALF RAISE MACHINE (pp. 128-29)

3. DYNACAM SEATED CALF MACHINE (page 129)

4. LEG PRESS MACHINES FOR CALF RAISES (page 130)

5. LEG KICK MACHINE (use the collar as you would the ankle weight) (page 84)

SEATED CALF RAISE: BARBELL

DORSIFLEXORS: TIBIALIS ANTERIOR (page 158) TOE EXTENSORS: EXTENSOR HALLUCIS LONGUS (page 159) EXTENSOR DIGITORUM LONGUS (page 158)

EXERCISES: EXERCISES WITH IRON SHOES AND ANKLE WEIGHTS, TENSION BAND EXERCISES

Free Weights

1. EXERCISES WITH IRON SHOES OR ANKLE WEIGHTS When you bend the foot at the ankle so that the ball of the foot moves downward, it's called "plantar flexion." When you bend the foot at the ankle so that it comes back toward the shin, it's called "dorsiflexion." Plantar flexion and dorsiflexion refer to a movement of the foot as it hinges at the ankle. Furthermore, when the toes are flexed as they are in the Tension Band toe flexor exercise described above, it is still called "flexion." But when the toes come back toward the shin (in a movement that is really independent of dorsiflexion), it's called toe extension. Don't let the terminology confuse you. Here it is in a nutshell:

PLANTAR FLEXION: foot hinges down at the ankle
TOE FLEXION: toes hinge down at the metatarsal joint
DORSIFLEXION: foot hinges up at the ankle
TOE EXTENSION: toe hinges up at the metatarsal

Now that we know which direction is which, we can do some exercises. To accomplish dorsiflexion with resistance, fasten an ankle weight around the toes instead of around the ankle. Sit in a chair so that you can start with the foot in a plantar flexion position. Hinge the foot at the ankle, and bring it up as far toward the shin as it will go. You can do the same thing with an iron shoe, but the weight will be distributed over the entire foot, instead of around the toes.

2. TENSION BAND EXERCISES Again, the Unique Tension Band gets at the hard-to-get-at-muscles. Loop the band across the tops of the toes, letting the rest of the band dangle below the foot. Stick your other foot through the loop, and hold the end of the band down against the floor. Now pull your foot into a dorsiflexion position, then extend the toes back toward the shin. If you want more resistance, lift the foot you're working on higher so that the band will be more taut.

Machines

DYNACAM LEG KICK MACHINE (page 84) Loop the collar of the leg kick machine around your toes as you would the ankle weights described in (1), immediately above. Sit on the floor facing the machine, and pull the foot into dorsiflexion. You can also do toe extension by moving only the toes.

DORSIFLEXION: ANKLE WEIGHT

A NOTE ON HYDRA-GYM AND MINI-GYM MACHINES

Many of the exercises listed above can be performed on Hydra-Gym and Mini-Gym equipment. Please refer to pp. 135-37 for a description of relevant equipment.

So much for the exercises. Now let's move on to the programs that you can develop with them. First, let's cover a few things you need to know before you start your own program.

5

DEVELOPING YOUR OWN PROGRAM

Section One: Things You Need to Know About Before You Start Your Own Program

You've got your exercises lined up, you know how to use all the equipment, and you've bought all your workout gear. But you're still not quite ready to start on a program. You need to know some of the pitfalls and problems that can plague beginning, intermediate, and advanced weight trainers alike. Let's take each of these common problem areas one by one and see how each can be overcome or avoided altogether:

A. SLOW GAINERS, SLOW LOSERS: A FEW TIPS FROM THOSE WHO'VE BEEN THERE

In training, as with everything else, the grass is always greener on the other side of the fence. The slow gainer envies the slow loser's ability to hang onto his bulk without the constant daily battle of trying to put on weight. The slow loser looks enviously at the slow gainer and envies her ability to eat everything in sight without gaining a pound, without the constant daily battle of trying to lose weight. And so it goes.

It's no secret that there are people who simply seem less prone to retaining or collecting body fat than others. We all know these people—usually long, lean, wiry, often hyperenergetic—who seem capable of eating the proverbial fatted calf without putting on an ounce of weight. And there are, in equal or greater numbers, people who seem to gain at the mere sight of food.

The two trends aren't always problems for the individual. The slow gainer may be perfectly satisfied with his/her lot if he/she is a fashion model, an actor or actress, or in any other field where superthinness is an asset. Similarly, the slow loser may be a powerlifter who both needs and wants the extra bulk—or perhaps he/she is a long-distance runner or cyclist who finds the extra weight necessary to avoid depleting energy stores in a race.

The problem comes when the "slow gainer" is a man who's trying to gain muscle size, or when the "slow loser" is a woman who is desperately trying to lose inches. Then the process seems maddeningly slow, and, likely as not, both parties end up frustrated and depressed.

What to do if you're either of these types? Persistence and patience help most in the end, but here are some tips to get you started:

If you're a slow gainer:

1. First of all, let's talk about weight gain. You want to gain lean body weight, not body fat. The ideal for anyone, man or woman, is to have the maximum amount of muscle mass, or lean body weight, and the minimum of body fat. Some athletes, according to Dr. Paul DeVore (March 1979 *Iron Man*), simply have more difficulty than others increasing both size and muscularity. Others accumulate excess body fat whenever they try to gain muscle mass. These tendencies are simply givens of individual physiology and metabolism. You have to recognize the problem, learn to compensate, and then set yourself a firm goal: increasing muscle mass while avoiding increased fat accumulation.

2. It helps to keep some detailed records for yourself. Start keeping a daily log of calorie intake, carbohydrate grams and protein grams ingested. Each day record your weight, and every week take your measurements. It won't take long to determine exactly how many calories you need to maintain your present weight.

Then start adding calories. Remember that to put on one pound of lean muscle mass you need to take in 2,500 extra calories, or about 750 calories a day to gain 1–2 pounds a week. Any excess weight gain will be either fat or water retention. Take in the extra calories in the form of protein, complex carbohydrates, and a few fats, but avoid high-fat foods, junk and processed foods, and refined carbs. One excellent way of getting the extra calories without the bulk of too much food is through a protein powder or weight-gain supplement.

There are many delicious, nutritionally balanced powders and liquids on the market now.

3. Another rule of thumb: Don't overtrain. There's a myth in some quarters that if you're a hard gainer, if one set is good, two are better, and ten are best. Don't succumb to this myth. Both hard gainers and losers, incidentally, fall for this one. They do excessive amounts of work, break down too much tissue, overexert their systems, and prevent their recuperative powers from taking effect. Remember that training in small amounts stimulates growth. Too much stimulation becomes overwork, and your already underweight body responds by tearing down even more tissue.

4. If you want to gain muscle mass, the right *kind* of training is just as important as the right length of time or the right diet. Leg and back muscles, as the largest muscles in the body, are usually strongest and thus grow in size and strength relatively fast. When properly worked, these muscles will trigger reciprocal growth in lesser muscle groups.

5. The traditional way of gaining is to use heavy weights and low reps to gain muscle mass. But there are other ways, according to Bill Pearl in an interview in *Muscle,* July 1975. Pearl believes that low reps with heavy weights and numerous sets done quickly are the fastest way to make a muscle coarser and larger. But other bodybuilders and weight trainers find that relatively light weights and "pumping" reps can also give muscle mass. In fact, there simply is no absolutely correct method for building muscle size, since individual response to training varies so greatly.

6. One final note for the slow gainer: Remember that for you, as for the slow loser, weight in pounds is only a small part of the story. You want to gain, all right—but lean body tissue, not fat. Don't make the mistake that so many slow gainers do and turn into a human garbage disposal, devouring all the junk food in sight, and then some. In many ways, we really *are* what we eat. Quality food and good nutrition produce quality gains in muscle and vital tissue. Sugar and fat will produce quick weight gains, but usually the gains are 90 percent or more fat and water. Protein, complex carbohydrates, and low-fat dairy products together with vitamin and mineral supplements will give you the kind of slower, lasting, quality gains you need. So resist the urge to gain those 20 pounds by shoveling in the chips and dips, sodas and sweets. Take it slowly, but watch yourself get more muscular and stronger—not fatter. There really *is* a difference, as your mirror, if not the scales, can tell you!

If you're a slow loser:

Now what about the slow loser? More often than not, this person is a woman who's on her hundredth diet, trying to lose those same 10 (or 20, or 30, or 40 . . .) pounds she's lost so many times before. Or she's a person who always seems to plateau out at a certain point and never get beyond it. Or sometimes our "slow loser" is a man who puts on fat when he tries to bulk up and gain body mass. Or he's simply an average man who'd like to look trimmer and train for definition but finds he gets those cuts at a discouragingly slow pace. Unfortunately, there's no royal road to weight loss, but here are a few things to keep in mind:

1. First of all, stop feeling guilty. Some people *do* lose weight much more slowly than others. That's fact, and there's little you can do about it except keep on your program and wait for the results to come. But on the other hand, be honest with yourself. Most "slow losers" are either eating a little more or moving around a little less than they think they are.

2. As with the slow gainer, meticulous record keeping is a must. Get yourself a small notebook or diary and record every mouthful you eat, with its calorie, carbohydrate, fat, and protein counts. Do this for three to five days. Also record your weight daily to see if you're losing, gaining, or maintaining the status quo. If you're just maintaining, then remember that in order to lose a pound of fat, you'll have to cut back 3,500 calories. So start cutting. But while you're counting calories, also start reducing grams of fat and carbohydrates. Do this slowly, at the rate of perhaps 5–6 grams a day. Continue to cut until the scales register a loss. Then monitor your progress closely until you find the level at which you're losing the desired two pounds a week (anything over and you're probably losing muscle tissue as well as fat). What you've just found is your critical carbohydrate and fat level, which then gives you a baseline for determining daily intake.

3. Have you cut your calories to a minimum, dropped back on your carbohydrate intake, and reduced fats—and still aren't losing? Then you may be suffering from water retention (edema). It's more common in women than in men, although both sexes suffer from it to one degree or another. If your fluid retention is not caused by high blood pressure, diabetes, heart disease, or another serious ailment, then a simple reduction in salt may do the trick. Also cut back on carbohydrates, since they bind twice to three times their weight in water. Drop high-sodium and processed foods from your diet. Avoid even low-calorie sodas (because of the sodium content), and beware of foods containing MSG and other preservatives. Women may also need to go off the Pill or find one that contains less estrogen.

4. You're on a low-cal, low-carb diet, have cut out salt and preservatives, and *still* can't lose? Then check out your exercise levels. Are you skimping on your workout periods? Doing too little and resting too much between sets? Keeping the weights too light or the sets too short? Try stepping up both the length and intensity of your workouts and see what happens. "Shock" the body by working out twice a day for thirty minutes each, instead of your usual hour-long once-a-day routine. Run a mile, cycle, swim, or skip rope on "off" days. Walk where you usually ride. Increase your activity level in some small but significant ways and see if you can break through that sticking point.

5. In a very few cases, there really is a medical problem at the core of your "slow loser" syndrome. While people love to blame their thyroid for weight loss and gain, it's the culprit in only a small percentage of cases. If you're one of those unlucky ones who seems to gain weight at the sight of food, have a basal metabolism test run. You may be mildly to severely hypothyroid and not know it. Or you may have a severe case of edema that needs medical attention. In any case, get the medical attention you need before you proceed with the diet and exercise program.

6. Remember that weight loss is a slow, often uneven process. Dr. Barbara Edelstein, in *The Woman Doctor's Diet for Women,* says that women lose weight from the head down but redistribute from the feet up. That is, they lose in the face, neck, arms, bust, and midriff/waist area first, then in the hips and thighs, and finally in the calves and ankles. But they "redistribute" the remaining subcutaneous fat from the lower legs up—which is why, after an initial period of looking haggard, drawn, and tired with a disappearing bust and skinny arms, you can look forward to regaining some weight in your face and upper body while those stubborn hips and thighs finally shrink down to size. (Valerie's own pattern of weight loss followed exactly this model—we even made a series of slides to record the story on film.) Remember that the whole process may take six weeks or longer, so be patient. Often it seems that nothing is happening, while in fact the redistribution process is going on—literally under your nose!

7. Read our advice for the slow gainer carefully. Some of it applies to you, too. Remember that what you want to lose is fat, not lean body mass. Crash dieting is not the answer. Indeed, researchers like Mark Friedman of the University of Massachusetts (cited in Toby Cohen's article, "Why Diets Don't Work," *New York* magazine, May 21, 1979) have found that immediately following a severe crash diet, there's a runaway tendency for the body to produce fat. If you diet too severely and lose 20 or 30 pounds in a month, then return to "normal" eating and regain the weight you lost, the pounds will return, all right—and a larger proportion than before will be pure fat. That's true because much of the original loss was tissue, muscle, and water loss, and very little was fat. Result: You're now "fatter" than before—that is, you have a higher percentage of body fat—although you may weigh exactly the same on the trusty bathroom scales.

Remember that in dieting, as in anything else, slow and steady wins the race. The recommended maximum of 2 pounds a week is a safe limit for anyone and is about all the body can handle. If at the end of a five-month period, you've lost 20 pounds of real fat—not fluid, not muscle tissue—you're well on your way toward solving your weight problem for good.

8. Remember that the real end of weight loss is not just a temporary drop that will get you through a wedding (yours or someone else's), a vacation, or a special party, but a lifelong, genuine process of re-education. You've not only got to lose the weight but also keep from re-gaining it—far harder, if we are to believe some current statistics. According to the 1979 *New York* article cited above, 95 percent of those who lose significant amounts of weight gain it right back—some within six months or less. Others experience a constant, frustrating, and debilitating yo-yo syndrome—fat one month, thin the next.

Weight loss is like many other "cures": The longer the patient is in "remission of symptoms," the better the chances for survival and cure. If you can maintain that new reading on the scales, give or take a few pounds, for six months, a year, two years, you give the body a chance to readjust to the lower weight, let your appetite (or "appestat," as the popular jargon goes) readjust to lowered demands for feedings and also let the fat redistribution go on. If you continue to exercise while redistribution occurs, you also continue increasing lean body mass while decreasing fat and surplus fluid.

9. By now, it should be obvious why exercise is of value to the slow loser. Weight loss by dieting alone, as we've already noted, brings a decrease in pounds but not in inches. By contrast, if you're on a carefully planned diet, with adequate protein and complex carbohydrates, and also work out with an exercise program, you're losing mostly body fat and excess fluids, with very little tissue loss. So you lose more slowly according to the scales—but you also look leaner, trimmer, lose inches, and shrink down a dress or pants size or two. An added plus: Researchers have found that your body continues to burn calories for four to six hours after an exercise period. If you work out for an hour, that means five to seven hours during which your revved-up metabolism burns calories, with a corresponding loss in fat.

10. Finally, if you're a slow loser, cheer up. The slow, steady loss allows your mind and psyche to keep pace with the changes that are taking place in your body. Too sudden and dramatic a change in body size, shape, and general image can be unsettling to anyone (more about this later), and as a result, you may start overeating again in a subconscious desire to return to your old safe, familiar body weight. Losing more slowly lets your head and psyche readjust along with your body and makes it more likely that you'll maintain the loss.

B. STUBBORN FATTY DEPOSITS: CELLULITE AND OTHER CONTROVERSIES

If you're on a diet and exercise program—particularly if you're a woman—you've probably read about that stubborn fat called "cellulite." Then perhaps you've glanced down at your own thighs, which look like a rippling mixture of oatmeal, cottage cheese, and orange peel, and delivered a horrified self-diagnosis: You too are a victim of "SELL-you-leet," as current pronunciation has it.

It's a controversial subject, and no one, including us, seems to have found the definitive answer. All we can do is to present both sides of the controversy and make a few observations about the nature of this stubborn, dimple-textured fat that's made so many dollars for so many "specialists" in the last decade.

Nicole Ronsard, probably the first cellulite "authority" to surface (her *Cellulite* first appeared in hardcover in 1973), defines cellulite as "more than simple fat . . . a gel-like substance made up of fat, water and wastes, trapped in lumpy, immovable pockets just beneath the skin." She calls the deposits "fat gone wrong" and says that the pockets act like sponges to absorb large amounts of water, blow up and then bulge out, resulting in rippled, flabby flesh.

Ronsard is adamant about one thing: Cellulite, she says, is not regular fat and thus will not burn like normal fat when a diet is undertaken. The treatment, she maintains, consists of a special diet to "purify" the body of excess water and toxic wastes. Her program is designed to return the connective tissue to its normal elasticity and suppleness, free the trapped waste materials, and drain and remove them.

Ronsard's diet is basically a balanced one, stressing raw fruits and vegetables; salads; low-fat milk, yogurt and cheese; lean meat and fish; six to eight glasses of water throughout the day; and a program of nutritional supplements, minerals, and vitamins. The diet stresses natural diuretic teas, herbs, and foods (asparagus, cucumbers, watercress, spinach) and eliminates foods high in sodium and preservatives. Other elements of the program: proper elimination, frequent saunas and dry sand baths, friction rubs with a loofah or friction mitt, breathing and relaxation exercises, special herbal baths, water gymnastics, and massage.

Anna Blau and Celestina Wallis of the Anushka cellulite salons (New York and Houston) also recommend special diets and massage. Their salon treatments begin with a total physical examination and progress to elaborate sessions with pulsed ultrasonic waves, hand massage by trained masseuses, immersion of the body in steaming turbo baths, and therafin wraps (a special type of paraffin). The Anushka diet is somewhat more restrictive than Ronsard's. Anna Blau believes that many women plagued by cellulite also have some carbohydrate intolerance—their bodies simply cannot properly metabolize carbohydrates. The diet stresses protein (14–16 ounces minimum per day); keeps fruits, vegetables, and starch to a minimum. Dairy products are confined to skim-milk cheeses, 4 tablespoons of plain low-fat yogurt a day, and 4 ounces of unsalted buttermilk a week. Vegetables are to be eaten lightly steamed (less likely to cause bloating) and should be confined to a small leafy salad and a small serving of steamed vegetables a day. Fruit portions are strictly measured, and pineapple, papaya, melon, and strawberries (low in carbs, high in digestive enzymes) are stressed. Sweets, sodas (diet or regular), alcohol, beer, salt, breads and cereals (except for plain bran, wheat germ, and gluten bread) are strictly forbidden. Special diet menus are provided for the faithful to follow.

Other "cellulite systems" available on the open market are largely home-massage devices—for example, the Lancome treatment pack, the Elancyl method, and the Horley treatment, all of which are basically rubber mitts or sponges, special soaps or gels, and after-massage lotions. The treatments' chief benefit is that they stimulate the circulation in the affected area—usually the top of the thigh and hip—and thus promote waste and fluid removal while preventing "pooling" of fluid in the legs or hips.

But medical orthodoxy, for the most part, continues to deny the existence of cellulite. Most MDs stick to their guns: Fat is fat, a calorie is a calorie, and people lose weight (and body fat) at a fairly constant rate all over the body. If stubborn fat continues to cling to one spot or another, simply continue with your diet and exercise program, and the unwanted flab will eventually disappear.

Only two current writers concede that cellulite may exist. One, Dr. Anita Columbu (a chiropractor, not an MD), who is the wife of bodybuilder Franco Columbu and co-author of their *Starbodies,* blames cellulite on junk food and other poor nutritional habits, a sedentary life-style, chemicals, preservatives, additives, caffeine, tobacco, drugs, and hormonal imbalance. She identifies two kinds of cellulite: hard cellulite (which she says appears on generally overweight women and can only be treated by massage) and soft cellulite (can appear on women of any weight and is treatable with vigorous massage and high-repetition exercises with light weights), according to her article in *Muscle* magazine in October 1979.

A more conservative view is that of Dr. Jonathan Zizmor, one of *Mademoiselle* magazine's team of consulting physicians. Zizmor prefers not to use the word "cellulite" but to talk about "maldistribution of fat," since he finds that with microscopic examination, the dimply puckered fat cells look just like any other kind of fat cell. Yet he does concede that some women do have problems with "a particular kind of nasty, bulgy, badly distributed fat that is very difficult to shed . . . definitely harder to get rid of than other fat" *(Mademoiselle,* June 1978).

As usual, the truth probably lies somewhere between the two extremes. Whatever we wish to call it, there is some fat on some bodies—especially women's bodies—that is "definitely harder to lose," as Dr. Zizmor says. We seldom have trouble losing from the shoulders, back, or, alas, from the bust, but nearly every woman over twenty-five has a touch of the orange peel on upper thighs, hips, upper arms, waist, knees, and sometimes calves or ankles. Precisely *what* it is, is a mystery, but the best research on the subject suggests that it's related to poor circulation, disorders of the lymphatic system and/or connective tissue, stress, heredity, elimination, water retention, use of certain medications, lack of exercise, and/or general overweight. Couple two or more of these factors with generally bad nutrition and a genetic predisposition to collect the nasty stuff, and you're in business.

It's true that if you were overweight and lost, say, 30 pounds, the "cellulite" would be affected—that is, the deposits would become thinner and less rippled in texture. But some deposits might remain even after you had reached your weight-loss goal and gone on a maintenance program. (Dr. Myles Pohunek, chief investor and president of the Sports Fitness Institute, reports seeing even *underweight* women—marathon runners and champion weight trainers—who still hang onto their cellulite deposits). What to do? We've no final answers, but here are some rough-and-ready practical solutions that you might try:

1. Cut down on salt intake. If the problem is linked to water retention, a strict salt-free diet with plenty of water and uncarbonated liquids is a first step toward solving the problem. Stay away from MSG and other preservatives that favor water retention. Choose salt-free, water-packed tuna and salmon, but skip the smoked meat and fish. Also pass up the Fritos, potato chips, pickles, olives, saltines, bleu cheese, pretzels, and sausages at your next buffet. Give up alcohol and diet sodas, and stay with plain mineral water, skim milk, fresh vegetable juices, herb teas, and decaffeinated or weak coffee.

2. Don't overdo the water cure, either. Instead of the usual recommended six to eight glasses for dieters, try four glasses drunk in small portions throughout the day. Drink no more than a half-glass at a time (use a straw to prevent bloating), and lie down for a half-hour or so (the body loses more water when you're lying down than when you're in an upright position). Use a mild diuretic, or, better yet, take naturally diuretic foods and teas.

3. Try cutting carbohydrate grams to 25 (or less) per day. Keep strict records, and if your "oatmeal fat" doesn't respond, keep cutting until you notice a change. If you have a problem with carbohydrate metabolism, the side effect of general weight loss will be a plus. Remember that carbohydrates bind water, as does salt, so some of the loss will be excess fluid.

4. Do try an exercise program that stimulates overall circulation and steps up circulation in the affected area. If you collect "orange rind" on your buttocks, a program built around a high-repetition squat program, combined with leg curls and extensions, hack or sissy squats, and jogging in place or riding the stationary bicycle will increase circulation to the hips.

5. For best results, try massage with a loofah, sponge, or one of the cellulite "systems" mentioned earlier. Again, the massage is nothing magic—it simply stimulates circulation to the affected area. Always work with long, upward strokes that move the blood back toward the heart. The kneading and pounding and "knuckling" motions that Ronsard describes are also good. But work gently—no need to injure yourself in your fight with the Cellulite Demon.

6. Make sure you stimulate regular elimination and perspiration. Gone are the days when women tried to avoid sweat. Now we recognize that perspiration is the body's "disposal" system through which it detoxifies itself. Work out in a sauna suit or with plastic wraps if necessary (only indoors, never outside or in hot weather). Add bran, raw vegetables, and brewer's yeast to your diet to insure proper elimination.

7. Finally, remember that some patterns of "cellulite" collection are hereditary, especially if you gather the stubborn stuff in odd areas like the ankles, calves, upper arms, or high on the upper hips (the chief place where men are cellulite-prone). Remember, too, that cellulite isn't the only kind of controversial, hard-to-lose fat. Some diet and weight-control experts now have begun to talk about "brown fat" (more stubborn, hard-loss areas), "hard" vs. "soft" fat, "new" vs. "old" fat. Controversy rages around all these terms and classifications, and probably will continue for some time. The only reliable treatment now consists of patience, persistence, a sensible diet, and a regular exercise program. Stimulate circulation, keep moving, and let your tapemeasure be your guide!

C. INJURIES: WHAT TO DO TO AVOID THEM, WHAT TO DO WHEN THEY OCCUR

Weight training is among the safest of all the contemporary sports. With tennis elbow, racquetball wrist, runner's knee, and jogger's shin splints all making news, weight training lags far behind in producing a set of similarly chic injuries. Nevertheless, there are some things you should and should not do in order to assure yourself the most injury-free workouts possible.

1. Always warm up adequately before you work out. You may be in a hurry and eager to start the workout, but take the time to warm up. Do some simple limbering exercises, flexing each muscle against its opposite to get the circulation going and promote flexibility. Or do the weight-training movements that you'll use in the actual exercise, either without weight or with very light weights (for example, do a squat warmup by doing perfect-form deep knee bends with no weight at all). Or simply jog in place, run around the track three to five laps, or ride the stationary bike. But make sure that you're adequately warmed up before you start. In the wintertime, extra clothing helps. Try leg warmers over your tights or sweat suit, an extra shirt or top you can shed as the workout progresses.

2. Don't go for maximum poundages without working up to them first. You may have trained with weights in high school or college—but that was years ago. Don't expect to top your record after a decade-long layoff. Build up gradually to handling the heavy poundages. Remember that progressive-resistance exercise means just that—progressive resistance built up in small increments over a period of time.

3. Always work with a spotter if you're doing a heavy lift—or any lift, for that matter—that involves raising the weights overhead. Make sure your training partners are around for the bench press especially. Even if you don't need them, it's comforting to know that there's someone around to rescue you if you can't get the bar up that one last time. Do squats with a heavy-duty rack that will handle your weight safely. If you don't have a spotter or partner you can depend on, look for a gym with a safety bench-press rack so that you can train independently.

4. Make sure you're doing each exercise in proper form. Even pros can get lazy or sloppy about form. Make sure that you periodically check your form in a mirror or, better still, have your training partner or coach check it for you. Bad form leads to injuries, pulls, sprains that result from overcompensation for weak areas of the body.

5. Make sure you're using a lifting belt if you're doing heavy squats. Lifting gloves aren't a bad idea either, if you are doing heavy bench presses and your hands perspire a good deal. Keep your lifting belt tight around your waist when you squat, and practice proper form at all times.

6. Don't overtrain or work out when you're overtired. Drugs or alcohol may give you a sort of euphoric illusion that you can handle more weight than you actually can and so lead to injuries. Or they'll encourage sloppy form, which itself leads to injuries. Either way, staying straight for the workout will greatly increase your chances of coming out uninjured.

Dr. Gabe Mirkin in *The Sportsmedicine Book* provides the best comment: "In the 1968 Olympics, Japanese weight lifters were widely rumored to have used drugs to overcome their fear of lifting very heavy weights. True, they weren't afraid of the bars, but they couldn't lift them either." We rest our case.

7. What to do if you are injured? The first order of the day is to rest. Don't work out—at least, not with exercises that involve the injured area. For example, if you have a knee injury, switch to an upper-body or abdominal routine for a workout or two—however long it takes the injured area to heal. The point of training is not to injure yourself. The old maxim "No pain, no gain" should become "Train, don't strain."

8. When you do begin to train again, put yourself on a "rehabilitative" program for a short time. Work with light weights and high repetitions until the injury is completely healed. Don't expect to return to the level of training you had achieved before you were injured. Instead, stay with the light weights until the pain and stiffness leave. If the injury is serious, you should work with a physician or sports rehabilitation therapist such as Dick Hoover who specializes in treating sports injuries. Meanwhile, do movements that don't involve the injured parts so that you don't lose conditioning totally. And most of all, be patient and wait for the healing to take place before you swing back into your old routine.

D. HEALTH PROBLEMS: TEAMING UP WITH YOUR PHYSICIAN FOR MAXIMUM PROGRESS

All right, let's say you're already on your program. You made your initial check with your physician and got a clean bill of health as far as your current physical condition goes. How do you now continue working with the doctor for best results? Here are a few ideas to set you thinking of your program as a cooperative effort:

1. Remember that you need to start on the program with some fairly well-defined goals, which can fall into any of three categories: *somaesthetic* (body-oriented); *somahygenic* (health- or fitness-oriented); or *somadynamic* (performance-oriented). Remember, too, that every exercise program is, to some extent, rehabilitative. We exercise to look better, lose weight, lose body fat, prevent or reverse some illness or injury, lower blood cholesterol or triglycerides levels, build strength, or increase cardiovascular fitness—or sometimes all of the above.

So knowing what your specific goals are and being able to set priorities are helpful both to you and to your physician. If you want to lose 20 pounds *and* look better *and* lose your shortness of breath *and* cure your foot or back problems *and* also work on your chronic edema, be sure to let your doctor know of all the goals, not just one or two. Give him or her a complete medical history with as much detail as possible. Don't omit details, lie, or cover up. You're putting both you and your doctor at a terrible disadvantage if you "neglect" to mention your family history of diabetes or forget to mention that you smoke three packs a day.

2. As for goals, it helps to be able to sort out your primary, secondary, and tertiary goals. If you're our mythical early-thirties overweight patient, male or female, it helps in planning an intelligent program to know that your primary goals are to eliminate your shortness of breath, foot and back problems, and chronic edema, while your second order of priorities is to lose 30 pounds and look better. A third goal might be to increase performance to improve or start a new sport (running, tennis, cycling, swimming, whatever). But it always helps to tell your physician these things. If your chief goal is just to look better and fit into your new clothes, then speak up and communicate this, too. Don't feel that your primary goal always has to be health-related.

3. Keep in mind that your goals will change as your program continues. Valerie herself began with the modest goal of slimming down so that she could fit into a pair of faded-blue denim jeans. Now five years later, this former fatty shrugs off the size four designer pants in her closet and concentrates on improving lower-back definition and adding weight to her bench press. Same for Ralph: The skinny kid who hated the Charles Atlas ads today works on improving form in his 455-pound squat and experimenting with rotational movements.

So *your* goals will change, too. Don't be intimidated by superathletes who laugh at your 5-pound Executive Bells or, even worse, your sedentary co-workers who think a night out on the town will get all this exercise foolishness out of your head. Start with a modest goal and work toward it; in a year you'll surprise even yourself.

4. Don't be afraid or ashamed to approach your doctor with goals that are "merely" cosmetic (somaesthetic) ends. If you're a woman, this is particularly important. *You* may want to lose 20 pounds in order to look better, while your doctor assures you that you're in generally good health, that being "chunky" runs in the family, and that you should concentrate on health problems and forget your fashion-centered ideal. If this happens to you, run, do not walk, in search of a doctor with some more specific training in bariatrics (weight control), diet, or nutrition. *You* know when you're ashamed or uncomfortable with your body weight, and you'll eventually try to do something about it, safely or not. So you might as well do it right, with proper medical guidance from someone who is knowledgeable about, and sympathetic to, your problems.

Often, too, what passes at first glance for "just 20 extra pounds" can be traced to an underlying medical problem. Valerie herself is a case in point. For years she was unhappy with the shape of her lower body—her "piano legs," as she called them—and went to doctor after doctor for help. The answers ranged from "just hereditary" to "chronic overeating" and "lack of discipline." It was only after she got into a regular weight-training program that she traced her problems to chronic edema, a disorder of the connective tissue, a borderline hypoactive metabolism (which the exercise stimulated), circulatory problems in the lower leg, and a rather severe carbohydrate intolerance. Quite a complex medical history for someone who was told for twenty years that she was "just vain" and "born to be plump!"

The moral of our little fable is simple and obvious. Don't feel that losing a few pounds is beneath your doctor's notice. Both lay people and physicians today, thank goodness, are increasingly savvy about weight loss, so the "born-to-be-fat" theory no longer works for either side. No competent contemporary physician looks down on a man or woman who wants to look and feel better.

5. Plan to meet with your physician periodically during your program to evaluate your progress. Don't look on this as a session where you'll be punished or scolded for slow progress or "rewarded" for "being good." Instead, it is (or should be) a meeting between two intelligent, rational adults for the purpose of evaluating the results of a mutually agreed-upon program.

If you've failed to lose the required two pounds this week, don't go on a fast or take a ton of diuretics or laxatives to fake a loss. Instead, make a careful record of everything you've eaten, the liquids drunk, the exercises done each day. If you're a woman, a chart of your menstrual cycle is helpful, too. Then sit down with your doctor and try to find out why the weight loss isn't coming faster. Faking results will only make the fact-finding that much harder.

6. A word about goals, too: A physician can be a great help in aiding a beginning dieter or exerciser to set realistic goals. *You* may want to lose 5 pounds a week, lift heavy weights, and become an athletic superstar the first day of your program. You're aided and abetted in your starry-eyed idealism by all the popular literature and Dr. Whoosit's Quick-Weight-Loss Diet that your best friend swears took off ten pounds in three days. But your friendly MD, if he or she is current with the latest research, can show you that your goals are unrealistic and will help you set realistic, achievable goals. It's invaluable help; take advantage of it.

7. It also helps to choose your doctor from among the ranks of the specialists in the field. Choose according to your most serious or obvious problem. If you're overweight, find a doctor whose field is bariatrics, nutrition, or a combination of the two. If you suspect your overeating is psychological, then visit your psychiatrist first and your internist second. See the internist first if you suspect heart, lung, or circulatory problems. If injury rehab is your goal, look for an osteopathic surgeon, or consult the local AMA listings or a reputable hospital or clinic for an MD whose major field is physical therapy. Or find out who trains a local team or consults with a local high school, college, gym, or athletic center. Check out the local grapevine at the gym for someone who's simpatico with your sport. (A note of warning here: Doctors who are runners are often unsympathetic with weight training; your best bet is the MD who consults with, or is on the advisory board of, your local health club, gym, or fitness institute.)

8. Finally, once you're on a program that you and your physician both can live with, stay on it. Don't deviate too radically without a medical OK. It's all a part of seeing you and your physician as a team, working together for your best health, looks, and well-being.

E. GENERAL BULKING UP: GOING FOR THE HEAVY METAL

For many years—until quite recently, in fact—bodybuilders talked about "bulking up" as a particular theory of training for muscle size. The principle was simple: Eat as much as you can, use heavy weights, and pack on the bulk. Then "trim down" by going on a "high-definition" diet, mostly protein and liquids and little else, to get the "cut-up" (high-definition) look so popular among current bodybuilders.

The difficulty with this theory of "bulk up/trim down" is that any gains you make by overeating are in body fat, not in muscle tissue. You're "bulking up," all right, but the increase in size is more fat than muscle. Also, when you trim down, you may lose muscle tissue, with the result that you're trim and well defined, but not as muscular as you thought you'd be.

The modern method of bodybuilding is first to trim down and reduce the total amount of body fat to as low a point as possible. Then eat and train specifically for increases in muscular size. We'll give specific routines in the next section.

If you're building for strength as well as size, your diet should be higher in calories, obviously, than for the person who's interested in burning fat and losing weight. But some of the same rules apply. Go for good nutritional value, rather than just more calories. Take in your total number of calories for the day in six to eight small, spaced feedings, rather than one or two giant meals. Concentrate on high-quality protein—lean meat, fish, eggs, poultry, low-fat cottage cheese and cheeses, plain yogurt and skim milk or low-fat buttermilk, and complex carbohydrates (whole grains, fresh fruits, vegetables, and juices). Since your aim is to build muscle tissue, not to add body fat, you'll do well to forget the high-calorie temptations—the junk and processed foods and sugary snacks. Although your gains will be slower on this nutritionally balanced, high-protein diet, they'll be genuine gains in muscle without the increase in body fat.

Remember that the stress is on high-quality nutrition and systematic gains in muscle strength and size, not a mere increase in body weight. If building strength to handle the heavy metal is your aim, get set for a long, rewarding program. Concentrate on maximum poundages, perfect form, maximum performance, and good nutrition. Then watch yourself handle the heavy weights!

F. GENERAL SLIMMING DOWN: SCULPTURING YOUR BODY

There's been a good deal of ink spilled on the controversial subject of what weight training will do for the bodybuilder, the powerlifter, and the Olympic lifter. We know its obvious benefits for these groups: The "pro" magazines are full of magnificent pictures of men and women who've gone this route. But what about the person—often a woman—who just wants to lose weight, trim down, reduce body fat, and start looking decent for a change?

We've already told you one true story—about Ralph's change from the 94-pound weakling to a strong, healthy, active adult. There's another success story behind this book—the chronicle of Valerie's transformation from a 185-pound, sedentary fat girl to an active, strong, attractive woman who weighs 110 to 112 pounds. Check out our previous book, *Bodysculpture: Weight Training for Women,* for the details. Valerie, like many women, for years was afraid to train with weights—afraid that they would give her big, bulging muscles; unfeminine contours, and little or no weight loss. She objected whenever Ralph suggested that she might defeat her "Fat Demon" by doing weight lifting. "I really don't want to turn into the Hulk; I just want to be *thin.*"

Now, five years later, hundreds of women are discovering, as Valerie did, that weight training is the fastest way to build strength and stamina, shape (or reshape) the body, get rid of excess body fat, and at the same time preserve the vital lean muscle tissue. Weight training will help you change that much-touted muscle/fat ratio so that you not only weigh less but look leaner, trimmer, shapelier, wear smaller sizes, and generally decrease your measurements.

If you're starting a weight-training program for the purpose of slimming and trimming your body, start by rereading our tips for "slow losers" in the early part of this chapter. Then go to work, keeping in mind these do's and don't's:

1. *Don't* rely on diet alone to do your slimming for you. (Valerie had tried diet after diet and lost weight from the waist up, while her hips and legs continued to *gain* size.) Remember that your problem is much more complicated than simply "being overweight." You weigh more than you should, yes, but you also lack muscle tone and have too much subcutaneous fat (that's the fat that collects beneath the skin, over the muscle). Remember that athletes store fat in their muscles; ordinary people under the skin. That's why an active person and a sedentary person may weigh the same and yet look vastly different.

So you will certainly need to diet, but you also need a well-designed exercise program. Result: You'll lose pounds as well as inches, and you'll also reproportion the muscle and fat in your body.

2. *Don't* expect miracles from your diet. If you try to lose more than two pounds a week, you're on too severe a regimen. Plan to lose no more than two pounds a week, and maintain that steady pace until you reach your goal.

3. If you're working out primarily to slim down, *do* break down your goal into small, manageable segments. *Don't* think in terms of losing 50 pounds. Instead, resolve to lose 8 pounds this month, then give yourself a small reward.

4. *Do* plan to use clothes, makeup, hair styling, and accessories to enhance your new slimmer image and keep your spirits up. Makeup and clothes will keep you motivated and "psyched up" to finish the program with flying colors.

5. *Don't* increase poundages on either machines or free weights to the max you can handle. Rather than going for heavy lifts, add more repetitions, up to twenty, twenty-five, thirty, or more. Work as if you were working for "high definition," as indeed you are.

6. *Don't* panic if after a week of intensive exercise you show a very slight increase in measurements. You may slightly hypertrophy (swell) the muscle in the thigh or upper arm, say, after several intensive workouts—especially if you're unused to any exercise at all. Not to worry. In a day or so, the hypertrophy will go away, and you'll notice a decrease in the measurements.

7. *Do* be consistent and regular in your workouts. This doesn't mean that you should work out with the flu or any other illness that involves a temperature, nausea, or general weakness and fatigue. But don't make lack of time, energy, or motivation an excuse to skip workouts. Start your session with the idea of doing *something,* even if it's only for ten minutes. Chances are you'll finish the workout.

8. *Don't* look on your diet and exercise routines as something temporary that you "go off" at the end of three months, six months, or whatever. Learn to think of these as long-range programs that help you maintain the progress you've made. Re-educate yourself about food so that you form healthier, saner eating habits.

9. The same goes for exercise programs. *Do* learn to value your program for itself, not just for its results. Savor the time on the running track, bicycle path, health club, or gym as time that you dedicate to yourself and your physical well-being. Think of your exercise period not as a chore or a burden, but as a time saved for yourself, when you get both mind and body in order for the coming day or evening.

10. Finally, give your body time to adjust to your new body weight and image. *Don't* rush it. Years of being overweight and out of shape take their toll, often disastrously, in our general condition, our self-image, the way we walk and move and relate to the space and people around us. We've done intensive work with overweight women at the Sports Fitness Institute to help them overcome years of negative conditioning about their bodies and ways of moving. If you lose weight and inches slowly, your body and mind, we've found, will have time to readjust gradually to the wonderful and dramatic changes that are taking place within you. So take it slowly, and enjoy every minute of it!

G. CARDIOVASCULAR FITNESS: MYTHS AND LORE, FACTS AND FANCIES

Cardiovascular fitness! The very phrase has a magical ring to it for a nation of people as fitness-conscious as we've become. Ever since the publication of some of the key works on fitness of the seventies and eighties, "cardiovascular fitness" and "cardiovascular conditioning" have been on the lips and minds of everyone, from the pro athlete to the paunchy executive, male or female, who just wants to lower his/her blood pressure a few points.

Let's try to separate the lore from the facts. First of all, remember that "fitness" is often used in a sort of popular sense, as "the state of being 'fit' or in good shape, healthy and active." We see the word used a good deal in this popular general sense—especially in magazines that feature articles on how "fit" Cherry, Cheryl, Harry, or Rachel is. Or we find the word emblazoned in orange or yellow on the cover of a book telling us that we can become "fit" in ten minutes a day "without unpleasant dieting or exercise."

"Fitness" in the more technical—and hence controversial—sense has to do with "cardiovascular fitness." It's a term that came into common parlance from medical terminology and surfaced in popular literature in the mid-seventies, when suddenly we had a whole host of doctors, therapists, coaches, champion and amateur athletes, writers, bodybuilders, and fitness "experts" of every imaginable kind arguing endlessly about what exercises did or did not produce cardiovascular fitness.

Dr. Gabe Mirkin in *The Sportsmedicine Book* advances a simple yet accurate definition: Cardiovascular fitness, he says, "is the capacity of the heart to do work." Dr. Paul DeVore in an article called "Cardiovascular Benefits of Strength Training Exercises" (*Iron Man*, July 1979) extends this definition a bit. "Cardiovascular fitness," he writes, "is a bodily condition that encourages economy of effort on the part of the cardiorespiratory system when it is placed under physical stress." He goes on to characterize the state of cardiovascular fitness: We recognize it by a relatively low resting pulse rate which will remain low even during strenuous exercise.

So far, so good. A simple definition and a simple way to recognize it. Where the whole matter becomes complicated is in the exercise—kind, level, and amount—that various authorities find necessary to achieve this fitness. Mirkin states that "to achieve cardiovascular fitness, you must push your heartbeat to more than 60 percent of its maximum for at least 30 minutes three times a week."

DeVore says that a trainee's heart rate must be maintained somewhere between 70 and 85 percent of maximum heart rate (which he figures according to age-adjusted maximal-heart-rate charts), for at least twelve minutes consecutively. He adds that though ten to twelve minutes will suffice, twenty minutes are usually better.

Dr. Kenneth Cooper has a slightly more complex view of the matter. He states in *Aerobics* that "if the exercise is vigorous enough to produce a sustained heart rate of 150 beats per minute or more, the training benefits (i.e., the effect that produces cardiovascular fitness) begin about five minutes after this exercise starts and continue as long as the exercise is performed." (If the exercise isn't sufficient to produce this 150-beats-per-minute rate, the exercise has to be prolonged over five minutes.)

Again, simple enough. Despite the controversy over how long the exercise must be sustained, the frequency of the exercise, and the exact level of the heart rate, all three authorities agree that the heart must be working at a fairly high percentage of its capacity for a fairly sustained period of time and that this must happen frequently (at least several times a week) for any sort of training effect to occur.

The real controversy, then, centers around what *kind* of exercise it shall be. Mirkin, citing the President's Council on Physical Fitness and Sports, gives highest honors to jogging and running, bicycling, swimming, skating, skiing, handball, and squash, in that order. Weight training doesn't even place. Cooper's famous point system awards points only for running, swimming, cycling, walking, stationary running, and handball/squash/basketball (in that order). He cites a story of three men who were given stress tests, including one cyclist and one weight trainer. The cyclist won the competition hands down, thus proving Cooper's contention that weightlifting (notice: lifting, not training) "builds you up to an unnatural degree and . . . has but little training effect on the heart and lungs." Other champions of purely aerobic exercises (exercises that work the heart and lungs and work red muscle cells, which use more oxygen than white cells, as opposed to supposedly "anaerobic" pursuits like weight training that work white cells for the most part and thus don't work the cardiovascular system as much as long-range endurance or "aerobic" exercises) claim that working with weights just will not cut it as far as cardiovascular fitness is concerned. Indeed, some even argue that it's counterproductive.

Dr. DeVore, however, comes up with a solution. The problem, he says, is that with strength-training exercises it's been traditional to rest between sets to allow for maximum hypertrophy of the muscle fibers. The secret, according to DeVore, is to modify your strength training in such a way that a cardiovascular training effect can be achieved. "You simply reduce the rest period between sets . . . and you will become increasingly more cardiovascularly fit."

So here's the secret, then: not the *kind* of exercise, after all, but the pace at which it's done, the amount of rest between sets. Both of these factors influence the amount of effort that the heart must expend in order to get through the exercise. To put it another way, weight *lifting*—that is, traditional powerlifting or Olympic lifting—is not fitness-producing. But weight *training*—working with lighter weights with sustained effort, more reps, more sets, and little or no rest between sets—can be aerobic and thus can produce cardiovascular fitness, with muscle toning and dramatic increases in strength as fringe benefits. (See our sample programs in section two of this chapter for details of PHA [Peripheral Heart Action] programs specifically aimed at producing fitness.)

DeVore's contention is supported by a Syracuse University study called "Circuit Weight Training." The study, which used Dynamics health equipment (fifteen different machines), observed twelve female and ten male participants during thirty-six sessions of circuit weight training (thirty seconds on each machine with no rest between machines). The study extended over a twelve-week period. The results reported showed significant reductions in body fat, substantial skin-fold reductions, increases in body-strength measures, and, most important for our purposes, "significant increases in cardiovascular respiratory endurance."

Then, there are other fitness myths that need to be dispelled. Let's look at a few final ones with a critical eye. For example:

1. You can achieve fitness by working out for only a few minutes a week.

Wrong! Much as we'd like to support this one, it just doesn't work that way, although the experts differ widely on the amount of time it *does* require. Mirkin says thirty minutes at least three times a week; DeVore ten to twelve (preferably twenty) minutes "several" times a week; and Cooper that you should simply aim for earning at least thirty points on his point system, spread over at least three days a week. Most weight trainers or bodybuilders work out for forty-five to seventy-five minutes three to five times a week. The Syracuse study had the participants working for a half hour a day three days a week. So don't expect to become "fit" in the cardiovascular sense if you go in, hit the machines for ten minutes, take long rests, and then head for the sauna or steam room. Sorry, but that's just not enough to get you in shape.

2. If three times a week for thirty minutes is good, seven times a week for two hours is better.

Wrong again—unless you're training to be the youngest dropout from your exercise program. While undertraining is bad, overtraining can be worse. And yes, Virgil or Virginia, there is such a thing. Whenever you exercise vigorously, your muscle fibers are damaged, anywhere from slightly to severely, and the muscles themselves burn up fuel and are depleted. You must allow some time between workouts for your muscles to recover. If you don't, you become susceptible to injuries, minor infections, and other by-products of overtraining. When this happens, you'll have to take a layoff anyway—so why not give yourself a rest day between workouts and prevent the overtraining effect altogether?

3. You *have* to run or jog in order to achieve cardiovascular fitness.

Wrong again. We've already seen that weight training can be aerobic in effect, depending on how it's done. Even if you are on a strength or power program (see section two of this chapter), you can assure aerobic conditioning by working in some days where you do PHA (Peripheral Heart Action) endurance training. Swimming, bicycling, brisk walking, even aerobic dancing can help supplement your program to ensure cardiovascular fitness. Even in the dead of winter or on a tight fitness schedule, a short morning or evening ride on a stationary bike will give you the cardiovascular workout you need—as will a brisk run up your stairs. Then go for the heavy poundages on "heavy" workout days, and you'll find yourself growing both strong and fit without the potential for knee and foot injuries that running brings with it.

4. If you train for a long period of time, you can't ever get out of shape again.

Would that it were so! But whether you weight-train, run, play tennis, or swim, you'll find that after a layoff of even a few weeks, you simply can't handle your usual workout.

No, fitness, like freedom, must be won and rewon every day. The effect we're talking about is called *reversibility*. Dr. Mirkin says the term "describes the fact that your muscles—including your heart muscle—quickly lose their ability to utilize oxygen efficiently if they are not stressed constantly." You simply don't have the same capacity for work after a layoff. Don't feel too badly about it—Mirkin tells the story of O. J. Simpson who once couldn't finish a half-mile run because he had been on the banquet and tour circuit and was out of training!

Two more studies on weight training and its effect on cardiovascular fitness before we stop and recap our findings. In a study reported by George R. Parulski, Jr., in *Muscle* magazine (November 1979), researchers at the University of Rochester, led by Dr. Fallon, studied both weightlifters and bodybuilders. The findings confirmed that the bodybuilders' resting heart rates were lower, their oxygen consumption greater, and their endurance better not only than the non-exercisers' but than other athletes' as well. The bodybuilders' general fitness level was found to be second only to that of runners. And the bodybuilders' blood pressure was lower, cholesterol and triglycerides lower, coronary arteries larger in size, and proportion of fat cells smaller than any other athletes'.

Finally, Al Thomas, a runner plagued with osteoarthritis, who was forced to give up his running for a winter, reports in *Muscular Development*, (April 1978) that by doing high-repetition squats with a medium-heavy weight, he reduced his blood pressure and resting pulse rate far below even the levels he'd achieved as a runner.

To summarize: Cardiovascular fitness is a controversial subject among doctors, athletes, exercise experts, writers, and gym owners or instructors. Much as all the sources differ on precise requirements, all seem to agree that the exercise must be: 1) aerobic (oxygen-burning); 2) sustained for between twelve and thirty minutes; 3) repeated several times a week; and 4) done with the minimum of rest between sets in order for the training effect to occur. Weight *lifting* (power lifting and Olympic lifting) do not qualify as cardiovascular conditioners, but weight *training* does, done with little or no rest between sets.

Remember, too, that cardiovascular fitness is not to be achieved without at least three training periods a week, can be done too little (undertraining) or too much (overtraining), is reversible, and can be achieved from a variety of activities—not just from running, as many experts claim. Current research now suggests that both bodybuilding and weight training, practiced specifically with cardiovascular ends in mind, can achieve and maintain this type of fitness. So get out the barbells, ladies and gentlemen, and pump that iron to your heart's content—literally!

Section Two: A Few Sample Programs That Can Be Combined to Meet Your Individual Needs

A. SOMAHYGIENIC, SOMAESTHETIC, SOMADYNAMIC: THE THREE KINDS OF PEOPLE YOU'LL MEET IN GYMS AND HEALTH CLUBS

Everybody has an exercise program. Stop by the local supermarket or drugstore magazine counter and you'll see what we mean. You can't buy groceries or get a prescription filled without being assailed by exercise programs. Most of them are marginally effective. Many of them are worthless. If you gathered a collection of the magazines together as we've done, you'd see that they have many things in common. They all tell you to do a certain number of repetitions of certain movements a certain number of times a week. In most cases, the movements are the same. Rarely are you advised to use progressively heavier weights, or to think in terms of exercise *intensity* instead of merely accumulating repetitions.

This is because most of the people who create exercise programs for popular magazines have only a limited knowledge of what exercise is, what it does, or how it affects the people doing it. It's appalling to see some magazines, especially women's magazines, offer the same old programs over and over, each time done up in a different package, not because they are effective but because they follow editorial policy. That's right. Some magazines simply will *not* run programs that feature progressive-resistance exercises because they feel that their readers would react negatively to them. So they don't print the exercises that have proven to be the most effective. They print the exercise programs that they know their readers will buy. The assumptions are twofold: that readers are gullible and have closed minds about exercise; that they are under no obligation to tell their readers the truth if it will endanger sales.

We think they're selling their readers short. Women and men are far more knowledgeable about exercise programs than they've ever been in the past. It's time to make the next step. It's time to get down to cases and talk about effective programs that will accomplish what you want to accomplish.

If we're going to help you achieve your goals, we have to talk about what those goals are. Let's look for a few moments at the kinds of people who go to health clubs, gyms, and family fitness centers. It'll help you to locate yourself and focus your activities.

People who go to health clubs fall into three broad categories. We've invented names for those categories. Here they are:

SOMA-HYGIENIC: people who are primarily interested in fitness, health, and well-being.

SOMA-ESTHETIC: people who want to look a certain way, to conform to some idealization of what the human body should look like.

SOMA-DYNAMIC: people who want to excel in the performance of some physical activity.

Each of these categories has a soft-core and a hard-core version.

The hard-core *somahygienic* person is the guy you see out jogging in the park every day at dawn, rain, shine, sleet, or snow. He's knowledgeable about nutrition, food additives, cardiovascular conditioning, slowing down the aging process, and the long-term benefits of diet, exercise, rest, etc.

The soft-core *somahygienic* is your garden-variety health nut, who is a yogurt- wheat-germ- honey- granola-muesli junkie, who has a Sunday-supplement knowledge of all the latest fads in diets, exercises, mental attitudes, and the right words to say to your plants before you kill them and eat them. If he's determined and intelligent, he'll eventually become a hard-core *somahygienic,* and that's when he'll begin to make some real progress.

The hard-core *somadynamic* person is the competitive athlete. He or she is performance-oriented and will do anything to win, even if it endangers health and ruins looks. The soft-core *somadynamic* person is the weekend athlete, the person who has been coasting on high school phys ed or college football for several years, and who erroneously thinks that a weekend round of golf or an evening with the company sandlot team will give him genuine *somahygienic* results and will also let him retain for an indefinite length of time the title, "athlete." He's kidding himself and is probably heading for a coronary when he stops coasting.

The hard-core *somaesthetic* person is the competitive bodybuilder, male or female. The goal is to actualize the current extreme ideal of the bodybuilding world, to enter physique competition and to *win.* Like the hard-core *somadynamic,* this person will do *anything* to win, even if it means sacrificing his health by gobbling aspirins before a workout (dilates the peripheral blood vessels and helps achieve a pump faster); guzzling coffee after a workout (increases definition); shooting anabolic steroids (promotes edema and muscular hypertrophy); megadosing mineral supplements, vitamins, and esoteric substances that will jack up the metabolism; all to put that extra fraction of an inch on the delts, lats, biceps, or pecs.

The *somaesthetic* is interested in form, the *somahygienic* is interested in substance, and the *somadynamic* is interested in performance. The hard-core cases in each category will neglect the goals of the other categories in order to achieve their own goals. The *somahygienic* will sacrifice looks and performance for health, the *somaesthetic* will sacrifice health and performance for looks, and the *somadynamic* will sacrifice looks and health to win.

Furthermore, there is a lot of enmity among the categories. Competitive athletes tend to look down on bodybuilders, fitness buffs look down on both groups, and both groups tend to dismiss the fitness buff as merely a harmless health nut.

Whether they like it or not, each member of each category has just as much right to his or her goals as the members of the other groups. There's certainly nothing wrong with looking good, nor is there anything wrong with being healthy or able to perform athletic feats. The key here for the average person is that it's possible to look good, feel good, and perform far better than average, without going to any of the extremes cited above.

How do you do it? By following a good, sensible, systematic exercise routine, accompanied by a reasonable diet. There's nothing magic about this.

Most of the people who go to health clubs are soft-core types. Welcome to the club! There's nothing wrong with being a softie. There's less wrong with being a softie than putting your body through the kinds of abuse that some of the hard-core types indulge in. If you really get into exercise, you'll probably wind up somewhere between soft-core and hard-core. You'll look, feel, and perform above average, but you probably will not wind up in competition events. On the other hand, some of you will catch the bug and will go all the way.

We've prepared some sample programs that will help you go as far as you want to go. If it's a certain look you're after, we've got a program for the look you want. If it's fitness and health you're after, we've got endurance and cardiovascular programs. If it's enhanced athletic performance you're after, we've got a program based on one of the most successful athletic training systems in the country.

The beautiful thing about it is, the decision is up to you as to how far you go with any of this.

Now, let's make one last digression before we outline the individual programs. You need to know which programs produce what kinds of results; otherwise you'll still be in the dark over designing a program specifically for your goals. You know all the major muscles. You know all the important machines. You know how to do the exercises for those muscles both on the appropriate machines and with barbells and dumbbells. You've got the pieces; now let's put them together. Once you know what you need to do and why, you can tailor-make a program specifically for your needs.

Training programs fall into several categories, depending on the goals of the program:

B. FIVE BASIC KINDS OF TRAINING ROUTINES

Strength training is the development of raw, brute muscular strength. Strength is measured in terms of being able to push a resisting body or force from one place to another. The obvious example would be the bench press: the ability to extend the arms while holding a heavy weight in the hands. Strength here is defined by kinesiologists in terms of being able to push that weight from your chest to arms' length.

Endurance training involves being able to perform a large number of repetitions of movements over a long period of time. You must do a particular exercise movement for two minutes or more for it to qualify as endurance training. Endurance training works the red, slow-twitch fibers and is usually aerobic. You can improve your cardiovascular fitness by endurance training.

Stamina training involves being able to perform many repetitions of a particular movement in a relatively short amount of time. If you did twenty calf raises in the space of thirty seconds, you would be giving your calves stamina training.

Power training involves making an all-out, explosive movement during the contraction phase of an exercise, then letting the weight back down slowly, resisting all the way.

Muscular hypertrophy training is any type of training that will increase muscle size. This kind of training is limited in effectiveness for women but always works to some degree for men. Men grow bigger muscles as they become stronger. Women don't grow appreciably big muscles but become stronger and leaner. Muscular hypertrophy results from a combination of three elements:

1. The amount of weight lifted.
2. The number of repetitions performed within a given duration of time.
3. The duration of time within which the movements are made.

The correct combination of these three elements yields what is called "exercise *intensity*." The three elements are also variable:

1. You can decrease the weight if you increase the reps during a given time.
2. You can increase the weight and decrease the reps within a given time.
3. You can increase the reps and keep the weight and the duration the same.
4. You can decrease the amount of time and keep the reps and the weight the same.

However you do it, the three elements have to be there if your muscles are going to get bigger. People usually start with eight to twelve reps for arm movements, ten to twenty reps for torso and leg movements. We wish we could give you a simple preset formula, but everybody is slightly different in the response to this sort of activity, and "intensity" will mean different things to different people. You'll have to try it and see how much weight and how many reps are required within that amount of time for you to achieve muscular hypertrophy.

To sum up, using the bench press as an example and starting with the bar down across the chest (see page 178 for a description of the bench press):

STRENGTH TRAINING

1. Slow movement up from the chest and slow movement back down.
2. Do three repetitions.
3. Don't worry about how long it takes you to do the three repetitions. You aren't racing the clock when you do strength training.

ENDURANCE TRAINING

1. Make the up-and-down movements rhythmically and at a uniform, moderate rate of speed.

2. Use a "submaximal" amount of weight: whatever you can lift continually for two or more minutes.
3. Work for a certain heart rate as you would for any cardiovascular routine.

STAMINA TRAINING

1. Make the movements up and down as quickly as you can.
2. Make them over and for thirty seconds. Work up to two minutes over the span of several workout periods. Then add weight and drop back down to thirty seconds.
3. Use as much weight as the rapidity and duration of the exercise allows.

POWER TRAINING

1. Make the upward movement as fast or "ballistically" as you can. Give it all you've got as fast as you can go.
2. Pause at the top of the lift, then let the weight back down to the chest slowly, resisting all the way.
3. Do one to three rep sets. Work up to six sets, adding weight each set.
4. Once a week, use the maximum poundage you can handle, with one-rep sets.

MUSCULAR HYPERTROPHY TRAINING

1. Use a weight that will fatigue the muscles within eight to twelve repetitions.
2. Do those eight to twelve repetitions in as short a time as possible, with as much weight as you can handle in strict from.
3. Increase the weight, shorten the time, or increase the number of repetitions progressively. Changes should be made about every third or fourth workout.

C. PUMPING AND PHA: TWO FUNDAMENTALLY DIFFERENT ROADS TO MUSCULAR HYPERTROPHY

There are two basic theories about the best way to achieve muscular hypertrophy, given the three elements that yield exercise intensity. The most popular theory is the "pump" or "congestion" theory. The other is the Peripheral Heart Action or PHA theory. Both theories will yield bigger muscles, but for different reasons. Let us describe both of them, and you can decide which one or combination of the two is for you.

Although practiced by bodybuilders for many years, the pump method was introduced to the general public by Butler and Gaines's book, *Pumping Iron.* Arnold Schwarzenegger is the best example of the results of pumping and is one of the foremost advocates of it. In simplified form, here's how it works.

Let's say that you want to make the biceps larger. There are many exercises for the biceps: two-arm curls, dumbbell curls, bentover concentrated curls, machine curls, incline-bench curls, etc. A pumper will do a set of curls, rest for a minute or two, then do another set. He'll continue to do sets of curls until his biceps are literally pumped up with fluid and blood. Sometimes, especially if he has spongy connective tissue and responsive muscle tissue, the pumper will gain the better part of an inch in upper-arm measurement during a single workout. That's why he measures his arm "cold" (before pumping) and "hot" (after pumping—and uses the latter measurement for press releases.)

When he's pumped and pumped and pumped some more, the muscle will begin to feel as if it's burning. That comes from the lactic acid that's coursing through the muscle, telling it to stop and rest. For the pumper, this is the time when he should do several more reps or sets. It's called "blasting through the pain barrier." If you're an advanced bodybuilder, working out five to six times a week, and if you are force-feeding mineral supplements, shooting anabolic steroids and other pharmaceutical products, the result is extreme muscular hypertrophy. Some of the top bodybuilding stars have stretch marks where their skin has torn when the muscle enlargement exceeded the ability of the skin to grow or stretch to accommodate the increase in size.

A by-product of pumping is the concentration of "exodates" (lactic acid and waste products) in the muscle tissue and the connective tissue that surrounds the muscles. These are the by-products of the process of muscular contraction. In cases of extreme muscle stress, as in forced repetitions past the pain barrier or repeated pumping sessions, the buildup is significant enough to add eventually to the total girth of the muscle.

Consequently, the increase in the size of the biceps, for example, is not only in terms of hypertrophy of the individual muscle cells, it is in terms of edema of the muscle and the connective tissue as well. Try an experiment. Find a pumper (make sure he's a friend), and ask if you can press hard on his pumped-up biceps. Do it with the end of your finger. You'll find that the impression made by the end of the finger remains after the finger is removed.

Whether or not this is a healthy state is a matter of dispute among bodybuilders. There's no dispute among physicians. They consider it a mild form of insanity. Why is it the premier method for achieving muscular hypertrophy? Simply because it is the method that gives the fastest results. And besides, it's the method that the body-building superstars use. Who can argue with a superstar?

The pumping theory grew out of an older theory that was abandoned several years ago, but has recently begun to come back into favor. When Ralph first heard about weight training, it was from his father. Randal J. Carnes was born in 1890, was 5 feet 4 inches tall, and could do a one-arm snatch (bringing a barbell from the floor to a position overhead in one smooth motion) of 167½ pounds at a body weight of 135. In the old days, long before strongmen had caught up with cell physiology, the prevailing theory was that intensive muscle stress actually broke down the individual muscle cells, and that they grew back bigger or, if literally destroyed, multiplied. This accounted for the increase in muscle size and strength.

So the old-time strongmen trained with heavy weights, tried to break down as much tissue as they could, and gave themselves a day between workouts to recover and rebuild. The purpose of pumping a muscle was to send to it the vital nutrients in large supply. The cycle was: (1) tear the tissue down; (2) send in the blood and nutrients; (3) take a day off to rebuild.

This process is called *hyperplasia,* and involves the development of additional cells. The theory was discredited several years ago, as tissue samples seemed to indicate that the total number of cells was not increasing. The prevailing view is that we are born with a certain number of muscle cells, and that the enlargement of a muscle is due not to *hyperplasia,* but to *hypertrophy.* In short, you don't grow additional cells, the ones you already have swell up under stress.

Recently, the hyperplasia theory has been revived and new research is underway to settle the question once and for all. The truth is that right now, nobody really knows the exact mechanism by which muscles get larger under stress. The first physiologist to find out, and to market a product that will enhance such growth without the dangers inherent in overdoses of steroids, will be able to retire young and spend the rest of his or her life clipping coupons and jetting around the world to inspect properties and investments.

For the purposes of this section, let's dodge the issue of hyperplasia vs. hypertrophy and use "hypertrophy" to describe an increase in muscle size. This is the language that is currently used in the physiology textbooks, and there is no reason to confuse the issue more than it already has been.

Suffice it to say that whichever theory is correct, muscles do seem to grow under stress and in the presence of other factors such as proper nutrition, rest, and systematic progressive resistance exercise. And as greater and greater poundages are used, there will be other changes in the body as well.

There is a neurophysiological component here, too. As we related earlier, when you lift a small amount of weight, a relatively small percentage of muscle fibers or cells contract. If you add weight, a greater percentage of the total number of cells in a particular muscle (for example, the biceps) contract. As you develop strength and size, two things are happening: (1) you get better leverage from the increase in the size of the muscle as a whole; (2) more and more "dormant" muscle fibers "learn" to contract. There's nothing mysterious about this process. It's a matter of conditioning your nervous system to lift heavier weights (read: trigger off a larger number of individual cells).

If your goal is muscular hypertrophy, you may not make commensurate gains in muscular strength. It depends on how you train. Take a look at some of the lifters (as opposed to the bodybuilders). Underneath the body fat they carry around, some of the strongest ones have small muscles in comparison with the bodybuilders. Accordingly, some bodybuilders (Franco Columbu is a notable exception) have huge muscles but aren't all that strong.

The other end of the spectrum from pumping is Bob Gajda's PHA theory. Here you do not go after a pump but try to keep the blood circulating *through* the muscle. You don't try to congest the area with fluid, blood, and waste products. Instead, you try to carry the fluid and blood through the area and carry the wastes out of the area where they can be eliminated through excretion.

This is done by planning your exercise sequence carefully. The pumper will do multiple sets of a single exercise, with long rest periods in between. At best, he'll walk around between sets. The PHA trainer will go directly from a set of, say, bench presses, to a set of calf raises. Then he'll move to a set of curls, followed by a set of abdominal crunches. He'll follow a set of behind-the-neck presses with a set of leg extensions, or follow a set of shoulder shrugs with a set of wrist curls. The idea is (1) to keep the circulation going; (2) to use the rest periods actively, instead of sitting around encouraging the blood and fluid to remain in the area pumped.

The result is muscular hypertrophy with a minimum of edema and waste-product collection. Since this hypertrophy is not dependent on congestion and fluid retention, according to Gajda, muscles developed through PHA don't tend to disappear overnight when the muscles aren't kept pumped up.

We have a friend at a local health club who works out six days a week. He's a pumper. He says that if he misses three days in a row, he'll lose as much as five pounds, with a corresponding loss in size. He's not losing muscular *hypertrophy;* he's losing fluid and waste products. His size isn't so much a product of true muscular hypertrophy as it is a product of swelling or edema.

Ralph stumbled onto PHA quite by accident. Because of the heart murmur, he didn't have the stamina enjoyed by the other guys in the gym. In order not to be embarrassed when he was left huffing and puffing after a hard set of squats, he would do a set of abdominal crunches between sets. This gave him time to recover so he could do another set of squats. He didn't know that he had been doing a PHA routine all along. Now Ralph still does the abs work, wrist work, twists, calf raises, and other "lesser" exercises between the big ones. It's not because he has to recover from the heavy metal, but because it has proved to be the best way to make gains in muscle size, stamina, strength, and power without becoming too tired to get a good workout. The workouts he presently does would be horrendous for a beginner or intermediate weight trainer *without* a heart anomaly. The benefits of the method are no accident.

Why isn't PHA the most popular method of gaining muscular hypertrophy? The reasons have to do with that vast, amorphous environment of surfaces called popular culture. PHA is complex, and its results are not as immediately spectacular as pumping. And remember, most of the superstars are pumpers. The superstars sell magazines to the hopefuls. By the logic of the traditional syllogism, therefore, pumping sells magazines to the hopefuls. Get the picture?

While the bodybuilding superstars pump away, the PHA routines are being used by professional athletes in all sports to gain strength, size, power, endurance, stamina; and also are proving to be effective in injury rehabilitation. Why the latter? Because PHA carries waste products away, increases circulation, and thus promotes the healing process.

However, there's a catch. While some people respond well to pumping, others respond well to PHA training. Some will make gains from one kind of training but get little or nothing from the other. You have to experiment with the two extremes, and with combinations of both, until you find a routine that will work best for you. Remember: There is no single, absolutely correct way to make your muscles grow.

D. CORE TRAINING, STRUCTURAL INTEGRITY, AND SYMMETRICAL PERFORMANCE ABILITY

That brings us to a final topic before we begin to construct programs. Many people, especially competitive and weekend athletes, want to improve performance as well as enhance their looks and their health. This has a number of implications, most of which are neglected in books on sports training. Let's go to the core of sports training.

It's called "core training," another one of Bob Gajda's training techniques.

One of the most important prerequisites of enhanced performance in any sport is the ability to work as well with one side of the body as with the other. You may throw a ball with your right hand, but you run on both legs. You may pass a football with your right hand, but you have to block in all directions, pivot and run whichever way there's an opening. You may hit a tennis ball with a racquet held in your left hand, but you must zoom around the court in every direction with equal facility. If you're a powerlifter, you have to work both sides of your body in a coordinated effort to push the metal.

Technically, this is called "Symmetrical Performance Ability." It means, simply, to be able to use both sides of the body equally well and in unison.

Core training is a method of developing symmetrical performance ability by the development of certain "core" muscles. Those muscles are the ones that surround the waist area, both inside and outside the body cavity. The muscles are (1) the *sacrospinalis;* (2) the *external* and *internal obliques* and the *transversalis* muscles that lie under the obliques (page 154); (3) the *rectus abdominis* (page 154) and the *ilio-psoas* muscles (pp. 155-156). These are the muscles that keep us upright, and these are also the muscles that help us to stay bilaterally symmetrical in our performance ability.

While these muscles can be developed by spinal extensions (page 199), twists, and side work (pp. 197-98); leg raises, situps, and crunches (page 196); leg raises and straight-leg situps (page 199) respectively; they can be given *coordinative* development by learning to walk and hop on a balance beam or by learning to stand on teeter-totters or kinesthetic primer boards.

Lest you think that this sort of thing is insignificant in comparison to the "real" training that comes from squats, bench presses, and deadlifts, you should know that this is the kind of training program that got people like Gary Fencik of the Chicago Bears out of the sidelines and back into the game. It's the difference between the "fine tuning" done by certified athletic trainers, physical therapists, and corrective therapists and the brute-force techniques of the old-time iron pumpers.

Along with core training goes the concept of "Structural Integrity," which means that you develop not only the core muscles but all the stabilizer muscles that coordinate and assist the big muscles in what they do, while paying special attention to maintaining the strongest possible symmetrical stabilization of the bones and their joints. When you put it all together, you take with you to your respective sport the most efficient, strongest, tightest package of bones, ligaments, tendons, and muscles, forged into a bilaterally symmetrical set of movements. In short, you've really got it together.

* * *

You've got it all. Now let's outline some sample programs. Remember, given the cross-referencing of exercises, machines, and muscles, you can develop any routine that your special circumstances call for. With what you now know about the basic theories of muscular hypertrophy, you can get big quickly and keep what you get once you get it. With what you now know about what's going on inside, you can avoid injuries and unhealthy training methods. With what you now know about the difference between training for strength, endurance, stamina, and power, you can make your own decisions about how much you want to lift, how much fat you want to burn, how much power you want to have, how lean and mean you want to look. With your knowledge of core training and structural integrity, you can enhance your performance in any sport.

In short, you're your own boss. If you've got this book, you don't have to depend on the good graces of your local health club instructor, who may or may not know what he's doing.

Let's first outline a general exercise routine that can be used as both a cardiovascular and a muscle-conditioning program. Everybody should do this one, especially if you're new to weight training.

E. A GENERAL CONDITIONING ROUTINE

EXERCISES

SQUAT pp. 110-118, 126
ABDOMINAL CRUNCH pp. 84-89
BENCH PRESS pp. 93-96, 178
CALF RAISE pp. 127-31
SHOULDER SHRUG pp. 70, 172
SPINAL HYPEREXTENSION pp. 81-84, 199
CURLS (ARM) pp. 104-107, 187-90
LATERAL RAISES pp. 71-72, 152
PULLDOWN BEHIND NECK pp. 76-78
SIDE LEAN/TWISTS pp. 195, 197-98

Use enough weight to fatigue the muscles after eight to twelve reps on the arm movements and twelve to twenty reps on the torso and leg movements.

Remember, you can make this set of exercises a general conditioning program for strength, stamina, endurance, power, or muscular hypertrophy, merely by using the reps and time limits as outlined on pages 236-243. If you want to increase your endurance, use submaximal weights and do each exercise for two minutes or more. If you want to train for strength, do three reps for each exercise. For stamina, do each exercise for two minutes as fast as you can go. For power, fast up, hold, then slow down. For muscular hypertrophy, do your eight to twelve reps quickly, with as much weight as you can handle in strict form.

If you want cardiovascular conditioning, do it as an endurance program. If you want to build muscle size, do it as a muscular hypertrophy program. If you want strength, act accordingly. Look back to pages 236 through 242 and get to work.

The exercises are in a planned sequence. Each "heavy" exercise is followed by a lighter one. Consequently, you can use this routine for PHA training. If you want to pump, do multiple sets of the exercises, resting between them. If you want to do PHA, don't rest between exercises, but go right on to the next one. If you still want to do multiple sets, go through the entire sequence, and then begin it over again.

Regardless of your training goals, you should increase poundages and repetitions on a regular basis. One way to do this is to increase the arm movements one rep every third workout, and increase leg and torso movements two reps every third workout. When you reach twelve reps on the arm movements and twenty reps on the leg and torso movements, drop back to eight and twelve and add weight. You'll have to use trial and error to find out how much weight you should add.

The exercises listed will start you toward a solid foundation for future progress. They should remain a basic part of your workout routines from now on. Use either free weights or machines for the exercises. Consult the appropriate pages for information on how to do the individual exercises.

It is also possible to use this program as a circuit-training routine. All you have to do is move from one machine or station to another without rest. Stay at each station for thirty seconds to two minutes for stamina training, two minutes or over for endurance training, etc. Remember that circuit training is made effective by the sequence of exercises, not by what happens to be available on a particular machine. If you circuit-train with this list of exercises, keep them in sequence.

Now let's try a core training routine.

F. A CORE TRAINING ROUTINE

CORE TRAINING EXERCISES FOR STRUCTURAL INTEGRITY

SPINAL HYPEREXTENSION pp. 81-84, 199
ABDOMINAL CRUNCH pp. 84-89
SIDE LEANS AND/OR TWISTS pp. 195, 197-98
SITUPS p. 196
LEG RAISE pp. 90, 93, 201-202

BALANCE BEAM p. 131
KINESTHETIC PRIMER BOARD pp. 116-117

While the first five exercises listed will work the core muscles individually or in groups, the balance beam and the kinesthetic primer board will work all of the core muscles together as they keep the body erect.

The same rules for strength, power, etc., apply for these exercises as applied for the general conditioning exercises.

G. HOW TO GRIND AWAY THE FAT

As you progress in burning fat, building muscle, gaining power and strength, endurance or stamina, you will want to expand your program to include other exercises in the long list that starts on page 168. You should vary your program from time to time. The first one, the general conditioning program, should be followed for about ninety days. Then you can branch out and add more specialized exercises.

If your goals are somaesthetic, you'll be burning fat or building muscle. If your goals are somahygienic, you'll be building endurance and gaining cardiovascular fitness as well as muscular tone. If your goals are somadynamic, you'll be gaining strength, stamina, power, and structural integrity.

If you want a fat-burning program, start with the general conditioning routine, and do it as an endurance program. As you begin to lose those inches, you'll begin to see where you need special work. Here it's important to utilize the PHA method. Why?

It's part of medical orthodoxy that fat metabolizes at an equal rate all over the body. This is why "spot-reducing" programs get so much flak from the medical community. Also, as we've discussed earlier, few physiologists believe in the existence of "cellulite," which is supposed to be a special kind of fat that is difficult to get rid of. Fat is fat, they say, and they're right as far as biochemistry is concerned.

On the other hand, some fat deposits seem harder to get rid of than others. We've seen runners who've pared their body fat down to a few percentage points but still have mealy-looking fat sitting right up on top of their stringy muscles. What's happening?

There does seem to be fat in certain parts of our bodies that doesn't respond well to diet but responds well to exercise. In these cases, everything else being equal, the fat will just sit there if you don't exercise and will go away if you do.

It will go away, that is, if you exercise the very dickens out of the area where the fat is hanging on. We're not saying that you can eat to your heart's content, exercise your hips alone, and lose the fat off your hips. We are saying that if you're on a diet and are on a regular exercise routine already, you can enhance the probability of getting rid of particular fat deposits by drastically increasing the circulation in the area where the deposit is located. The muscles underneath the fat are toned, circulation is improved, and (remember the PHA theory) waste products and excess fluids are carried out of the area so they can be eliminated.

The importance of the sequence of exercises should be stressed if you tend to collect fluid in the lower limbs. This is a problem most women have, as the steady sales of diuretics demonstrate. Let's say that you collect fluid around your feet and ankles, as Valerie does. Never, *never* do exercises in such a way as to congest the area of the calves and leave it congested. You'll just compound the problem. For people who collect fluids in certain areas, pumping the muscles in that area alone is about the worst thing you could do.

Instead, you should sequence the exercises. Start off with ankle rotations, dorsiflexion, plantar flexion movements, and then progress up the leg to seated and standing calf raises. Follow these with abdominal work or leg extensions—anything to increase the circulation right on up the line. This will help carry the fluid out of the area instead of further packing it in.

Massage seems to help some people rid themselves of hard-to-get-at fat. Medical orthodoxy maintains that fat deposits can't be "broken down" by massage. This is correct, but it's a red herring. Massage helps circulation if it's done correctly (squeezing and rhythmical movements, always in a direction toward the heart and away from the affected area). Few people still think that massage breaks anything down.

On the other hand, some physicians scoff at the notion that massage aids the circulation. A recent article in *Forum* magazine contends that massaging veins and arteries will not make blood flow faster. Jumping on a garden hose is cited as an analogous situation: It won't make the water flow through the hose any faster.

But veins are not garden hoses, and the blood doesn't flow through them in a continuous stream the way water flows through a hose. Veins, unlike garden hoses, have little flaps or valves that assure that blood moves through the veins in one direction only: toward the heart. It is the action of the muscles, as they contract and thus squeeze the veins, that makes the blood go back to the heart. The muscles themselves are "massaging" the veins. That's how the system works. Consequently, massage *does* help local circulation, in the same way that the muscles do.

So don't give up on massage. Try

it and see if it works for you. If it does, do it.

When you've begun to slim down by using the general conditioning routine as an endurance program (and hence as a fat burner), you'll want to take a good look at yourself in the mirror and check out where you need extra work. Take a look, then consult the anatomy chart to see which muscles lie under the fat, then look in the exercise section for the exercises that work those muscles. Do a stamina routine for those muscles. You'll really smoke 'em as far as circulation is concerned, and you'll see the results pretty quickly.

H. AN ADVANCED GENERAL CONDITIONING ROUTINE

Using the general conditioning routine as your basic list of exercises, you can branch out and specialize on particular parts of the body. Remember, it's the way you train that makes the difference between, for example, strength, endurance, stamina, or power. The same exercises that jack up the circulation in a particular area when you do them in a stamina-training style can become muscle builders if you keep the poundages up. Try to keep the sequence of exercises such that you go from a heavy exercise to a light one. Don't follow heavy squats with maximum bench presses.

Here's a sample of a longer, more advanced routine, based both on the basic exercises of the general conditioning routine and the PHA method of going through that routine.

EXERCISES

LEG EXTENSIONS pp. 121–22
LATERAL RAISES pp. 71–72, 152
SQUAT pp. 110, 113, 126
WRIST EXTENSIONS p. 191
BENCH PRESS pp. 93–96, 178
CALF RAISE pp. 127–31
WRIST CURLS p. 191
SHOULDER SHRUG pp. 70, 172
DORSIFLEXION EXERCISES pp. 209–210
CURLS (ARM) pp. 104–107, 187–90
SIDE LEANS/TWISTS pp. 195, 197–98
PULLDOWN BEHIND THE NECK p. 76–78
ABDOMINAL CRUNCHES pp. 84–89
PRESS BEHIND THE NECK pp. 98, 174

Here we've covered all the bases, and we've added a few more exercises. Again, you can do this routine for stamina, endurance, strength, or power, depending on the way you time the exercises and the way you handle the repetitions. If you want to pump, do multiple sets.

The list is getting long, however, and if you use heavy weights on all the exercises, you may wind up too tired to get the full benefit from the routine. Slow down and take stock. Many people, when they reach the point where it is impossible to allocate either the time or the energy to several hours in the gym, will split up their routine from day to day.

If you work out on Monday, Wednesday, and Friday, you can do half the routine on one day and the other half on the next. Or you may want to divide up the exercises so that you never do two really heavy exercises on the same day. You could, for example, do arms and upper body on Monday, legs and back on Wednesday, and arms and upper body on Friday. The next week, do legs and back on Monday, arms and upper body on Wednesday, and legs and back on Friday. That would give you an average of three workouts per body area over a two-week period. If you're over thirty-five, this might suit you to a tee.

If you're younger and full of spit and vinegar, you may want to try working out every other day, or perhaps four times a week. That way you can get in at least two workouts on each body area each week. Depending on the sequence, you can get more.

Many people work out five and six days a week, especially if they're training for a contest and they want to get into top contest condition. Some work out every day because they love it. The rule of thumb is to test yourself and see if you are undertraining or overtraining. If the former, you won't lose fat and you won't gain muscle. If the latter, you'll look drawn and you'll be tired all the time.

Nobody can tell you how much to train but yourself.

I. GOING THE WHOLE TEN ROUNDS: A NO-HOLDS-BARRED, PRE-COMPETITION PHA ROUTINE

Now let's go to a full-fledged PHA routine, with modular sequences within the routine. Here's a sample course suggested by Bob Gajda. Remember, this is a universe away from what we ordinary guys would do just to shape up.

EXERCISES

First Sequence

PRESS BEHIND THE NECK pp. 98, 174
ABDOMINAL CRUNCHES pp. 84–89
CALF RAISE pp. 127–31
CURL (ARM) pp. 104–107, 187–90

Second Sequence

BENCH PRESS pp. 93–96, 178
LEG RAISE pp. 90–93, 201–202
ROWING pp. 172–73
CALF RAISE ON ONE FOOT (use only one foot) pp. 127–31

Third Sequence

SQUAT pp. 110–113, 126
LEG RAISE pp. 90–93, 201–202
PULLOVER pp. 74–75, 178–79
TRICEPS EXTENSION pp. 100–104, 184–87

Fourth Sequence

DEAD LIFT pp. 199–200
UPRIGHT ROWING pp. 172–73
LEG CURL pp. 122–24, 206–207
WRIST CURL p. 191

Do ten repetitions of each exercise, and don't rest between the exercises in each sequence. If you do multiple sets, do *sequence* sets, not multiple sets of the same exercise. For example, do the first sequence three times, then do the second sequence three times, etc.

Work out three times a week. For a strength program, do the exercises slowly. For power, remember to go fast on the way up, hold the weight for a moment, then let it slowly back down. You know by now how to vary the timing and the number of reps for different training goals.

Without getting overly complicated, you can develop this routine into an intermediate program simply by increasing the number of sets from one to three all the way up to four or five sets per sequence, still working out three times a week.

For a really advanced program, work out six days a week, and develop four or five sequences for each day, training with heavy weights on one day and light weights on the following day. Vary the exercises so that you don't repeat exercises done the day before. Also, don't do more than one really heavy-weight exercise per day. Don't combine heavy squats, heavy bench presses, and heavy deadlifts in the sequences for a single workout.

It can become a rigorous program that will involve a lot of time in the gym, but you'll find that you have more staying power with the PHA routines than if you were pumping through exactly the same set of exercises. That's because you're not accumulating waste products in the muscles but are keeping the circulation going and eliminating the waste products. With fewer wastes congesting specific areas, fatigue is avoided. You'll come away from the gym exhilarated instead of knocked out.

Whatever you do, don't try advanced routines at the beginning. We're trying to be constructive here, right? Start slowly, and the progress you make will stay with you.

Try the routines we've listed, play around with them for a few weeks, and you'll find out readily how much weight to use, how many days a week to train, and what to do to get the best results. Your body will tell you. Look at yourself critically, then do what produces the best results.

Again, it's easy to develop your own program. All you have to do is take a good honest look in the mirror, admit to yourself what you need to do, and then do it. The sequence goes like this: What area do you want to (check one) build up ( ), trim down ( ), strengthen ( )? Find the muscle on the chart, note the number of the muscle, look up the number and get the name of the muscle. Look up the exercises that work that muscle, and plug the exercises into your program.

Simple.

Also, take your copy of this book with you to the health club, gym, or family fitness center. Familiarize yourself with the machines in your club, and look them up in the book. Maybe you live in a condo, and there's a gym with exercise machinery on the premises. You're prepared. With this book you'll probably know more than the instructor does. If there's no instructor, you're prepared for that, too.

J. WRAPPING IT UP: A FEW LAST WORDS ON PUTTING YOUR OWN PROGRAM TOGETHER

So good luck with your programs. Use the general conditioning routine as the foundation. Stay on it for ninety days, then start adding exercises. Vary your routine. Increase the number of sets of each exercise. Work until you feel right with the way you are making progress. Remember, nobody can tell you how much weight to use. You have to find that out for yourself by trial and error. Here are some rules of thumb:

1. Add reps every third workout if you are working for general conditioning and development.

2. Add weight whenever possible if you're doing strength routines and are thus limited to three reps per set.

3. If you're going for stamina, work up from thirty seconds to two minutes. Then add weight and drop back down to thirty seconds and work your way up again.

4. If you're going for endurance, start at two minutes and work up to five minutes for each exercise. Add weight and drop back down to two minutes. Remember, use submaximal weights. The idea here is to sustain a heart rate that takes you into aerobic or cardiovascular conditioning territory. The object is *not* to lift heavy weights but to use enough weight to accomplish your endurance goals.

5. If you're going for power, add weight whenever you can as your power develops.

6. If you're trying to improve your athletic ability in any sport, look up the muscles that are used in that sport, and work for strength, stamina, endurance, or power in the exercises that work those muscles. Remember, exercise is specific. Try to simulate as precisely as possible the exact movements that are required by that sport, and you won't go wrong.

7. Whatever your sport may be, whether competitive or recreational, you'll enhance your performance by working your core muscles and by developing structural integrity.

Finally, make a habit of carrying this book around with you so you'll really have a chance to familiarize yourself with what's in it and internalize the parts that are most relevant to your particular needs. It's your body. Use this book to get to know it, and it'll be a joy to you all your life.

But don't forget to shift the book sometimes from hand to hand. You wouldn't want to ruin your bilateral symmetry by developing one side of your body to the exclusion of the other!

6

COPING WITH THE NEW BODY IMAGE

A. AT HOME

Families are either the weight trainer's best friends or worst enemies. There seems to be no in-between ground: They are either totally supportive, bursting with pride, loving and bragging about your "new self"; or they're nagging, constantly trying to sabotage your diet and exercise program.

Part of the sabotage is unthinking. Some is, unfortunately, intentional—and for a variety of reasons. The intentional sabotage is, strangely enough, the easiest to deal with since it's open warfare: the husband who can't live on "funny food" and sincerely *misses* his steak, potatoes, and apple pie; or the "dutiful" wife who insists that you clean your plate and is close to tears when you can't eat that lovely meal she spent all afternoon preparing. Then there are the kids who constantly mourn the loss of their chocolate-chip cookies and are upset that Mommy and Daddy have taken to lifting those "gross" chrome things over their heads every evening. And the parents who are genuinely distressed when their once-tubby child starts melting away—or turning into the Hulk—before their very eyes.

Remember that it's all a matter of relative values, and try to deal with it on that level. To *you,* you're finally shaping up that flabby body; trimming down or building muscle; cutting out the junk food, booze, and cancer sticks. But your friends and family fear that roly-poly, familiar, fun-loving George or Georgina is about to be replaced by a humorless tofu-and-sprouts eater who doesn't drink, smoke, stay out late at night, nosh on bagels and cookies like any normal soul—and will spend inordinate amounts of time on intimate terms with gyms filled with torture racks.

So meet the open sabotage with good humor and a spirit of compromise. No, you will *not* snack on the Famous Amos chocolate chips or the wonderful box of Fannie Farmer Chocolates, but you will relent and keep one shelf at the top of the pantry for their sweet-tooth needs. No, you won't go to the gym six days a week, but your hour three times a week is off limits to any other engagements. Invite the family to join in your workouts. If you can get spouse, children, parents, friends, roommates involved, so much the better. Do try to explain your regimen in plain English to them—some of the propaganda just might work. While you may not convert the whole family to your Spartan diet all at once, if you can quietly reduce the household intake of salt, sugar, fat, and preservatives by, say, 10 percent during the next year, you'll have done your loved ones a great favor. Serve some attractive diet meals, and substitute low-calorie fare for higher-calorie dishes or ingredients.

Howls and yelps for cookies and Big Macs are one thing, but the quieter, more insidious kind of sabotage is quite another and often much harder to deal with. You know the signs: the condescending little digs at your diet; the sneers at your workout program; the not-so-friendly jokes and jibes of friends who love to poke fun at "weight lifters" while they pour their fourth martini of the evening.

It helps in dealing with this more insidious sabotage to know that its prime motivating forces are fear and jealousy. A husband or wife who is himself or herself putting on weight, getting soft around the edges, drinking and eating a tad more than is recommended is secretly angry at you for your courage and self-discipline. Or he is jealous of the new person you're becoming. Or she is afraid of being left behind, of being the dumpy, plain, unattractive one while you burst out as the sudden new superstar. And the kids are just plain bewildered when Mommy or Daddy sheds those comfortable rolls of flab and starts to resemble an image from the TV screen. Sometimes they react by howling for a trip to the local ice-cream parlor or junk-food emporium. (Teenage girls can get particularly nasty when Mummy isn't Mummy anymore but starts sporting skinny jeans and tight knit tops.) Worst of all, Mother and Dad—*your* mother and dad—really yearn for their plump baby boy or girl. They aren't in the least impressed by the thin/muscular stranger who comes to visit and extols the delights of marathon running, PHA training, low-carb diets, and cardiovascular fitness. Their natural urge is to feed, comfort, and nourish their emaciated child.

Friends? Ah, that's another—but similar—story. If you're male, you'll be laughed at, called a jock, a muscle boy, and asked if you're in training as a double for the Hulk. People will say you're gay (if you're straight) or straight (if you're gay). Everyone has his theories about weight trainers: They're either super macho men or refugees from the set of *Cruising*. But secretly many of them will be envious—especially if they're on that late-twenties-into-early-forties downward spiral composed of cigarettes, booze, late nights, long hours, the obligatory commute, and the weekend disco ritual.

Same for your girl friends if you're female. The ladies you lunch, work, or coffee-klatch with will envy your stamina, self-discipline, and energy. Your real friends will love the new you as much or more than the old and will rejoice over your new trim body and good looks. The cats in the crowd will drop snide comments about (choose one) lady jocks, Wonder Woman, hormonal imbalances, and women who try to be sex objects by slimming down or "can't be really feminine" for lifting "those heavy old weights." They'll laugh at your new skinny pants and that smashing knit outfit and tell you to "dress your age." Or they'll remind you to quit trying out for the "Charlie's Angels" look-alike contest if they're secretly offended that you had a figure lurking beneath all the fat. Just keep on with your program. You'll know you're successful as long as the sarcasm keeps up.

So much for the reactions. Everyone has to cope with them differently, according to the situation at hand. But here are some general do's and don'ts to remember:

1. *Do* remember that your weight is often part of a complex power game that other people—your friends, husband or wife, children, parents—play with you. A popular ploy among women is for a thin, chic woman to reassure her chubby friend that she's "just right," "has a beautiful face," or is just "pleasingly plump." It's a way of maintaining control—the balance of power will shift if a thinner you gets the upper hand. Same thing for a husband-wife relationship—the better-looking, thinner one is usually the more powerful, popular, and successful of the two. Your new self-discipline is threatening. So he/she will often try to sabotage the other's attempts to change. Recognizing their state of mind for what it is—anxiety, not necessarily hostility—makes it easier for you to deal with it.

2. Be prepared for sabotage from children as well. The fact that they're small doesn't make them less likely to intefere with your program. Often they can be diverted with a trip to the zoo, ice-skating rink, movies, or museum—a healthy way to teach them that "fun" doesn't necessarily mean calories!

3. It helps to remind spouses, parents, and children that you'll not only look better but be healthier, more energetic, and live longer as a result of what you're doing. It doesn't hurt to show them some statistics on longevity, the rate of cardiovascular disease-related deaths, etc., if they laugh too long and hard.

4. *Do* try to make the changes in your life style gradual. If, in a six-month period, you lose thirty pounds, pitch your entire old wardrobe, change hairstyles, change jobs, start running ten miles every morning at dawn, become a vegetarian, take up yoga, and start training with weights, it can prove disconcerting to your near and dear ones. Your family and friends want desperately to hang onto a shred of the old familiar you. Try to find some middle ground between your radicalism and their conservatism, and you'll both be a good deal happier.

5. *Don't* talk endlessly about your diet and exercise program. Nothing is more tiresome and offensive to the non-fitness-conscious. Do your thing, but *quietly*.

6. On the other hand, if they're interested, give them information. Tell them why and how you do those mysterious rituals in the gym. Take them along on a visitor's pass. Whip up some diet dishes for a weekend dinner. Try to get them involved, and they may end up converts to your program.

7. Don't try to impose all your diet reforms at once on the family. Often the changes are so slight and so flavorful no one will notice until long after the changes have already sneaked past them.

8. *Don't* flaunt your new attractiveness at an insecure mate, a plump adolescent child, an aging parent, or friends who dread the thought of the scales. If you have to gloat, do it alone or with a supersvelte friend.

9. *Don't* become the family (or office) spoilsport—you know, the one who can't stay out past 8 P.M. because he/she has to get up at 6 to get to the gym. Or the one who never orders anything more than plain salad with lemon dressing and an herbal tea, while everyone else pigs out on pizza and pasta. You don't have to eat the forbidden goodies, but you might take a token slice and leave half on your plate. That's especially important at a party in a private home when your hostess has obviously cooked a Big Production for her guests. Taste, nibble, and stay quiet about your latest diet. Ask to pick the restaurant, and then lead the pack to some watering hole where you can sip Perrier-with-a-twist and munch spinach salad and sprouts, while they have their fries and pies—but stick to your maintenance routine.

There's also a special category of "problem" that happens to the person, male or female, who suddenly becomes attractive—either for the first time in his/her life or for the first time in many years. All at once, you have people responding to you in very different ways. Some of the changes are positive; some are threatening and anxiety-provoking.

First all, remember that fat for a woman and shapelessness for a man are symptoms of powerlessness. They are, in their own ways, physical flaws quite as much as an obvious deformity or handicap. They signal the other person that, at least in this one area, he or she has got the upper hand. While this sort of thing is a little less obvious with men, as a rule the better-looking, shapelier person will tend to dominate the less attractive one. We seem almost always to assume that fat people are less intelligent, interesting, aware, and *au courant* than leaner ones.

As you start to get your body in shape, you can look for a definite change in the way you affect people, the way strangers and casual acquaintances respond to you. Part of the change will be sheer pleasure. You will get better tables in restaurants, better service in stores, more respect and cooperation from co-workers, admiring stares from strangers.

But part of the change will be a mixed blessing. For suddenly now you are no longer invisible under your cloak of flab or fat, but a Force to be reckoned with. Co-workers suddenly view you as competition and start scurrying to protect their turf at work. The boss begins to consider you as direct competition, perhaps a potential threat.

If you're unmarried, you're suddenly fair game in the meeting and mating wilderness. There will be a sudden rush of dates and would-be dates, matchmakers, hustlers, talkers, and walkers. No more going out with your friends to the local singles place to hang out. You're now the new kid in town, and you're about to be besieged with every line known to woman or man. If you're female, learn to cope with whistles, hoots, catcalls, hustles from everyone up to and including your oldest friend, your oldest friend's husband, the hardhats on the corner, and your boss and co-workers. Some of the attention will be welcome and flattering. Some will be unwelcome, unsettling, and downright frightening. Much of it you simply won't know how to assess. You won't feel as safe—or be as safe—on dark streets or deserted corners. Take proper precautions: It's simply a fact that pretty women are more frequent targets of crime than plain ones.

If you're married, the changes may be even more unsettling. You have to cope with altered responses from your mate and also from the rest of the world. You're suddenly a sexual object and are getting all the delayed attention you never experienced in all your years as the town Georgy Girl or the local ninety-seven-pound weakling. You secretly love the whistles and stares and hustles, although you may not want to respond in kind. But your mate is envious, angry; or feels unwanted, insecure, and left out. You're torn in two directions: You want to get out and boogie, get dressed up and enjoy the belated strokes you earned with all those hours in the gym. But a part of you also wants to shrink back, stay at home, and keep George or Georgina happy in familiar surroundings.

The best solution as usual is a kind of compromise. Enjoy all the harmless, inconsequential attentions: the hardhats' whistles; the fluttering eyelashes of the secretarial pool; the stares of an attractive stranger across a crowded room. But take it slow—whether you're male or female, married or single—realize that you've belatedly stumbled on the wonderful world of flirting, hustling, coming on, putting down, preening, showing off. Enjoy it all as a tribute to your new image, but don't feel you have to *act* on any of it. If your present situation is unhappy, all the attention may give you the confidence to make a move. But if you're happy at home with your present friend or spouse, learn to smile and say, "Thanks, but no thanks."

B. AT WORK

Throughout this book we've used the term bodypower in one sense—namely, the physical power of your new body, the force it can exert, the vitality and energy it can feel. In this section, let's expand our definition to mean also the psychological power—the "psychic energy," if you will—that this newly trimmed, toned, shaped, revitalized and energized body can give you. It's the personal, day-to-day body power that comes with being in the best of shape, knowing it and showing it.

In the last several years we've heard a great deal about winning through intimidation, playing the games that people play in the office, dressing for success, jockeying for power on the job—all the "obnoxious success games," as one writer called them. Now consider another kind of power that you acquire on the job when you shape up, trim down, and become healthy and fit. You gain Bodypower, the power of the new "physical elite," as they've been called. You become a force to be reckoned with, suddenly: You're attractive, energetic, bursting with self-confidence and new ideas—in short, a perfect spokesperson for both yourself and your business.

So how do you take advantage of this new body of yours? How do you turn all this fitness to your advantage at work without coming off like the office Muscleman or Wonder Woman? Here are some ideas to get you started:

1. Some of the same rules apply as with the family and friends. Don't proselytize and don't preach. Everyone expects the new fitness convert to deliver himself/herself of endless sermons on tofu, sprout culture, yogurt, mineral water, and resting pulse rates. So surprise them and don't yield to the temptation. Share your information if asked, but don't give out free advice. Your co-workers will love you for your restraint and good taste. This applies to smoking as well—or to any other fitness-related reform!

2. Don't turn into the office vamp or Casanova. It's the oldest story in the world—the thirtyish (or fortyish) person who loses weight, shapes up, and overnight turns into a hot sex symbol, complete with cleavage and stiletto heels (hers) or shirts open to the navel and the obligatory gold chains (his). Flaunt the new shape if you wish, but do it tastefully. Everyone will notice, sooner or later, that your new suit really is three sizes smaller.

3. Do give your fellow workers time to adjust to your new image. You'll have to put up with a certain amount of curiosity, staring, questioning, kidding, and general disorientation on their parts. After all, they have always known you as Georgina-of-the-big-hips or George-the-flabby. It takes a bit of adjustment to shift over to Georgina-of-the-fabulous-cheekbones or George-of-the-incredible-biceps. Be patient. They'll make it.

4. Do be prepared for a certain amount of hostility and resentment from co-workers. Part is simple jealousy. They wish they could do it themselves, and at the same time they're scared to death they never will. Especially if you're a woman, be prepared for some mixed reactions. There are some women who will be totally supportive, loving, and enthusiastic toward another woman who fights off the Fat Demon and wins. On the other hand, you'll also hear yourself called a shallow, self-seeking, and vain woman/sex object; a woman who's prostituting herself for fashion (or men, or success, or vanity, or whatever). You'll also hear it said that you're sleeping your way to the top (never thought you'd hear that said about yourself, did you?). Especially if you're promoted or receive favorable attention about the time you remake yourself, get ready to hear (from both males and females): "Well, if I had all that money/time to spend on myself . . ." You know the rest. But be ready to hear it all again anyway.

5. About those promotions, new committee appointments, and other favorable notices at work: It's heady, exciting, but complex stuff to handle. A dramatic change in your physical appearance is a strain of sorts on your psyche that requires some adjustment of your old habits. You just can't continue thinking of yourself as a chubby lady or a flabby middle-aged man when suddenly you're the most attractive, vital, fit person in your office. Your boss, if he/she is smart, will latch onto you as a valuable person to have around.

You're learning, all of a sudden, that being good-looking carries with it some responsibility. People excuse dullness or ineptitude in unattractive people more than in good-looking ones. Beautiful women can't just be beautiful—they also have to sound intelligent, be well-informed, active, sociable, supermoms, good wives, and ambitious working women. Handsome men have to be top executives, civic leaders, exemplary family men, and relaxed, sporty socializers, all rolled into one. What you're discovering, belatedly, is the high premium society places on looks and the high expectations of beautiful or handsome people.

6. If your response to item five above is, "Duuuuh . . . who, me?" then start acquiring some of the skills you'll need to bolster up those new looks. If you need extra courses, an advanced degree, or knowledge of languages, management, math, or computerese, then get thee to the nearest university or community college in the area and sign up. It's another way to emerge from your cocoon and get the skills to support your growth from powerlessness to power.

7. Don't slide onto the martini and five-course expense-account luncheon circuit. You've just come from a long struggle to keep your body in shape. Why blow it all now? Choose a maintenance diet and exercise regimen that you can live with, and stick with it. Pass up the martinis after work in favor of a trip to the gym. Walk or shop or head for the gym during your lunch hour. Or brown-bag your dietetic goodies while you finish a big project at your desk.

8. *But note:* We're savvy enough about the world of work to know that there are occasions when you need that two-hour lunch at an important restaurant with the boss or a client. Or when the only (or best) way to pick up on the office grapevine is over Happy Hour after work. If that's the case, don't panic. You can stay on your diet nicely, but unobtrusively, with a light salad, a grilled fish or poultry entrée, and a wedge of melon for dessert. Now that Perrier-with-a-twist is the In drink, you can order it, and sip and gossip with a clear conscience. Remember: No health-nut lectures or sermons, and no one will be the wiser. They'll just assume you have to eat lightly and drink nothing because you're so important you need to stay fresh for more meetings later in the day!

9. The best weapon you have in the office fitness battle is to convince some coworkers to join your workout. If you're a woman, you'll probably find it easy to get other women in your own or nearby offices to join you in a lunchtime or post-work exercise class. Better yet, convince the company personnel officer to organize a corporate "Fitness Break" for break times or lunch. If the company has its own gym or has access to one, so much the better. If not, shop around for trainers or fitness experts who might offer an on-site workshop (as we do for both Chicago and suburban firms). Many companies are now starting regular fitness programs for their personnel as part of the "perks" of the job—among them, such notables as Xerox, Bonne Bell, and Texas Instruments. Check out the possibilities in your own firm.

10. If you're sent on the road, either on a sales trip or on conventions, don't panic. Invest in a Unique Tension Band, a good jump rope, some running shoes, a pair of "Executive Bells," ankle weights, a lightweight collapsible bar (we travel with ours on tour), and take to the road. After the day's work is done, head for the hotel sauna, gym, or pool, or take a short jog or run around the motel grounds. Jog in place while you watch the morning news. Run up and down the stairs instead of taking the elevators. Go through a short maintenance routine before you go down to breakfast. Maintain your fitness program on the road, and you'll find yourself less prone to jet lag when you return home.

11. If an occasional rush job keeps you working late for a week or so, don't give up your workouts altogether. Bring some light weights from home (your "traveling weights" will do nicely) and stash them in your desk. A twenty-minute workout before the day begins, a lunchtime break, a couple of ten-minute "fitness breaks" during the day, and a short energizer at 5 P.M. add up to a good deal of fitness with little time lost from the big project. You can't make dramatic gains (or losses) this way, but you can maintain the status quo until the big push is over.

12. Have energy to burn? Put it to work for you on the job. You'll find that you are now a valuable property in the company because you can do so much more than before. Don't let them saddle you with all the scutwork, but instead, learn to use the energy to your advantage. When everyone else is in the midst of low-blood-sugar slump at 4 P.M., or suffering advanced nicotine withdrawal symptoms, you're still awake, alert, and running the meeting. When everyone else at the convention is past going because they hit the Happy Hour room before the keynote address, you're asking intelligent questions and keeping the speaker on her toes. Supervisors and colleagues notice this kind of superenergy and often reward it later.

13. Finally, use your exercise periods to help relieve and work off tensions accumulated at the office. Use an early-morning workout to get cranked up for the day: You'll be bright-eyed when everyone is skulking around the coffeepot. Relax and work out the neck and back kinks with a lunchtime session. Unwind after work with a session at the gym. Use these times constructively to get rid of tensions and anxieties, think through problems, and generally re-energize. Try it—you'll be a more valuable person to your company as a result. And best of all, you'll become more valuable to yourself!

One area that you *can* enjoy with no reservations is the whole wonderful world of fashion. Clothes may not make the man or the woman, but they certainly can help us understand and define our new selves. Here are a few ideas for the newly svelte and shapely to help revamp your wardrobe while you're getting—and staying—in shape:

1. Don't discount fashion as frivolous and beneath the notice of a serious fitness buff. Men and women who feel they aren't looking their best often quit "seeing" new styles, fashion changes—with the result that even when they've shaped up they still look drab and outdated. Learn to use clothing intelligently to make the kind of statement, create the kind of image, that you now want to convey to the rest of the world. Get some help putting together one or two super outfits, and the rest of your wardrobe can be built around them. A few new outfits can help you create a new, healthier, younger, more energetic image and thus can pay big dividends in business, social relations, and personal life. What do you think all those "dress for success" books are really about?

2. Do use clothing to "keep you honest"—to help you stay with your diet and exercise regimen until you've lost those last hard-to-lose five pounds. Often a new, well-fitted suit, shirt, blouse, or pair of pants is all the inspiration you need to stay with the program one more week. Don't make the mistake of keeping all your "out-of-shape" clothes in the closet. Have them altered to size or pitch them: When you have too many ways out, the temptation to backslide is ever-present.

3. Do consider making those alterations to keep pace with your gains and losses. We know: Alterations cost money and time. But baggy, ill-fitting pants or skirts, a shirt that's ripping at the shoulders because your well-muscled arms have outgrown it, or jeans that fit another, heftier version of yourself aren't conducive to a good self-image. The biggest incentive, as we said before, is a wardrobe that fits exactly, with no room for cheating. Even when your program is just getting underway, keep at least three or four perfectly fitting outfits for work and play, and let them shrink along with you. Keep your spirits up by looking good while your program is in progress.

When you've reached your goal, then alter everything that works, pitch what doesn't—and give the rest to a friend who hasn't yet discovered Bodypower.

4. Do consider making some of your new purchases in a style or color you've never dared wear in your earlier incarnations. If you've always wanted fuschia jeans or a tight polo shirt, skimpy tops or sleek fitted pants, now's the time to indulge yourself. Don't change your entire fashion image overnight. But do make some small, inexpensive changes in your wardrobe, and give yourself an incentive to change your body even further. Show off that small waistline and those newly defined muscles!

5. Do use clothing to camouflage your physical flaws, and look even slimmer and trimmer than you are. Women can use overblouses, vests, cardigans, unfitted blazers, and other "third layers" to make heavy hips and waistlines disappear. Men can use vested suits, straight-cut jackets, narrow dark belts, narrower collars and ties for the same purposes. And both sexes can use vertical lines, thin vertical stripes, long ties or scarves, V-necks, and slenderizing accessories to advantage. Remember that the rule of thumb for dressing slim is to maintain an unbroken line. Dressing in a one-color outfit—especially a darker tone or a neutral, toning in with several shades of the same color, makes you appear slimmer than breaking the line with violent contrasts. If you yearn for the hot colors, use them in small doses—in belts, inexpensive tops, scarves, accessories, T-shirts, sporty and casual clothing.

6. Don't feel compelled to try out every new fashion or fad, or feel that now you should be able to wear every style. Some styles will probably never be flattering to you, no matter how much you slim or build. Don't become what *WWD* calls a "Fashion victim." Dress to suit *your* body type.

C. AT LARGE

And now for the most important part: the difference that your new shape (and shapeliness) can make to and for you, and the way you relate to the larger world. For all the effect the change has on your friends, family, co-workers, boss, job, school, and home, the person who is most affected by the change is *you.*

Tom Wolfe christened the seventies the "me" decade. This "me" orientation has extended into the eighties, and the change isn't all bad. We've learned over these past years of fitness consciousness that the most successful shaper-uppers are those who do it for themselves, out of a healthy sort of higher vanity. They don't shape up to please their husbands, wives, children, or friends, or even the world at large. The act of shaping up, slimming, building, getting fit, then, becomes a healthy, positive vanity; the ultimate gesture of self-affirmation and self-esteem.

That's why shaping up can be such an important, even pivotal, event in your life. It can touch off a whole personal renaissance. That's true for at least two reasons. First, more opportunities are available for healthy, good-looking, fit, energetic people than to unattractive, out-of-shape ones. You'll find promotions, social engagements, business and personal opportunities, invitations begin to expand as you improve your image and start to move from powerlessness to real body power.

Second, your self-esteem will be reflected in everything you do—the way you handle your business and social life, your contacts, your friends and acquaintances. You'll find that your renewed self-confidence gives you the courage to move in directions and do things you never thought possible. (For example, Valerie, always attracted to fashion and design, watched it from afar when she was overweight; now she writes fashion articles and books, develops programs for modeling agencies, even does modeling and sales rep work for designer friends.) You may end up amazing yourself in similar ways.

So take stock of where you are, where you've been, and where you'd like to be. Dream a little. Imagine where you'd really like to live, work, travel in five years. Then set out to make those dreams come true. You got yourself in shape. Now you can get your life in shape. You *can* change careers/go back to school/finish your degree/move up in the company/start your own business/travel to exotic places. All you need is the same determination that got you through your exercise program.

In a 1980 interview Muppets superstar Miss Piggy, queried about exercise, responded: "Jog? Why would little *moi* want to jog? Certainly not for pleasure. I can do other things for pleasure, if you know what I mean." Perhaps Miss Piggy hasn't yet discovered the joy of running—but you can and probably will. Exercise really is addictive, in a positive sense. And one of the joys of trimming down and shaping up is the way it puts you in touch with your own body and its potential. Encouraged by your success with the machines and free weights, you'll probably go on to try another sport or exercise. Unlike Miss Piggy, you probably *will* jog for pleasure—and run and walk. You may also bicycle; swim; play tennis, racquetball, or squash; ride horseback; roller skate; ice skate; or try your luck at aerobic, tap, ballet, or modern dance. But almost certainly you'll keep moving. Once having discovered the joys of propelling your body through space, you'll probably keep it up. And you'll discover new capabilities for physical action you never thought you had.

It's a well-known fact that many people who drastically change their body image continue to think of themselves as living in the "old" body. Fat women tend to think of themselves as fat even when they've slimmed down to size. (Valerie hardly recognized her own photos or reflection in store windows a month or two after her greatest weight loss.)

It's all too easy to continue visualizing yourself as fat, shapeless, or lacking in muscular development. But take the time to get reacquainted with yourself as you look *now*. Often our heads and psyches can't keep pace with our body's sudden changes, so we literally don't remember exactly how we look "this week." If that's the case with you, spend some time looking in mirrors or at photos, or, better yet, slides of yourself. Try to realize that you really do look different now. Then you can act in ways that fit that newly attractive person you see reflected in the mirror each morning.

There's another point worth remembering with regard to weight loss especially. Fat people use their fat as a sort of armor to protect them against the rest of the world. When they lose that armor, they feel naked, exposed, vulnerable, fragile, or small. (Weight training helps immensely here: You feel and look smaller, but in fact you *are* stronger—and that helps counteract the feelings of powerlessness and vulnerability that massive weight loss can bring.) It's often this feeling of being exposed that makes people start regaining the weight slowly until they reach a state where they're comfortable and "covered" again.

This is a complex set of reactions, but the simple fact of becoming aware of them will help. Realize that you will be tempted to eat your way back to a comfortable weight, and try to resist the temptation. Begin to see the fat as a padding or "insulation" from the world. And realize that you no longer need that insulation; you can cope on your own, thanks to your increased good looks and health.

In our image-obsessed culture, we expect too much even of dramatic changes in our bodies. We expect a shape-up program, if it's successful, to change our entire lives for the better, and are frustrated and disappointed when that doesn't happen. In point of fact, changing your body image sometimes creates more problems than it solves. Don't be ashamed if you need professional help to get you through this period of adjustment. A good psychiatrist, image counselor, career guide, or exercise therapist/trainer is invaluable at this time. Speech or acting lessons can help you learn to project the image you want. A wardrobe or fashion consultant can help you learn to make the most of your new physique. Special training in body awareness, such as the balance beams or kinaesthetic primer board (described in chapter five), can also help; we've found in our seminars that they aid previously overweight people in readjusting to the body's new center of gravity.

Finally, when you've taken all the steps outlined here, do one more thing. Use that new body image to develop a new mental outlook. We're not talking about simple-minded "positive thinking" to the exclusion of critical judgment, rationality, or realism. We *are* talking about the renewed enthusiasm, optimism, and energy your new body and its potential can give you. So look on the completion of your program not as the finish of something, but as the beginning of a whole lifetime of health, strength, vitality, and effectiveness. That's real Body Power!

Good luck to all of you!
RALPH AND VALERIE CARNES
Chicago, Illinois
February 1981

EXERCISE EQUIPMENT MANUFACTURERS

The following list is obviously not exhaustive. As a quick glance at any muscle magazine will show you, there are literally hundreds of small companies all across the country, each grinding out some sort of weight-training equipment. The companies listed below are the major manufacturers, or they are small companies with a unique concept. The equipment that these companies manufacture is what you'll find in health clubs and gyms anywhere in the United States.

BODY CULTURE EQUIPMENT COMPANY
P.O. Box 10
Alliance, NB 69301
(Iron Man free weights and machines)

DIVERSIFIED PRODUCTS
Opelika, Ala/Compton, CA
(DP Olympic barbells)

DYNAMICS HEALTH EQUIPMENT MANUFACTURING COMPANY, INC.
1538 College Ave.
South Houston, TX 77587
(Machines and free weights, many accessories)

HYDRA-GYM ATHLETICS, INC.
2121 Industrial Park
P.O. Box 599
Belton, TX 76513

NAUTILUS SPORTS/MEDICAL INDUSTRIES
P.O. Box 1783
Deland, FL 32720
(Nautilus machines)

PARAMOUNT HEALTH EQUIPMENT CORPORATION
3000 South Santa Fe
Los Angeles, CA 90058
(Machines, free weights, and accessories)

SAF-T-GYM (RICK ADAMS PRODUCTS)
815 Alexander Vy Road
Healdsburg, CA 91364
(The Saf-T-Gym workout bench)

STRENGTH/FITNESS SYSTEMS
P.O. Box 266
Independence, MO 64051
(Mini-Gym machines)

UNIQUE TRAINING DEVICE COMPANY
P.O. Box 1094
Glendale Heights, IL 60137
(Tension bands, benches, accessories)

UNIVERSAL GYM EQUIPMENT CORPORATION
17352 Von Karman Avenue
Irvine, CA 92714
(Universal multistation machines, accessories)

WEIDER INSTITUTE
21100 Erwin
Woodland Hills, CA 91364
(Weider barbells and accessories)

YORK BARBELL COMPANY
York, PA 17405
(York barbells and accessories: the company that started it all)

Index